YOUNG PEOPLE AND CONTRADICTIONS OF INCLUSION

Towards Integrated Transition Policies in Europe

Edited by Andreu López Blasco, Wallace McNeish and Andreas Walther

First published in Great Britain in December 2003 by

The Policy Press
University of Bristol
Fourth Floor
Beacon House
Queen's Road
Bristol BS8 1QU
UK

Tel +44 (0)117 331 4054
Fax +44 (0)117 331 4093
e-mail tpp-info@bristol.ac.uk
www.policypress.org.uk

British Library Cataloguing in Publication Data
A catalogue record for this book is available from the British Library.

Library of Congress Cataloging-in-Publication Data
A catalog record for this book has been requested.

ISBN 1 86134 524 0 paperback

A hardcover version of this book is also available

Andreu López Blasco is Head of Research at the Association of Regional and European Analysis (AREA) in Valencia, Spain, **Wallace McNeish** is Lecturer in Sociology at the University of Abertay, Dundee and **Andreas Walther** is Senior Researcher at the Institute for Regional Innovation and Social Research (IRIS) in Tübingen, Germany.

Cover design by Qube Design Associates, Bristol.
Front cover: photograph supplied by kind permission of www.third-avenue.co.uk
Printed and bound in Great Britain by Bell & Bain Ltd, Glasgow.

Contents

List of figures and tables

Figures

Tables

Acknowledgements

All across Europe, governments are increasingly concerned with young people's transitions from school to work. This concern was illustrated by the development of the European Employment Strategy in 1997, and was reinforced again in 2001 by the EC's White Paper on youth policy. It is common sense that 'something has to be done' for the younger generation – for individuals' personal development and for the future cohesion of society as a whole. However, consistently high rates of youth unemployment and significant drop-out rates of young people from education and training, or their withdrawal from the formal transition system altogether (so-called 'status zero' youth) indicate that vulnerability and risks of social exclusion are more complex than is commonly assumed and that they are highly resistant to institutional 'cures'.

Young people and contradictions of inclusion aims to critically assess contemporary transition policies, to improve the dialogue between researchers and policy makers concerned with all aspects of young people's transitions, and to explore the perspectives of a more holistic approach towards this area of social development than that which appears in dominant social and political discourses.

The book is centred on the proceedings of a European conference held in Madrid during the summer of 2002 under the title 'Young people and transition policies in Europe'. The findings of seven EU-funded research projects were presented and discussed with policy makers from EU member and candidate states. The conference was jointly organised by the Institute for Regional Innovation and Social Research (IRIS) in Tübingen (Germany), the Association for Regional and European Analysis (AREA) in Valencia (Spain) and the Spanish Youth Institute (INJUVE) based in Madrid (also Spain). Its main source of funding was the EC under the research programme 'Accompanying measures', while additional funding came from the Spanish Ministry for Employment and Social Affairs.

Like the conference that brought together more than 100 participants from 20 countries, this book is a genuine pan-European endeavour. It is written by authors from 11 countries working in research institutions or policy administrations and its contributions are based on research findings from 13 European countries – mostly EU member states, but also candidate countries. We hope that this makes the book useful, challenging and provocative for a broad readership both within and outside of Europe.

We should like to acknowledge our gratitude for the production of this book first to the authors involved for sharing their ideas, time and creativity. Without the funding of the EC, the whole project would not have been possible. We thank, therefore, Angelos Agalianos especially, the scientific officer responsible at DG Research. We also want to thank Antonia Freijanes Benito and Julio Camacho Munoz from INJUVE for their efforts in making the conference happen on which this book is based. Finally, a warm thank you goes to the staff of The Policy Press, especially Karen Bowler and Dawn Rushen for their support, and to the anonymous referees for constructive comments and the recommendation of publication.

Andreu López Blasco, Wallace McNeish and Andreas Walther
October 2003

Notes on contributors

René Bendit, psychologist and sociologist, is Senior Researcher at the German Youth Institute in Munich (Germany) and responsible for international research cooperation. His research themes are youth in Europe and European youth policies, comparative research on youth transitions and transition policies, and young immigrants and members of minority ethnic groups in EU-Europe.

Paul Burgess is Director of the Social Science Degree in Youth and Community Work at the Department of Applied Social Studies, University College, Cork (Ireland). His research centres round themes of lifelong learning, community education and youth work. He has also undertaken research concerning community relations, community identity and social policy in Northern Ireland.

Lorenzo Cachón Rodríguez is Professor in Sociology at the Complutense University of Madrid (Spain). His research themes are the labour market and public policies, especially in the fields of young people's transitions to work and immigration.

Manuela du Bois-Reymond is Professor for Education and Youth Studies at the Department of Education, University of Leiden (Netherlands). She is a member of EGRIS (European Group for Integrated Social Research) and has collaborated in several EU-financed projects. Her fields of interest are intercultural childhood study and intergenerational relationships as well as comparative transition research with special attention to new forms of learning.

Thomas Kieselbach is Professor for Psychology and Head of the Institute for Psychology of Work, Unemployment and Health at the University of Bremen (Germany). He is chairman of the Scientific Committee 'Unemployment and Health', International Commission on Occupational Health and of the Commission 'Psychology of Unemployment', International Association of Applied Psychology.

Siyka Kovacheva is Lecturer in Sociology at the University of Plovdiv and Director of the New European Centre for Regional Studies, Plovdiv (Bulgaria). She has participated in national and comparative research projects on young people's transitions, unemployment, self-employment, political culture and youth policies.

Patricia Loncle, political scientist, is a Senior Researcher at the National School of Public Health in Rennes (France). Her research themes are youth policies at local, national and European levels, comparison of territorialisation and regionalisation of health and social policies.

Andreu López Blasco, sociologist, is Head of Research of the Association of Regional and European Analysis Group (AREA) based in Valencia (Spain). His research themes are sociology of age, family, youth, social services and local policies, mass media, migratory movements, and evaluation of training and employment programmes.

Wallace McNeish is a Lecturer in Sociology, University of Abertay, Dundee. His key research interests include sociology of youth transitions, employment, unemployment and labour markets, citizenship, rights and the state (political sociology), social movements and political protest.

Steven Miles is Head of Research at the Centre for Cultural Policy and Management at the University of Northumbria. He is a sociologist and has a particular interest in young people's identities, lifestyles and cultural consumption.

Sven Mørch is a sociologist teaching Social Psychology at the University of Copenhagen (Denmark). He has been involved in European youth research through the Council of Europe and EGRIS (European Group for Integrated Social Research) network. His main research fields are social integration, educational theory and practice, development and competencies, action research and 'practice research', and the planning and evaluating of youth projects.

José Machado Pais, social scientist, is Principal Researcher at the University of Lisbon (Portugal) and has been Visiting Professor in several South American universities. He has conducted research in the fields of youth, culture, leisure and social structures and has been coordinating the Portuguese Youth Observatory since 1991.

Axel Pohl, educational scientist, is currently working as a Researcher at the Institute for Regional Innovation and Social Research (IRIS) in Tübingen (Germany). His research interests consist of young people's biographies, transitions to work and migrant youth. His main areas of work are the evaluation of transition policies from a youth perspective and related fields such as youth and community work.

Amparo Serrano Pascual is Senior Researcher at the European Trade Union Institute in Brussels and Associate Professor at the Complutense University of Madrid (Spain). His primary topics of research include comparative employment policies, transition of young people to the labour market, gender mainstreaming and evaluation of the European employment strategy.

Barbara E. Stalder, psychologist, is a Senior Researcher in the Ministry of Education of the Canton of Berne (Switzerland). She is responsible for the coordination of research, evaluation and planning in the field of vocational education and training. Her main research fields are the transition from education to employment, risk and resilience in education and apprenticeship training.

Barbara Stauber is a Senior Researcher at the Institute for Regional Innovation and Social Research (IRIS), Tübingen (Germany), and at the Tübingen Institute for Women's Studies. Her main fields of interest are gender and generation relationships, youth cultures and transition research. She is founding member and coordinator of EGRIS (European Group for Integrated Social Research).

Dermot Stokes works on behalf of the Department of Education and Science in Ireland as National Coordinator of the YOUTHREACH programme. He has been centrally involved in a range of education and training innovations in Ireland and the EU regarding young people' transitions from childhood to adulthood. He has a particular interest in educational disadvantage and social exclusion.

Harm van Lieshout, sociologist, is Lecturer in Industrial Relations at the Hanzehogeschool Groningen (Netherlands). He was previously employed as senior researcher at the Hugo Sinzheimer Institute, Universiteit van Amsterdam. He specialises in comparative research on industrial relations, labour market governance, (vocational) education governance, and labour market and education and training policies.

Andreas Walther, educationalist, is a Senior Researcher at the Institute for Regional Innovation and Social Research (IRIS), Tübingen (Germany). His research themes are young people's transitions to work and adulthood and comparative studies on welfare, youth and transition policies. He has been coordinating EGRIS (European Group for Integrated Social Research) since 1993.

Ton Wilthagen holds a chair in Institutional and Legal Aspects of the Labour Market in National and International Perspective at the University of Tilburg (Netherlands), where he is also Head of Research of the Institute for Labour Studies. His research themes are labour law, social security and labour market policies, especially with regard to 'flexicurity' and 'transitional labour markets'.

ONE

Introduction: young people and contradictions of inclusion

Andreas Walther and Wallace McNeish

"I want a job where I am happy to get up in the morning and go to work. Money is important too, because you need it for your living. But I prefer if I have fun at work." (Male, 23, unemployed, Germany)

Young Europeans ... are precisely the people who are primarily affected by economic change, demographic imbalance, globalisation or cultural diversity. We are expecting them to create new forms of social relations, different ways of expressing solidarity or of coping with differences and finding enrichment in them, while new uncertainties appear. Despite the more complex social and economic context, young people are well equipped to adapt. It is up to the national and European policy-makers to facilitate this process of change by making young people stakeholders in our societies. (EC, 2001)

"I don't go to the employment service. The times when I have been there it was only trouble. I'd rather give up on the benefit .... You know, you feel they do not like their job." (Male, 22, unemployed, Germany)

"There's nothing in there unless you have a qualification.... You fill in forms and talk to one in there like, and then you hear nothing, unless they have a poxy job going where ... you're treated like a slave." (Female, 20, unemployed, Ireland)

The European Council draws attention to the particular importance of preventive measures to reverse the trend of youth unemployment ... through early identification of individual needs and tailor-made responses.... Member States will ensure that ... every unemployed young person is offered a new start before reaching six months of unemployment, in the form of training, retraining, work practice, a job or other employability measure. (European Council, 1997)

Government approaches towards young people's transitions to work are based on a shared assumption that social inclusion depends on labour market integration and that labour market integration depends on education and training qualifications. From this perspective, the 'success' of such policies is more or less strictly quantitative; that is, defined by the proportion of young people brought into paid employment through *some* kind of education or training. However, the constant failure of government policies in reaching, keeping and channelling a considerable proportion of their target group into viable and sustainable trajectories is strongly related to the fact that the notions of social integration that underpin such policies are too narrow and too inflexible to be concomitant with what young people themselves feel and understand integration to be.

Young people and contradictions of inclusion aims to:

- *challenge the dominant quantitative perspective on young people's transitions and to suggest a more holistic and qualitative approach as an alternative.* This means taking a step back from the reductive institutional focus on transitions to work in order to re-embed them within the broader perspective of transitions to adulthood with all the complex and contradictory implications that such an approach necessarily entails;
- *contribute to the development of a dialogue between transition policy and transition research.* As late modern societies grow ever more complex, it becomes more and more difficult to discern the specific effects of specific policies and to relate one to the other; hence, the demand for evidence-based policies is increasing. However, the relationship between policy and research has often proven to be fraught and structured by mutual misunderstanding and suspicion.

This book is based on the assumption that modernising transition policies on the basis of a more comprehensive understanding of social inclusion requires a dialogic restructuring of the relationship between researchers and policy makers.

Towards a holistic concept of social inclusion and the integration of transition policies

Transition policies are defined as the set of different policy sectors that, in one way or another, address young people's transitions from education to work. While recognising that policy sectors (economic, financial, transport and housing, or criminal justice policies, for example) have impacts on young people's transitions to work as well, but in a more indirect way, we mainly refer to:

- *education and training,* providing young people with qualifications that are required by the labour market (but also in the sense of channelling young people into taking different pathways of unequal status and recognition);

- *labour market policies* that regulate the relationship between supply and demand for labour by counselling and mediating, by shaping the conditions of labour market entry, by creating new jobs, or by providing training or employment schemes for the unemployed. The aim of young people's integration, however, does have to compete with employers' interests in cheap and flexible labour as well as with the state's political interest in keeping unemployment figures low and with fiscal pressure to limit public funding;
- *welfare policies* concerned with the income situation of those in fragile living conditions, as well as providing social services for other groups at risk. However, it also means the determination of social assistance depending upon involvement in education, training or labour market policies, and thus contributes to the 'normalisation' of young people's transition strategies;
- *youth policies*, where youth workers engage in career counselling – either in transition-related projects or as a side effect of leisure-related youth work activities.

The chapters of this book contribute to the development of a broader transitions perspective by critically assessing the rationales and success criteria underlying public transition policies, by comparatively evaluating their effectiveness, and by confronting them with young people's experiences, needs and orientations. One explanation for the lack of sustainability in such policies is the fact that many policies still struggle to reflect the complexity of socioeconomic and socio-cultural change that modern societies are currently undergoing. Often, single policies are not connected with one another and deal with individual biographies only from the compartmentalised perspective for which they are institutionally responsible (as labour, as a human resource, as a claimant of benefits, and so on).

The most significant shared empirical finding of the research projects involved in this book is that *young people's subjectivities are as much a part of social realities as labour markets and social structures, and therefore have objective impacts on processes of social and labour market integration*. A key to this is young people's motivation to participate or to stay in counselling, education, training or a job – or to drop out. Not only policy makers but also other social and economic actors in transition systems have neglected this important subjective factor and have failed, therefore, effectively to combat youth unemployment and the risks of social exclusion. The trend of a growing discrepancy between individuals and policies does not only concern young people, but also individuals and societies in general. From this perspective, the focus on young people's transitions serves a double purpose. On the one hand, it is a legitimate end in itself due to the increased risks with which a large section of the younger generation are confronted – something that may constitute a major threat to future social cohesion. On the other hand, young people also constitute a strategic group that can be analysed to understand broader trends of contemporary social and economic change due to the coincidence of their biographical transition from education (youth) to employment (adulthood) with a historical shift of societal constellations referred to as 'late modernity', 'post-Fordism', or 'globalisation'.

Therefore, the objective of this book is to analyse the potentials of – and prerequisites for – a more holistic approach suggested and discussed under the aegis of the broad category of Integrated Transition Policies (ITPs). In short, ITPs imply that there is a need to start from the biographical perspective of young people themselves, to include their subjective needs and orientations, and to coordinate policies across sectors in order to allow young people to become the key actors in their own transitions (see Chapter Two of this volume; also Walther et al, 2002a).

Analysing contradictions of inclusion and potentials of ITPs requires a European perspective considering the marked trends towards convergence in labour market-related policies promoted by the EU and concretised by the recent adoption of the European Employment Strategy (EES). One key aspect of the 'Europeanisation' of transition policies is that national approaches are increasingly challenged by comparison with other national policy models. The main instrument of convergence is the implementation of benchmarking indicators such as the guideline of the EES, which sets out the principle that all unemployed young people under 25 years of age shall be offered opportunities of orientation, education, training, work experience or employment after six months of unemployment.

The conclusions of the European Council's Employment Summit in 1997 leave space for a considerable diversity of policy approaches addressing the integration of young people. This 'open coordination' strategy for EU policies has been designed to be concomitant with the principle of subsidiarity, while national governments remain accountable to the established benchmarks. Comparisons show that there are considerable variances regarding just how much youth unemployment has been reversed in the different member states since the EES agreement, with policies of the more successful countries being promoted as 'best practice' (see Chapters Five and Six of this volume).

While there are differences in the success rates of bringing young people into jobs, there is nevertheless a common preoccupation regarding the long-term effects of transition policies and their efficacy in actually reaching all the young people addressed. It is clear that, although national governments have all attempted to address the problem in different ways, the sustainability of policy effects across Europe has been lower than expected. Therefore, the other aspect of Europeanisation that needs to be critically assessed is the *adequacy* of the concepts – and the underlying ideological assumptions – that have become dominant on the agenda of policy as well as of research concerned with youth transitions. The most current concepts and discourses that are generally referred to are as follows:

- The *active citizenship and participation* of young people can be seen as a consequent adaptation of young people's status to prolonged and risky transitions, the necessity of which on a general level is agreed upon. However, there are only a few ideas on how to concretise this. Most approaches, such as those suggested by the EC's White Paper *A new impetus for European youth* (EC, 2001), are limited to the area of youth policy and youth work. In contrast, in education and training, participation is reduced to mere qualification attainment or, in labour market-related contexts, to having a job (Walther et al, 2002b; see also Chapters Two, Eight, Nine and Ten of this volume).

- *Disadvantage* is the term by which the problems and risks faced by young people in their transitions to work are most often addressed; for example, 'disadvantaged youth'. In these discourses, the interpretation of disadvantage as resulting from unemployment has shifted to disadvantage as the *reason* for unemployment: young people are unemployed because they have more disadvantages compared with those who manage to enter the labour market. This perspective can be further differentiated into social disadvantage due to selective education or segmented labour markets, and into individual deficits such as learning disabilities, early school leaving and lack of qualifications or inadequate social behaviour. In most cases, it is young people themselves who have to compensate by further education or training, and indeed by compromising in terms of aspirations concerning wages or occupational choices. In order to recognise the 'constructedness' of so-called problem or disadvantaged groups, this volume has tried, therefore, to integrate the perspectives of *gender* and *ethnicity* in the different chapters in a cross-thematic way rather than dealing with them in separate chapters (see especially Chapters Two, Six, Ten, and Fourteen of this volume).
- *Flexibilisation* refers to the broader interpretation of labour market-related changes in contemporary transitions. Flexibilisation denotes the actual changes that are taking place in terms of the present dynamics of both job loss and job creation. At the same time, however, flexibilisation is promoted in dominant discourses as the remedy to meet current economic challenges. For example, from the free market economics perspective, policies must aim at adapting to flexibilised labour market dynamics rather than hindering them. In this perspective one can therefore speak of the normative power of social facts (see Chapters Seven and Thirteen of this volume).
- *Employability* of the labour force is the key concept in this regard, a term that has been introduced to the European scenario from the UK context. It means that individual skills and qualifications are evaluated less with regard to their formal – or subjective – relevance, and more with regard to the actual demands of employers. It implies that education and training or other forms of support first of all have to be quantified with regard to their success in bringing people into the labour market. Employability can be interpreted as the narrowing of an integration perspective in a labour society that struggles to provide its members with the central means for integration; that is, paid work (see Chapters Four, Six and Eleven of this volume).
- *Activation* is a concept that is often viewed as complementary to employability. Research findings reported in this book (see Chapters Five and Six) refer to

the increasing pressure under which individuals have to demonstrate responsibility for their own careers in exchange for being entitled to benefits and other kinds of state support. Other European studies, however, have shown that activation can also be – and, in fact, is – interpreted in a more comprehensive way by asking for the prerequisites of individual agency or activity such as choice and security and by including the activation of institutions as well (Lødemel and Trickey, 2001; van Berkel and Hornemann Møller, 2002; Chapters Eight and Nine of this volume).

- *Lifelong learning* is another key 'buzzword' that has been on the European policy agenda in recent years. While policy documents underline the increasing necessity to conceptualise learning with regard to the whole person as the 'subject' of learning, it appears as if such statements are largely of a rhetorical nature. When one analyses policies promoted under this heading, one finds holistic management training as well as low-level schemes for long-term unemployed that are aimed mainly at adaptation to precarious and low-skilled jobs rather than at real competence development. Manninen (1998) distinguishes reactive, proactive and innovative learning measures and argues that access to these different approaches is determined by categories of social inequality: previous education and labour market position, gender and ethnicity (see Chapters Two, Six, Seven and Nine of this volume).

- *Equal opportunities* is one of the main social policy perspectives referred to in current transition and labour market policies. It refers to providing opportunities (or access options) on the grounds of 'merit', while social protection – especially with regard to young people, and increasingly so in the context of activation policies – seems to be losing ground (Rifkin, 2000). 'Equal opportunities' refers to gender and class, as well as to ethnicity. Again, there are different interpretations. One such perspective would be to provide opportunities to reach the same goal through different pathways considering different starting positions and resources. Another implies – and this is the classic but prevailing liberal perspective – one chance for every individual and the meritocratic recognition of competition results. Although 'second chances' may be conceded, they rarely take into account the substantive nature of social positioning. In fact, in terms of 'secondary integration', they most often imply the downgrading and 'cooling out' of aspirations (Goffman, 1962; see also Chapter Six of this volume).

The concepts that have just been outlined are general ones that are used widely within current discourses surrounding education, training and integration. However, they mean quite different things and have given rise to different consequences and strategies in different contexts. Given its comparative nature, this book concentrates primarily on national policies and on government-operated programmes in Europe. The first reason for this is that, compared to enterprises, social work practitioners and training providers, public institutions have a legally defined responsibility to facilitate and care for the integration of the younger generation. Second, due to this responsibility they have a considerable power in this respect even if this power is not sufficient to solve the respective problems for which they are responsible (they do, however, have the power to designate who or who is not a 'problem', and who or who should not be granted social assistance and benefits). Third, it can be argued that policies always depend on other actors who have a more direct approach towards young people's subjectivities and motivations. However, in the case of employers, the recognition of individual subjectivities and motivations will always depend on the labour market situation and on their interest in those workers who best fit their needs, while the scope of professionals – such as youth workers, trainers or counsellors – to put their knowledge about young people's needs into practice is curtailed by the guidelines of funding programmes; that is, of policies. Due to this concentration on the public level, the perspectives of other actors (such as trade unions and employers) play a more minor role and are referred to rather indirectly through practical discourses like those surrounding 'local partnerships' or the 'marketisation' of transition policies. An important exception is made, however, with regard to third-sector organisations and this indicates something of the specific nature of the ITP perspective developed in this book. Starting from a position that recognises and reveals the inability of the actors in the formal transition systems to improve young people's chances of integration and their tendency to reproduce structures of selectivity and segmentation, ITP are especially interested in, and concerned with promoting, policies that recognise the informal side of social integration. Hence, important aspects of informal support and informal learning are given particular analytical attention with regard to their integrative potentials (see especially Chapters Eight, Nine, Ten and Twelve of this volume).

Towards a dialogue between transition policies and transition research

By structuring the discourses related to young people's transitions, the concepts introduced in the previous section of this chapter represent the arena where policy and research meet. While for policy makers they serve as an orientation mark for convergence towards 'best practice' (in most cases defined by quantitative indicators), research has either engaged in comparing different interpretations of these concepts, has evaluated changes and effectiveness of policies implemented under these headings, or has critically analysed underlying ideological assumptions.

Research can and does influence policy in a number of ways, but research communities and policy communities need to come to a better understanding of each other's worlds if so-called 'evidence-based' policy making is to be strengthened. Research can contribute at all stages of the policy cycle, from policy development, through implementation to evaluation – and not just at the latter stages. This latter stage collaboration, however, is the reality in most cases, and it is both sides that allocate the categories of ex-post evaluation. Researchers argue that scientific practice needs to be liberated from the straightjacket of the instrumental need for concrete and immediate application, and policy makers tend to experience (and thereby to devalue) academic debate as an irrelevant and abstract deviation from the administrative and political procedures structuring their reality. Researchers, however, also complain about the discrepancy – often based on research evidence – between policy objectives (such as social inclusion) and the bureaucratic structures of implementation that cause non-intended (but nevertheless often well-known) counter-effects in terms of exclusion risk being reproduced or even intensified (see Chapters Two and Six of this volume).

The impact of research upon policy cannot be understood in terms of a clear linear relationship; rather, it must accept that its place is as one of a number of competing logics that impact in a complex manner upon policy – that is, political, organisational and administrative rationalities as well as research. How research does impact, however, is through accumulations of research, and rarely through a single definitive study. Consistent with this, it is advisable that both policy and research communities should pay more attention to lessons that can be taken from the current knowledge base, which in many areas is substantial (as is illustrated by the many research projects presented and referred to throughout this book), than always looking to do further research. At the same time, however, it should be noted that structures of research funding continue to refer to a conventional study format rather than to more flexible and open forms of research-based, scientific policy consulting.

Research is useful for policy only at the specific time it is needed, and policy makers often cannot wait for the outcomes of new studies. It is through the time and space perspective that the difficult relationship between research and policy can be best characterised. On the one hand, policy makers, for different reasons (such as governance, legitimacy and power maintenance), need solutions for concrete problems and (have to) define appropriate costs with regard to given budgets and competing interests. On the other hand, researchers underline sustainable benefits and cost relations in the long run. They can afford to do this, since academic rationality is still defined by distance and long-term perspectives, and academic peer control maintains an academic codex by which applied research and science often struggle with being recognised within the scientific community[1].

The relationship between the two communities of research and policy may be characterised as two separate systems, while communication is normally organised in situations that both sides perceive as external or at best marginal. A positive rearrangement of this relationship would mean that the systems themselves are reorganised in a manner that allows for an overlap while at the same time preserving the integrity of each system; that is, without leading to the co-option, colonisation and loss of independence of science and research by the policy-making community. This requires a radical redefinition of policy making, a shift providing institutional space for acquiring knowledge and evidence. In fact, at a deeper level, this also means the redefinition of science and research in terms of including communication with, and dissemination to, the non-scientific world rather than making it an additional, external demand. This requires time, competencies (also the translation of scientific jargon into everyday language), and acceptance of the insight that publicly funded science may be asked to prove its societal use in a way that can be understood by wider society. Hence, the stress should be laid on synthesis, joint critical assessment, openness and 'communicative dialogue' (Habermas, 1987). In concrete terms, opportunities for ongoing face-to-face discussion are needed both to foster understanding of each culture, and to match what both sides need and can provide for one another and society in general. This is of course an ideal (speech situation); nevertheless, it is something that should be striven for, because only by the development of understanding between the two worlds of research and policy development can a progressive way forward be found.

This book represents only a minor step in this direction. Despite an academic format, the research projects presented here deal with concrete policies and, in most cases, do so in an applied perspective. This ties in with the perspective outlined earlier in this chapter, and at the same time represents one key criterion of EC research funding. In fact, the international conference upon which the book is based succeeded in providing a dialogic alternative to the conventional set-up in which policy makers simply provide a framework for academics on which to hang their presentations and debates. Therefore, in this book, the views of policy makers have been taken seriously and considered both directly and indirectly. For example, in Chapter Six, statements given in interviews are documented and analysed in a comparative perspective; Chapter Ten includes and reflects upon comments and statements made by policy makers during the conference; Chapters Eleven and Fourteen, meanwhile, have been co-authored by researchers working in policy institutions, and who, therefore, have personal experience of the difficult policy/research relationship. Finally, this segment of the introductory section has been inspired by the comments and reflections of a researcher working in a government department[2].

After so strongly stressing the relationship between transition policy and transition research, it is perhaps necessary to remind ourselves of the most important part of the equation – *dialogue*; that is, the young men and young women who have to be considered as the subjects of their own transitions. Dialogue must not be restricted to policy and research as an end in itself; rather, it must give the young men and women concerned a genuine voice, by appropriate design of research and policy as well as by direct involvement and citizenship rights with regard to research and policy.

Book structure and overview

This book is divided into three parts. The first part sets the scene by outlining the principal dichotomy that lies at the heart of the contemporary contradictions of inclusion; that is, the widening gap between the perspectives of the policy-making institutions and young people themselves. In the second part, research projects are presented that have analysed important aspects of both the design and implementation of European transition policies and the effects of these policies on young people's lives. The third section concludes the book by providing a discussion of policy dilemmas that have been identified across each research report.

The first part, entitled 'Risks and contradictions in young people's transitions to work', is begun by Manuela du Bois-Reymond and Andreu López Blasco (Chapter Two), who provide a theoretical framework for understanding the structural and biographical changes that have led to a destandardisation of young people's transitions. Illustrated by the metaphor of the 'yo-yo', the central concepts in this chapter are young adults' transitions and misleading trajectories. By comparative analysis, non-intended effects of integration policies for young adults are related to institutional structures and procedures that continue to be inspired by the assumptions of gendered standard biographies and the possibility of full employment. Setting out the policy context for this book, they introduce the perspective of ITPs that start from the basis of individual biographies and are coordinated in a cross-sector manner. Authors of the chapters that follow refer throughout to this perspective.

In Chapter Three, Thomas Kieselbach contributes a differentiated perspective towards integration and exclusion by presenting the findings of qualitative research into the *risks of social exclusion* faced by long-term unemployed young people in six European countries. Applying the multidimensional concept of social exclusion developed by Kronauer (1998) to varying European socioeconomic and socio-cultural contexts, this social relationship is found to take very different forms. The dimension of social isolation (more frequent in Northern Europe) in fact counteracts the more economic or labour market-related aspects of social exclusion. Also, the dimension of institutional exclusion is contradictory because the existence of state institutions (more so in Northern Europe) not only provides support but also causes stigmatisation, while young people in Southern Europe do not expect anything from institutions.

The second part of this book, entitled 'Young people and transition policies in Europe', deals with the trends in current transition policies and the effects of these policies. The European perspective here applies to both EU policies and a comparison between the national policies of EU member states.

In Chapter Four, Lorenzo Cachón Rodríguez discusses the findings of a study that compares the *strategies* of actors, market logics and policies regarding the employment of young people in six European countries. His focus is recent developments with regard to modernising vocational education and training. While identifying tendencies of convergence, he shows that structures of path dependency continue to influence the structural patterns of national transition systems. With regard to the two major trends of increasing professional qualifications and flexibilising wages, he shows that specific strategies are connected to different actors and complex processes of negotiation.

Following this, Amparo Serrano Pascual (Chapter Five) critically analyses the concepts and discourses related to the EES, which, since its adoption in 1997, has had significant influence on national, regional and local policies addressing young people's transitions to work. She reconstructs and at the same time deconstructs the process of the 'Europeanisation' of transition policies as one that coincides with a more individualising approach towards youth unemployment. Terms like 'employability' or 'activation' reflect a shift from a lack of employment opportunities for young people to a 'deficit' notion of youth.

With the background provided by the previous two chapters, it is useful to compare the recent policies against youth unemployment adopted in the aftermath of the 1997 Luxembourg summit. In Chapter Six, then, Wallace McNeish and Patricia Loncle critically analyse major trends, general and particular objectives, problems of implementation and the effectiveness of programmes in eight EU member states. They show persistent differences due to the path dependency of national institutions and policies, but also trends of convergence on both practical and ideological levels imposed by the EES process. While trends towards lifelong learning and individualised counselling appear on the surface to reflect the flexibilisation and diversification of transition patterns, the chapter's authors interpret them in terms of underlying differentiated pressure and control of adaptation of the individuals concerned.

The concept of transitional labour markets (TLMs) has been developed in the framework of another European research project. It conceives analytically of labour markets as not only constituting structures of supply and demand of labour but, by applying a life-course perspective, also as an arena for different kinds of transitions. Politically, this implies the regulation of transitions rather than employment statuses.

Harm van Lieshout and Ton Wilthagen (Chapter Seven) present the TLM concept and apply it to the situation in the Netherlands by discussing three case studies of transition policies in action: temporary work agencies, apprenticeship training, and the need to meet changing skill demands. They argue that only through a creative combination of flexibilisation and security can policies succeed in regulating transitions to the labour market.

The 'third sector' may be conceived of as a particular element of a broader transitional labour market. Due to the decreasing employment dynamics of both the private and public sector in the past decade, the EU (as well as national governments) has increasingly referred to the employment potential of the third sector. Referring to a study involving four European countries, Paul Burgess (Chapter Eight) assesses the potentials that third-sector initiatives may have for young people who face risks of exclusion in transitions to the labour market. The question 'ghetto for the disadvantaged or springboard?' refers to the vulnerable structure of third-sector organisations that may curtail these positive potentials, although cross-country comparison does show that this vulnerability may be compensated for by supportive legislation. Rather than acting as a 'job machine', the third sector serves as an empowering springboard for young people due to its informal structures.

In Chapter Nine, Steven Miles has a closer look at learning processes and empowering experiences in the more informal setting of projects for young people located in the arena of the performing arts. Based on the intercultural evaluation of three case studies (from Portugal, Germany and the UK), Miles shows that participation in the performing arts is a highly successful means to aid the development young people's self-confidence and social skills. However, the biographical effects of such experiences depend on how informal learning and non-formal education are recognised by respective national transition systems. It demands from policy makers an investment in programmes for which the outcomes are less predictable and measurable than those of formal education and training are normally assumed to be.

In this book's third part, entitled 'Dilemmas and perspectives of Integrated Transition Policies', an analytical reflection is provided on the research findings presented in Parts One and Two. Chapter Ten by Andreas Walther can be read as an overarching bridge between the three sections. By way of summarising the earlier chapters and integrating the reactions and comments made by policy makers during the Madrid conference, it becomes clear that policies themselves are driven by contradictory objectives or *dilemmas* that undermine their efficacy. One perspective in this regard may be the limited scope of empowering social and transition policies in modernised capitalist labour societies. Another perspective, which does not necessarily contradict the first, suggests that such dilemmas stand for a decreasing linearity between policies and effects in late modernity. This requires a fundamental shift from policies for social integration that rely solely on formal institutions and programmes towards policies that are open to complementary informal strategies and resources as well. This, however, implies the acceptance of uncertain policy outcomes. The most significant policy dilemmas introduced in this chapter are taken up and dealt with more in detail in the chapters that follow it.

The first dilemma analysed by Sven Mørch and Barbara Stalder (Chapter Eleven) is the tension between *employability* and *competence*, two concepts that have recently come onto the European policy agenda. At first sight, policy documents operate with the assumption that both of these concepts are compatible, with competence being a necessary prerequisite of employability. With a more detailed second appraisal, however, it can be shown that employability, as a labour market-related concept in most interpretations, is understood as an adaptation of the workforce to labour market demands, while competence is related to a more holistic view of individual capacity building and identity work. The authors of this chapter broaden the perspective in two directions, arguing that both social modernisation and individual personal development have to be considered as the necessary context for the conceptualisation of competence and employability.

The European discourse on lifelong learning and competence has increasingly referred to the potentials of *informal learning* as being broader with regard to both contents and access than formal education and training. The recognition of informal learning is seen, on the one hand, as a means for democratisation and equal opportunities. On the other hand, its connection to individual everyday life, with both its pragmatism and subjective meaningfulness, means that it constitutes a potential key to young people's motivation.

By drawing on this discourse, José Machado Pais and Axel Pohl (Chapter Twelve) reflect on the properties of informal learning and on the implications of recognising informal learning in a wider social context in a way that makes it a valuable resource of social integration. While they acknowledge approaches to validate job experiences in terms of vocational training, they are concerned about the limitations of the formal system of education and training and its bias against the recognition of the learning potentials of young people's everyday lives.

Flexibilisation is one of the major catchwords in all policy sectors related to young people's transitions to work: labour market, education and training, and even schemes for disadvantaged and/or unemployed youth. Flexibilisation is expected to increase access options and to allow for tailor-made pathways. Yet, both the driving factors behind the call for flexibility and the effects on labour markets, education and training suggest that flexibilisation is inseparable from increasing uncertainty and insecurity. In this context, Barbara Stauber, Siyka Kovacheva and Harm van Lieshout (Chapter Thirteen) ask how flexibility and security may be rebalanced in order to combine an increase of access options that meet young people's needs without at the same time making them individually responsible for coping with the respective risks of precariousness. Drawing on examples and experiences from different national contexts, and in particular Dutch temporary work regulations, they question the potential of 'flexicurity' to lead a way out of this dilemma.

The book concludes with a critical analysis by René Bendit and Dermot Stokes (Chapter Fourteen) of the notion of 'disadvantaged youth'. In the studies presented in the second part of the book and in most of research reports on transition-related risks, the specific needs of the most disadvantaged young people are highlighted and connected with the call for specific measures to address this group. However, the notion of 'disadvantaged youth' often serves to hide rather than to explain who is affected by transition risks, something that makes it difficult to address such risks adequately. In this regard, policy actors relate young people's vulnerability in transitions to work to the social construction of disadvantage through modes of ascription and compensation. For this purpose, the authors take up the distinction between structural and individual factors of vulnerability as suggested by López Blasco and du Bois-Reymond in Chapter Two. Before this background, they analyse recent policy and practice trends that are related to meeting the needs of the 'most disadvantaged' young people. This includes local partnerships and networks as well as holistic approaches addressing the whole person – something that requires increased funding rather than the curtailing of such programmes as is currently being experienced in most contexts across Europe. They also address the issue of the way in which specific policy approaches for the disadvantaged often also entail the risk of stigmatisation and demotivation.

As one participant of the conference upon which this book is based put it,

"Integrated transition policies require integrated transition research", and we hope that *Young people and contradictions of inclusion* makes some steps in this direction. One could continue that the dialogue between research and policy needs to be further integrated into the design and implementation of both transition policies and transition research.

In order to avoid misleading paths to traps and the dead ends of social exclusion, policies require constant feedback on their effects and efficacy. What is even more important, however, is that researchers and policy makers need to develop and to apply instruments – research methods as well as institutional mechanisms – by which the voices of the subjects concerned – that is, active young men and women – are heard and become relevant in evaluating the adequacy of existing policies.

Notes

[1] Interestingly, even scholars of such high reputation as Pierre Bourdieu, Ulrich Beck and Anthony Giddens have to face a loss of scientific credibility due to their involvement in politics and social movements, and therefore in discourses that, necessarily, do not take place on the 'heights' of scientific debate.

[2] Special thanks go to John Tibbitt, Senior Research Officer at the Scottish Executive, Enterprise and Lifelong Learning Department, Analytical Services Division.

References

EC (European Commission) (2001) *A new impetus for European youth*, White Paper (www.europa.eu.int/comm/education/youth.html).

European Council (1997) *Luxembourg Employment Summit of the European Council: Presidency conclusions* (www.europa.eu.int).

Goffman, E. (1962) 'On "cooling the mark out": some aspects of adaptation and failure', in A. Rose (ed) *Human behaviour and social processes*, Boston, MA: Houghton, pp 482-505.

Habermas, J. (1987) *Theory of communicative action*, Boston, MA: Beacon Press.

Kronauer, M. (1998) '"Social exclusion" and "underclass" – new concepts for the analysis of poverty', in H.-J. Andreß (ed) *Empirical poverty research in a comparative perspective*, Aldershot: Ashgate, pp 51-75.

Lødemel, I. and Trickey, H. (eds) (2001) *'An offer you can't refuse': Workfare in international perspective*, Bristol: The Policy Press.

Manninen, J. (1998) 'Labour market training strategies in late modern society', in A. Walther and B. Stauber (eds) *Lifelong learning in Europe, vol 1: Options for the integration of living, learning and working*, Tübingen: Neuling, pp 75-86.

Rifkin, J. (2000) *The age of access: The new culture of hypercapitalism, where all of life is a paid-for experience*, New York, NY: GP Putnam's Sons.

van Berkel, R. and Hornemann Møller, I. (eds) (2002) *Active social policies in the EU: Inclusion through participation?*, Bristol: The Policy Press.

Walther, A., Stauber, B., Biggart, A., du Bois-Reymond, M., Furlong, A., López Blasco, A., Mørch, S. and Pais, J.M. (eds) (2002a) *Misleading trajectories: Integration policies for young adults in Europe?*, Opladen: Leske+Budrich.

Walther, A., Mørch Hejl, G. and Bechmann Jensen, T. (2002b) *Youth transitions, youth policies and participation*, YOYO Project Working Paper 1 (www.iris-egris.de/yoyo).

Part One:
Risks and contradictions in young people's transitions to work

Yo-yo transitions and misleading trajectories: towards Integrated Transition Policies for young adults in Europe

Manuela du Bois-Reymond and Andreu López Blasco

Introduction

It is a normal facet of intergenerational relationships that adults complain that young people have changed compared to when they were young. Karl Mannheim (1970) described this as social conflict that arises from the different horizons and experiences separating generational layers, something that plays a key contributing role in social innovation. In this chapter, we argue that, in late modern societies, these changes are profound, perhaps more so than the older generation and the societal institutions they administrate have realised thus far. Hence, public policies persistently fail to address young people. We start from the hypothesis that young people's transitions to adulthood are undergoing a process of destandardisation, while institutions and policies addressing such transitions continue to assume a linear life-course model in which social integration is equivalent to labour market integration.

The chapter is based on the work of the European Group for Integrated Social Research (EGRIS) and particularly on the EU-funded project 'Misleading trajectories'[1]. It consists of three main sections. First, it outlines some general aspects and elements of the changes that have affected youth transitions during the past few decades. The second section concentrates on the relationship between young people's transitions and education and training, welfare and labour market policies. By simply reducing their perspective to school-to-work transitions and still assuming that 'normal' transitions are structured in a linear manner, such policies increasingly cause 'misleading trajectories'; that is, policies that intend to lead young people towards social integration but instead (re)produce social exclusion. Third, and finally, it suggests a new policy approach that takes these changes and risks into consideration: Integrated Transition Policies (ITPs), which attempt to overcome compartmentalisation and fragmentation in order better to deal with the complexity of contemporary young adults' lives.

Destandardisation of transitions: from linearity towards uncertainty

Over a number of years, a branch of social research has developed that is concerned with investigating young people in a comparative European perspective. In these studies, one can perceive some changes in what has come to be called the 'sociology of youth'. In the industrial era, the 'model of youth' has been conceptualised as a moratorium that follows childhood as a preparation for adult status. The transition from childhood to adulthood was perceived as a linear process resulting in gender-specific normal biographies structured by paid work for men and by the role of housewife and mother for women. In the last two decades, however, youth studies have made a decisive break with this model of a supposed 'natural' arrival in adult life after childhood and youth. Youth is now not only conceived as a phase in the life course, but also a life condition that is marked by unpredictability, vulnerability and reversibility (Cavalli and Galland, 1995; Bynner et al, 1997; Walther et al, 1999; Coté, 2002; Plug et al, 2003). Moreover, it has been recognised that, if we talk about youth, we must talk about very different situations and conditions. This talk must not only account for gender, class, ethnic groups or – in the European perspective – national contexts. It must also account for the fragmentation and individualisation of youth in terms of the weakening of collective patterns of socialisation and increasing self-responsibility, which does not mean less social inequality (Beck, 1992). Transitions have become uncertain, as the destandardisation of 'normal' standardised transition models – which contributed to reliability and predictability – reveals the end of the linear relationship of cause and effect, of before and after (Pais, 2002; Walther et al, 2002a).

At the same time, this new perspective has also been reflected by policy actors who, rhetorically at least, have taken notice of respective research findings. In its White Paper, *A new impetus for European youth*, the EC (2001) refers to three challenges concerning the analysis of the situation of young people as well as policies and interventions addressing young people:

> First, youth is lasting longer. Demographers have observed that, under pressure from economic factors (employability, unemployment, and so on) and socio-cultural factors, young people are, on average, older when they reach the various stages of life: end of formal education, start of employment, starting a family, and so on. A second point concerns non-linear paths through life. Today "our various life-roles are becoming confused" (Commissariat Général du Plan, 2001, p 33): it is possible simultaneously to be a student, have family responsibilities, have a job, be seeking a job and be living with one's parents, and young people now move increasingly often between these different roles. Paths through life are becoming less linear as societies no longer offer

the same guarantees (for example through job security, social security benefits). Third, the traditional collective models are losing ground as personal pathways are becoming increasingly individualised. "The organisation of individuals' family, marriage and career plans is no longer standardised" (Commissariat Général du Plan, 2001, p 35). This is impacting particularly strongly on public authorities' policies. (EC, 2001, p 9)

What do these challenges mean for the concept of youth and what are the repercussions on the policies addressing young people and their transitions to adulthood?

Youth as a socially organised phase in the life course

While, for a long time, youth has been conceptualised primarily as a socially organised life phase structured by conditions offered to young people (such as education, training, housing, welfare), the perspective of destandardisation increasingly focuses on the use that young people make of these conditions, individually and collectively. Young people are not simply determined by their society, nor are they mere 'objects' of socialisation. They are real actors who handle or at least influence the conditions of their lives (Gillis, 1981; Hurrelmann, 1993; Mørch, 1997). Young people behave in specific self-determined ways; they use certain biographical, economic, social and cultural resources. Hence, we can talk about 'youth' and 'youth life' as metaphors of different realities, and we must also apply other criteria such as gender, urban or rural environment, social class, cultural traditions and geographical regions to distinguish ways, styles and conditions of life. Due to the blurring of categories such as age, cohort and generation, the discussions focus on the *social construction* of youth. Age is no longer the fundamental parameter to distinguish one life phase from another; rather, more stress is laid on the condition under which transitions to adult life take place. Being 25 years old nowadays is not only different from 30 or 50 years ago: it also means different perspectives and conditions for different individuals.

Nevertheless, defining youth in terms of age is still usual in determining youth and transition-related policies. However, age limits do not only vary between countries but also depend on policy areas which leads to contradictions: in the educational framework young people are considered as adults when they have finished school and have learned a profession. In a work-related environment, they are considered as 'young' (unemployed) until the age of 25 in most European countries. As a consequence, young unemployed or young workers get half the benefits or wages of adults. The current definitions of youth adopted by the EU and its member states cover groups from 15 to 25 years or, in some cases, from 14 to 29 years. Regarding this extended interval of age, sociologists have preferred to subdivide the youth phase into 'adolescence', 'post-adolescence' and 'young adults', thus giving more leeway to each stage and allowing for the overlapping and blurring of age brackets. Policies, however, are still designed according to rigid age norms, especially concerning employment, education and welfare.

Normally, young people would not conceive of themselves in such terms either. It may rather be an important aspect of youth life to sequentially integrate oneself into these different institutional areas one after the other. In the recent past and especially in countries without a system of extended education and training such as Spain or the UK, the majority of young people tried to enter the labour market once they had completed education. This step was considered the last link of a chain that integrates the individual in society and was seen, therefore, as equivalent to taking part in the 'welfare' of the society. In the context of destandardised transitions, however, it becomes difficult for young people to feel either young or adult (du Bois-Reymond et al, 2002). Consequently, the concept of 'young adults' has become widespread and may extend until 35 years (Walther et al, 1999). The traditional dualism of young versus old, youth versus adult, student versus non-student, inactive versus active (in terms of employment), single versus married has been dissolved and substituted by a wide variety of intermediate and reversible transitory stages.

From linear status passages to yo-yo transitions

The concept of transition highlights the acquisition of abilities and rights associated with adult life and status. Here, personal development and individuation are viewed as processes that are based on learning and related to the internalisation of cultural and social rules that in turn are required to become a recognised member of society with all its consequences. This transition and socialisation process has been progressively extended into rather complex forms in current post-Fordist societies. The diversification of pathways to adulthood – a trend that in a more general perspective is referred to as 'individualisation' and pluralisation (Beck, 1992) – results from an extension of compulsory and post-compulsory education on the one hand, and the spread and variety of youth cultures and consumerism on the other (Mørch, 1999; Vinken, 2003). The concept of individualisation stresses that it is the young person who has to build his or her own biography without being able to rely on stable contexts or traditions. When the transition to adulthood changes from normality to uncertainty, young people are increasingly put under pressure. They must make individual choices in matters related to education and employment, as well as leisure, that may be of great influence in their futures, without being able to foresee the implications of their choices. Young people must make the right decisions and because of the increasing plurality of options in society they have to reflect about them and justify them (du Bois-Reymond, 1998). Taking decisions bears the risk of being wrong and as a result being socially excluded. Coping with uncertainties has become a new task in the transition to adulthood, aggravated by its prolongation: for many years now, young males and females do not know where they will end up with regard to work, housing, relational and other obligations. Individualisation does not mean, however, that the social structure in terms of origins and opportunities has become unimportant. Social inequality in resources and opportunities persists through individualised trajectories and leads to broader or narrower biographical options. The ability of the individual to negotiate his or her transition to adult life depends to a large extent on cultural knowledge, the support received by the family and the opportunities or restrictions related to education, gender and social (and ethnic) origin. These diverse constellations lead to different forms of *yo-yo transitions* (Pais, 1996; du Bois-Reymond, 1998):

- young adults with limited resources who are forced to switch between precarious jobs, unemployment and remedial training schemes;
- young adults with considerable resources who are free to make choices according to their needs and preferences;
- young adults who would like to try out new solutions in the combination of working and learning but are forced to submit their occupational and learning wishes to standardised and restricted vocational pathways;
- young adults who are forced into prolonged dependency on parental support because of insufficient social security in case of unemployment.

Nevertheless, we can observe that diversification and individualisation contribute to social change. This change is not only reflected in the emancipation process of young people, but also in their aspirations and demands. The result is an array of different situations, different opportunities, different spaces and environments that were sequentially organised before, and now appear as superimposed, interchangeable, progressive and regressive at the same time.

Transitions are not linear any more, in the sense of

education ➡ employment ➡ marriage ➡ children.

Rather, they can also be synchronised:

education + employment

or reversible, as in the movement of a yo-yo:

education ⬌ employment.

Many young people experience reversible steps in the process of transition: today they are trained, tomorrow they will find a temporary job that will keep them employed for some time; they will lose it on their way towards adulthood and will be led to a period of unemployment that may take them on to further training or to another (temporary) job. These are typical itineraries that reveal the phenomena of reversibility. Individual trajectories may turn from an advantageous direction into a negative and unexpected turn because of

Figure 2.1: From linear to yo-yo transitions

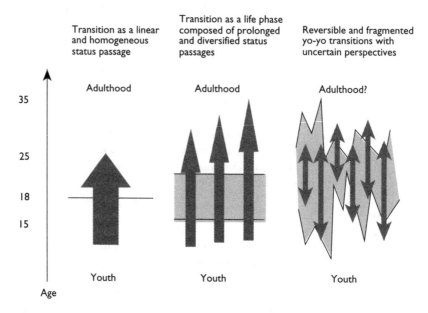

Source: Walther et al (2002a)

disadvantageous labour market developments or personal circumstances. At the same time, however, and yet less often, it can also happen that a young person compensates for his or her low educational level with invention, leading to a successful career. Figure 2.1 illustrates the recent changes in conceptualising youth transitions.

Individualisation of transitions means that young people's subjectivity gains increased importance, as decisions have to be taken to generate reliable collective patterns that fit into their personal life situations and experience. Prolongation and diversification of trajectories have decoupled the transitions that young people go through. While the institutional perspective focuses on the transition from school to work, transitions occur as well from family to independence, partnership and sexuality, from peer groups and youth culture to individual life styles, from child status to adult citizenship and so on. Fragmented transitions follow different timetables and have a variety of different rationales. They indicate the shift from modern to late modern or post-modern societies (Bauman, 1995). Young people must reconcile the different aspects of these broken or otherwise disrupted trajectories which tend to fall apart but which are nevertheless interlinked within their own biographies (EGRIS, 2001).

The concept of *biographisation*, which has been developed in the context of the debate on lifelong learning (Alheit, 1995), refers to increasing *reflexivity* in decision making and coping strategies: the young person constantly needs to assess the fit between individual needs and orientations and external demands

(Böhnisch, 1997; Beck and Bonß, 2001). Young people experience their transition period as an integral part of their life and are not willing to accept the instrumental measures of labour market integration that alienate them from their everyday lives and life plans. In young people's perception, the transition to work is linked with all the other decisions they take, or want to take: for example, where to live and with whom, what kind of work corresponds to their capacities and interests, and how they might continue with education while working.

Due to its comprehensiveness, the biographic perspective is a useful key to the *gender* dimension: young women have in some cases similar but in others different needs and wishes from young males concerning their educational and vocational or professional careers. The reconciliation of family and career poses a problem to all young European females, not only when they are actually confronted with that problem but even at the point when they begin to make educational and professional choices (Matthijs, 1998).

Biographisation is the other side of the coin of 'yo-yo-isation', in that it points to the internal processes of coping with new opportunities and new risks – and how to make sense of this intricate relationship in one's own life. As the 'normal biography' with clear gender and class roles and perspectives fades away, young men and women have to make decisions and legitimise their choices. This pressure is especially demanding for those who face precarious work trajectories. However, biographisation also refers to the manifold turning points in the lives of late modern subjects that make self-evaluation a constant task: why have I decided to do this instead of X? Should I have not done Y? Now I will have to Z, and so on. In sum, biographisation is in itself a complex and diverse notion that needs elaborate analysis, depending on the context within which it is situated. This is not only true for researchers, but is especially true for makers of adequate transition policies.

While biographisation is part of modernisation, it does not follow that this development occurs in each European country and region in the same way and with the same results. Differences with regard to the fundamental structural changes in transitions affect the forms and lifestyles young men and women develop. For example, it is undisputed that young women all over Europe are concerned with the problem how to reconcile family tasks with professional ambitions and job demands. Yet, research also shows great differences between countries, cultural and religious contexts, as well as individual preferences concerning this question. One obvious example is the difference between high rates of female employment in Northern Europe and low rates in Southern Europe stemming from different labour market structures. Another difference that is constitutive for the phenomenon of young adults is that young adults in Southern Europe live with their parents for longer and start building a family without being married less frequently than do their contemporaries in Western European countries (Biggart et al, 2002a). Such differences reflect variations in labour market structures, social policies and the relation between family regimes and education. This is especially important with regard to the support young people receive to cope with uncertain and insecure yo-yo transitions: in Southern Europe, it is the family; in the North it is the welfare state. However, as welfare provisions are currently shrinking and are increasingly tied to obligations in northern countries, the family is in fact being reconstructed as the main resource and safety net where young people go – or stay – when they have no job. Increasingly, young people in Europe are held in dependency or in an increasing variety of forms of semi-dependency for increasingly long periods of time (van de Velde, 2001; Walther et al, 2002a)[2].

The next part of this chapter deals with differences in education and training systems. It asks whether or not they provide sufficient and adequate structures for prolonged and destandardised transitions; do structural deficits reduce transitions to mere waiting phases?

Misleading trajectories

In spite of research findings that show non-linear yo-yo-isation of transitions, transition policies tend to *restandardise* young people's transitions. They create a fiction, or a:

> logical line of linearity that is not adjusted to the non-linear trajectories [that is, yo-to] existing in the life course of many young people. Many of these policies tend to create an artificial order in a social structure which is naturally chaotic. (Pais, 2002, p 88)

This means that the condition of young adults is constituted by being neglected and passed over by policies. This discrepancy between yo-yo transitions and the normal biography assumed by the institutions of transition systems leads to what in the framework of the EGRIS network has been conceptualised and analysed as 'misleading trajectories': (policy) structures that intend and promise to lead young people to social integration by way of counselling, education, training, welfare and labour market policies but in fact reproduce or reinforce the risk of social exclusion. Youth and labour market research gives evidence that many young people make (or are forced to make) educational choices that do not lead to stable jobs and to a socially accepted status; others drop out from schemes or withdraw from the system altogether and prefer a 'status zero' to what they experience as alienation and humiliation. This research is concerned with the effects of uncertainties and risks on young people's transitions in contemporary European societies and its implications for national and European transition policy agendas (Walther et al, 2002a).

Misleading trajectories in comparative perspective

As is the case with the destandardisation of transitions, we find in addition to general trends towards misleading trajectories across Europe differences between countries as well. A starting point for comparative analysis is the distinction of four broad types of school-to-work-trajectories that differ in status, qualification level and degree of precariousness:

- *unskilled trajectories* (labour market entry directly after compulsory school or after dropping out of post-compulsory education, including participation in remedial schemes that are mere 'waiting loops');
- *semi-skilled trajectories* (post-compulsory school and training qualifications that have no career value either for not being in tune with labour market demands or for the low quality of training);
- *skilled (vocational) trajectories* ([specialised] qualifications from post-compulsory [vocational] education or vocational training routes corresponding to relevant skilled occupational sectors in the labour market);
- *academic trajectories* (higher education certificates leading into highly skilled professional positions).

In terms of overall trends, it is probably the semi-skilled and academic trajectories that show the highest growth rates. Misleading trajectories are most likely in unskilled trajectories, although semi-skilled trajectories bear great risks of unemployment and social exclusion as well. In contrast, skilled and academic trajectories are more likely to result in well-paid, high-status and protected occupational positions without being a guarantee for a permanent safe and successful social position, however.

Apart from this *institutional perspective*, the 'Misleading trajectories' project aimed to include a *biographical perspective* in the analysis of young people's transitions to work. As a working hypothesis, *misleading* policies and trajectories were those that:

- do not take into account young adults' subjective perspectives by conflating social integration with labour market integration;
- function as 'containers' aimed at keeping young people off the street and lead to 'scheme careers' instead of helping young persons to build their own careers;
- disguise the structural misfit between the educational system and the labour market by personalising the problem of insufficient work and by defining problem groups who can be blamed for structural deficits (the scapegoat function);
- demotivate young people by demanding ever more education while at the same time not being able to make education worthwhile;
- regulate access to support according to bureaucratic criteria such as age, duration of unemployment, nationality, or gender rather than with regard to individual needs.

National differences between transition systems are accountable to different labour market structures, different education and training systems, different systems of social security and social protection, and of course different labour market policies for young people. What is clearly a risk trajectory in one country need not necessarily be so in another. For example, a Spanish university student has much less opportunity than a Dutch one to follow an academic career due to fewer academic jobs being available in Spain; thus he or she risks being over-qualified in an unskilled job with a fixed-term contract; in the UK semi-skilled young people have more chances of finding work than in Germany because of different job entry requirements. As mentioned before, countries also vary widely in how gender relations are perceived and dealt with. The same applies to policies concerning ethnic minority groups which vary according to the political will to provide equal opportunities and to the capability (especially of education systems) to deal with cultural differences. Finally, it is significant that social security should be constructed in such a way that young people with discontinuous careers are either protected (which seems to be especially the case in Scandinavian countries such as Denmark) or denied access to social security at all (as in Mediterranean countries such as Italy).

The method of comparative analysis developed and applied by the EGRIS network was to establish cross-country working groups consisting of three or four country teams:

- UK, Italy, West Germany;
- Denmark, Spain, East Germany;
- the Netherlands, Portugal, Ireland, immigrant youth in Germany.

The rationale of the group composition was to maximise differences of transition systems in order to engage in processes aimed at properly understanding structural differences and their consequences for young people's biographies. Comparative analysis was based on secondary analysis and literature reports and the groups were free to develop their own approach and perspective. The resulting group reports will be summarised in the following sections.

Misleading trajectories between flexibility and standardisation: UK, Italy and West Germany

On the basis of an inductive comparison of national research data, the group including the UK, Italy and West Germany arrived at three different interpretations of misleading trajectories:

- lack of social mobility and equality of opportunity for working-class youth (UK);
- lack of security due to a structural deficit between school and the labour market-making young adults dependent on the family (Italy);
- lack of individual choice due to cooling-out mechanisms in schemes for those who fail to pass the highly selective school system (West Germany).

In the UK, the transition system is structured by considerable flexibility, allowing for individual entry and exit options as well as the combination of, and shifting between routes. At the same time, however, risks are individualised and workfare policies put pressure on young people. Unskilled young people with working-class backgrounds and from deprived areas depend more directly on local labour market dynamics and may be forced into 'bad jobs'. In contrast, the West German transition system is highly standardised due to its much-praised dual system of apprenticeship. Opposing its many advantages – well-defined training, for instance – are, however, the disadvantages: a decline of training supply due to the lack of flexible adaptation of the dual system to the changing needs of the labour market. There is also the negative effect of clustering training, especially in manufacturing professions. Due to the lack of training in service jobs, young women especially feel pushed to choose training courses that are 'typically female', like hairdressing and sales. Young people who do not succeed in the highly selective school system (see the results of PISA; OECD, 2001) are pushed into pre-vocational schemes that do not provide them with recognised and accredited qualifications or into training courses that do not correspond to current labour market developments. A lack of individual choice leads to cooling-out mechanisms. Thus, in a system traditionally structured by a high share of skilled labour, the unskilled and semi-skilled trajectories increase significantly. Italy's situation must be located somewhere between the UK and Germany. Flexibility here is an unintended result of a structural deficit as regards transitions deriving from the misfit between school and labour market and the lack of access to social security. Young Italians are forced into prolonged dependency on their families, providing them with security and channelling them into jobs via family networks. The analysis of the relationship between flexibility and standardisation appeared to be crucial in identifying misleading trajectories, not only in these countries but in others as well (Biggart et al, 2002b).

Misleading trajectories by educational plans in segmented societies: Denmark, Spain and East Germany

The second group, representing Denmark, Spain and East Germany, moved in a deductive direction from the theoretical notion of segmented societies that they applied to the transition systems in question. Segmented societies are defined by occupational sectors differing with regard to their distance or proximity to the centre of qualified work. In a segmented society, young people move between the nucleus of qualified occupations and areas of social exclusion, and the model of youth transitions follows the educational logic of modern societies (see Chapter Three of this volume).

Modernisation in north-west European countries is almost synonymous with opening up the educational system for each and every person. A class-bound system over time has changed into a meritocratic system with new mechanisms of selection and allocation. Since the 1960s and 1970s, the meritocratic school has taken the lead and has shaped youth life and youth trajectories profoundly (see also Young, 1998). Supported by a dynamic labour market that demands qualified labour, 'education for all' in Denmark refers to, and is utilised to construct, individualised trajectories. In East Germany, the introduction of the West German dual-training system after the fall of the Berlin Wall is counteracted by a lack of jobs due to the thorough and still ongoing restructuring of the labour market. For young people, this means increasing frustration since they cannot invest their educational capital into careers. Many young people are kept in waiting loops or have to accept employment schemes for which they are over-qualified. Youth work and social security increasingly take the role of *secondary integration* (Böhnisch, 1994), yet without succeeding in providing the recognition and status of skilled work. In Spain, the situation is in some respects similar to Italy, where education and the family function as waiting halls for young people until they can enter the labour market (or not). Apart from general lack of work, the Spanish labour market continues to demand low-skilled labour; therefore, many young people are over-qualified.

When work is regarded as central in society as well as in the individual biography, lack of work and mismatch between education and labour market lead to tensions affecting individuals' identities as well as social cohesion. Educational and youth work measures are needed to prevent social exclusion by allowing for and helping to develop diversified and individualised trajectories (Böhnisch et al, 2002).

Misleading trajectories as contradiction between modernised transitions and disadvantage policies: Ireland, the Netherlands, Portugal and young immigrants in Germany

The group comparing Ireland, the Netherlands, Portugal and the situation of young immigrants in Germany adopted an intermediate approach by developing sensitising concepts: education, labour market, definition of youth, support, and disadvantage policies. Despite national and cultural differences, corresponding types of 'disadvantaged trajectories' were found in all four countries, threatening young people with, or actually leading to, social exclusion. Structural misleading elements emerged from the respective educational systems and programmes for the unemployed, which we have discussed already: vocational schemes leading to precarious jobs or unemployment; educational and labour market demands forcing young people to make choices that do not correspond to their subjective needs and interests. Overall, the misfit between education and labour market is especially detrimental to young immigrants and members of ethnic minority groups (especially Turkish, Moroccan and Surinamese youth in the Netherlands; young people from Turkey, former Yugoslavia as well as Russia, Ukraine, or Kazakhstan in Germany; youth with a Roma or African background in Portugal; travellers in Ireland). Although there is a tendency in all European countries to blame the individual for structural deficits, this is even more the case when it comes to immigrants and other minority groups. While there are countries where high overall unemployment rates prevent individuals from feeling guilty, as, for example, Italy and Spain, this is different for migrants and other minorities: they are held responsible for their disadvantaged social position, apparently due to a supposed lack of will to integrate (integration being most often interpreted in political terms of assimilation). Language difficulties, poor family support, traditional and gender-specific biographic perspectives and hidden as well as blunt discrimination by employers are real or ascribed obstacles for these young people making as much use of the educational system as indigenous youth. With regard to these groups of young people, transition systems produce, almost by definition, misleading trajectories in *all* contemporary European countries, be they economically advanced or relatively backward. Mechanisms channelling these groups onto tracks which do not lead anywhere in modern societies are important keys to the general conditions of social integration and social exclusion (Plug et al, 2002).

Subjective and systemic risks of social exclusion

In general terms, the identification of misleading trajectories requires a distinction to be made between systemic and subjective dimensions of social integration or exclusion. In a *systemic perspective*, qualifications and skilled jobs are indispensable assets of successful social integration. Furthermore, in a *subjective* perspective, social integration of trajectories is experienced as satisfaction. Trajectories missing one of the two – systemic success or subjective satisfaction – have to be considered as potentially misleading. Success without satisfaction may lead to dropping out, while satisfaction without success may work out in the short term but will run out of resources in the mid to long-term (Walther et al, 2002a). The systemic and subjective dimensions of integration coincided quite well in Fordist societies when the orientation towards the normal biography dominated. The demands of the system as to education and work fitted into subjective life plans, and it was felt by most members of society – young and old, men and women alike – that both dimensions were achievable. By contrast, post-Fordist societies develop a growing cleavage between the logic of education and training, the work and labour market systems, and the subjective perspectives and needs of (young) people. The change from Fordist to post-Fordist societies, with blue-collar work disappearing (or handed down to immigrant workers) and increasing emphasis on education and qualifications, leads to growing numbers of young people who do not meet the new requirements and are in danger of being excluded from social integration through stable jobs and family building.

Transition policies, however, tend to neglect the relevance of the subjective dimensions of social integration. The most common interpretation of 'transition problems' is that of the *disadvantages* of the young people showing such problems. However, there are considerable differences in how disadvantages are constructed and compensated for. The following scheme represents four different policy conceptualising and addressing disadvantage by different combinations of individual and structural factors.

Disadvantage as individual deficits (Field 1 of Table 2.1)

The first field of Table 2.1 relates to policies that ascribe failing social integration to individual deficits: lack of (or wrong) qualifications, learning disabilities, language problems, inadequate social behaviour, or dependency on welfare benefits. Such deficits may be real, as in the case of a physically disabled person. They may also be constructed by selective education and training and hard competition for a decreasing number of recognised occupational and social positions. Policy measures concentrate on traditional or modernised compensatory education and/or workfare (see especially Chapter Six of this volume). It is the individual who is held responsible for his or her inability to cope with risks, and the solutions that are offered do not aim to alter the system but are designed to reduce frictions on an individual basis. An example would be a young Moroccan male in the Netherlands who has failed in lower vocational school and has been in and out of the labour market for a couple of years. Eventually, he becomes unemployed and gets involved in criminal acts. In order to prevent further marginalisation, a special reintegration trajectory is worked out in cooperation with educational and youth welfare institutions. This reintegration trajectory is costly – requiring a welfare state that is able and willing to invest – but not very efficient, and the system as such does not change through the policy measures. In some cases, such measures may help

Table 2.1: Modes of constructing disadvantage in youth transitions

Consequences (policies) of disadvantage / Ascription of disadvantage	Individualising Deficit-oriented (adaptation to selection)	Structure-related Widening (or alternative) pathways of integration
Individual deficits	1. Compensatory pre-vocational measures; workfare policies	2. Broadened access to recognised education, training, and employment
Structural barriers	3. Compensatory pre-vocational measures; workfare policies; reorientation	4. Job creation through subsidised work; employment in the public sector or assistance of self-employment

Cooling out [   ] Empowering

Source: Walther et al (2002a)

the individuals concerned but they imply that others remain excluded – in effect, they simply change the order in the queue.

Structural approaches towards individual deficits (Field 2)

In this case, deficits are still ascribed individually but solutions do not depend solely on individual compensation and adaptation. Regular education and training are structured in a way that disadvantaged young people may succeed, or else government subsidies are given to create working places for less competitive young people. On the one hand, this means broader entrance options to the transition system, while on the other, availability of individualised support for those with greater difficulties. An example of this constellation is Danish Open Youth Education (which has since been closed by Denmark's conservative government), which gives demotivated students a second chance to obtain a qualification by tailoring education to their subjective needs and interests.

Individual adaptation to structural deficits (Field 3)

This constellation may be seen as the worst-case scenario of current transition policies. Although structural barriers such as labour market segmentation are recognised, the young persons concerned are channelled into measures that do not address these structures but force individuals to adapt and to downgrade their aspirations. An example would be a German young woman who wants to enter one of the few 'female' apprenticeship professions and, due to a lack of supply, is discouraged by the vocational counselling system and directed instead into pre-vocational training in home economics.

Structural answers to structural disadvantage (Field 4)

This is the most empowering scenario for young people in their transition period in terms of developing their competencies and providing opportunities to invest in them. Policies are aimed at removing barriers and assisting young people in progressing on their way through job creation with employers, either in the public sector or through self-employment. Such policies aim not only at short-term relief, but also at long-term solutions to structural shortcomings. New developments in the field of learning are incorporated into this approach, for example promoting dual trajectories of learning and working for young adults who want to upgrade their level of qualification, giving both subsidies and counselling for self-employment and enterprise creation, and recognising alternative forms of learning like non-formal and peer learning.

When one looks at the countries analysed, one finds all types of measures represented in Table 2.1's scheme in transition policies, yet to a different extent and with national and cultural modifications. We find pre-vocational measures to be very important in Germany, Denmark and the Netherlands. Workfare is especially relevant in the UK, but also in the Netherlands and Denmark; broader access to regular education and training features in Denmark, and to a lesser extent Ireland and the UK. Interestingly, approaches like assistance with self-employment, despite not being implemented systematically, prevail in contexts with a substantial lack of transition structures where high youth unemployment sets 'natural' limits to individualised ascriptions of disadvantage, as is the case in the Mediterranean countries. Moreover, job creation through incentives for employers and public employment schemes is also important in Eastern Germany, while in Southern Europe we find the most comprehensive reform plans for transition systems including education, training and labour market policies. Paradoxically, the extension and institutionalisation of transition systems through the subsequent differentiation according to target groups contributes to a shift from structure-related to individualising approaches.

Towards Integrated Transition Policies: conclusions in European perspective

Throughout this chapter, we have argued that transition policies that are to meet the requirements of post-Fordist societies must adopt a more holistic stance. Systemic and subjective dimensions of social integration have to be considered in relation to each other and attention has to be drawn not only to labour market needs, but also to individual motivations and experiences of the young persons concerned. As a result of the research on misleading trajectories, we want to suggest the concept of Integrated Transition Policies (ITPs). This means the coordination of policies that affect youth transitions in a cross-sectoral manner that starts from the individual's biographic perspective, especially policies concerned with *learning, employment* and *social support*.

Biographisation is essential in the yo-yo transitions of contemporary young people because the normal biography is eroding under the pressure of modernisation. In as much as young people are made self-responsible for their decisions, a prime objective has to be to *enable* young people to take such responsibility; *flexible support* and *active participation* in terms of real choice and influence are the main principles of ITPs. Individuals – especially children, women, pupils and immigrants – claim more rights to voice needs and frustrations and to participate in society. Across Europe, therefore, there is reference to the development of civil society; participation has become a leading principle in fighting social exclusion and guaranteeing human rights. It is the explicit aim of the EU and other European bodies to promote participation in all respects, and especially with regard to young people. In the EC's White Paper, *A new impetus for European youth* (the first document of the EU to lay down a commitment to build a framework for youth policy), the principle of participation is the most important one (EC, 2001; see also Council of Europe, 2003, for the attempt to establish youth policy indicators). However, youth policy is a policy sector in which participation is conceptualised in terms of influence and shared power, but in other sectors participation still means a rather passive attendance, such as in education and training or employment. This reflects a trend separating civil society from the welfare state and thereby undermining its integrative potential (Walther et al, 2002b). Integrated Transition Policies, therefore, may be understood as reshaping existing transition policies – especially labour market policy – in a youth policy perspective. The implications of this may be concretised with regard to learning: in knowledge-based societies the nature of learning and training has fundamentally changed. The following tendencies can be observed across Europe, albeit to varying extents depending on national and regional context:

- *From compulsory to voluntary learning:* although compulsory education is still the dominant form in education, non-formal learning and peer learning have gained in importance for the qualification of youth trajectories (Mørch, 1999; Coffield, 2000).
- *From extrinsic to intrinsic motivation:* for knowledge societies it is essential that the individuals acknowledge as early as possible that they learn for their own sake and will have to keep on learning; they have to build up a learning habitus which supports such an attitude (du Bois-Reymond, 2000; Alheit et al, 2002).
- *From exclusively learning in childhood and youth to learning throughout the lifecourse (lifelong learning):* many misleading trajectories begin in school. A learning habitus that is based on intrinsic instead of exclusively extrinsic motivation depends on learning experiences in the early school years and is further developed in the life course. *Active participation* of the learner in her or his own learning biography is therefore a prerequisite for a positive learning attitude (Alheit et al, 2000).
- *Integration of learning, working and leisure:* in as much as individuals are in charge of their own learning and working conditions, which is prominently the case with the self-employed and entrepreneurs, they tend to blur the borders between learning and working, and it is difficult for them to define when work or learning ends and leisure time begins. Under conditions of competition and precarious economies, this tendency may have negative effects on the lives of young persons such as self-exploitation and the stress resulting from the 'fear of falling' (Voß, 1998; du Bois-Reymond and Stauber, 2004: forthcoming).
- *Integration of vocational and general education:* one of the most discussed educational issues in Europe is deficits in school education, as the PISA study has pointedly shown (OECD, 2001). Young people lack general knowledge (especially in the fields of language literacy and science) and are often poorly prepared for further (higher) vocational and professional education and qualification. It seems that the traditional separation between general and vocational education is no longer adequate in post-Fordist societies.

These exemplary trends show that as the learning motivation of individuals gains in importance, they become the subjects of their own learning biographies. Such demands are posed increasingly by education and training systems while at the same time there is a lack of consciousness that individuals need to be enabled to be subjects which means to dispose of both contextual competencies ('learning to learn'; Mørch, 1999) and resources and opportunities. Moreover, these trends imply that institutions open up the learning spaces they have occupied by curricula and teaching settings that prescribe desirable learning outcomes. The individualisation of learning, therefore, requires *institutional reflexivity*. Institutions need to organise their feedback with regard to the biographical effects of their measures, accepting that what serves one person may contribute to the exclusion of another due to the subjective orientations of the young people concerned. This reflexivity is also necessary for a meaningful coordination of policies. For the central policy sectors this may have the following implications (among others):

* *Employment policies* creating jobs for young people or placing them in existing jobs or schemes must fit the lives and life plans of those for whom they are intended. This may mean support for young people to transform informal activities into paid activities or in helping them to 'sell' informally acquired skills in the labour market (see Davies, 2000). The activities of employment and work experience schemes need to be 'real' in the sense of providing, producing and selling goods and services that are in fact needed and called for by the local community; such recognition implies fair payment. A useful concept in this regard is that of *transitional labour markets* linking different activities such as education, full- and part-time employment, dependent work and self-employment, family and voluntary work in a comprehensive system (see Chapter Seven of this volume). Apart from this, *job counselling* will be more likely to be effective if organised closer to young people's life worlds and lifestyles. Institutional reflexivity in this respect means that young people are encouraged to comment upon job and training offers openly rather than keep silent for fear of losing their benefits.
* *Education and training policies* aimed at enhancing young people's skills, knowledge and competencies, as outlined earlier, should respect the fragility of their motivational careers. This also points to the acceptance of informal learning alongside formal education – despite the uncertainty regarding the outcomes of such learning processes. The starting point is the empowerment of young people's strengths instead of mere compensation for their learning deficiencies.
* *Youth policies*, especially youth work activities, in which experiences with more participatory approaches have been developed, should be acknowledged as important for the 'hard' sectors of education, training and employment, instead of being regarded and devalued as 'soft' areas of cultural and leisure-time activities. This also requires that youth work engages actively in young people's transitions to work.

- *Welfare policies* addressing young people's needs by conferring social benefits should be linked with employment, education and training policies in such a way that young people can make individual choices and have the possibility to experiment with different options (for example, young people who are tired of learning and do not use training measures but would like to do voluntary work in a foreign country). Given the fragility and precariousness of transitions, a basic income for young people while in (yo-yo) transition would increase their ability to cope productively with risks. It may also mean matching part-time or low-paid work with welfare payments to guarantee a decent living, especially in case of young parents.

As we have shown in this chapter, the transitions of young people are different across European countries and regions as a result of different educational systems, labour market conditions and welfare regimes. At the same time, young Europeans share some basic problems during their transition to adulthood and there are some overarching principles by which misleading trajectories can be identified, prevented and transformed. When one evaluates the spectrum of transition policies made and executed on the local, regional or national level in European societies, one finds a number of standard 'solutions': more education, more training schemes, more pre-vocational measures, labour market deregulation, and special treatment for minority youth. As one leaves the general level and approaches the local level, measures become more specific, geared to serve specific groups of young people in specific local labour markets. However, procedures are missing to transform 'good practices' of transition policies from the local to other contexts – they miss a *European dimension*. In that respect, the discourses developed around the EC's White Paper on youth (EC, 2001; see also IARD, 2001) and the Council of Europe (2003) may be seen as useful starting point for developing the institutional reflexivity necessary for ITPs. Rather than benchmarking processes that reduce the complexity of biographic transitions to quantitative indicators, we think of processes of intercultural communication by which national and European policy makers engage in processes of mutual learning and understanding what good practices mean, and for whom, and why they are successful in a given context[3]. The problem in research as well as in the field of transition policies is how to arrange a process of contextualisation–decontextualisation–recontextualisation in such a way that what is learnt through the analysis of particular cases/countries can be decontextualised to develop a valid theory of yo-yo transitions in contemporary societies. Such a theory may then be recontextualised to implement adequate Integrated Transition Policies.

Notes

[1] Since 1993, the EGRIS network has been concerned with analysing changing transitions between youth and adulthood. Between 1998 and 2001, it received EU funding from the Fourth Framework Programme, Targeted Socioeconomic Research,

for the thematic network 'Misleading Trajectories?' Evaluation of labour market policies for young adults in Europe' regarding non-intended effects of social exclusion, involving teams from Denmark, Germany, Ireland, Italy, Netherlands, Portugal, Spain and the UK.

[2] The EGRIS network currently conducts the project 'Families and transitions in Europe' (Fifth Framework Programme, Improving the Socioeconomic Knowledge Base, 2001-04), which investigates the role of the family in facilitating or constraining young people's life management in the transition from education to the labour market across different European models of state support for young people and their families. Teams from eight countries are involved: Bulgaria, Denmark, Germany, Italy, the Netherlands, Portugal, Spain and the UK (see www.socsci.ulster.ac.uk/policy/fate/fate.html).

[3] This is the objective of another project the EGRIS group currently is involved in – 'Youth policy and participation (YOYO): Potentials of participation and of informal learning for young people's transitions to the labour market' (2001-04) – which analyses case studies addressing young people's transitions to work in a participatory way (see www.iris-egris.de/yoyo).

References

Alheit, P. (1995) 'Biographical learning. Theoretical outline, challenges and contradictions of a new approach in adult education', in P. Alheit, A. Bron, E. Brugges and P. Dominicé (eds) *The biographical approach in European adult education*, Vienna: ESREA, pp 55-75.

Alheit, P., Becker, J., Kammler, E., Taylor, R. and Salling Olesen, H. (eds) (2000) *Lifelong learning inside and outside schools*, Collected Papers, Vol 2, Roskilde: Roskilde University, Universität Bremen, Leeds University, pp 360-75.

Alheit, P., Harney, K., Heikkinen, A., Rahn, S. and Schemmann, M. (eds) (2002) *Lifelong learning: One focus, different systems*, Frankfurt-am-Main, Berlin, Bruxelles, New York, Oxford, Wien: Peter Lang, Europäischer Verlag der Wissenschaften.

Bauman, Z. (1995) *Life in fragments: Essays in postmodern morality*, Oxford: Blackwell.

Beck, U. (1992) *Risk society: Towards a new modernity*, London: Sage Publications.

Beck, U. and Bonß, W. (eds) (2001) *Die Modernisierung der Moderne*, Frankfurt-am-Main: Suhrkamp.

Biggart, A., Bendit, R., Cairns, D., Hein, K. and Mørch, S. (2002a) *Families and transitions in Europe: State of the art report*, Working Paper, Coleraine: University of Ulster.

Biggart, A., Cuconato, M., Furlong, A., Lenzi, G., Stauber, B. and Walther, A. (2002b) 'Misleading trajectories between standardisation and flexibility – Great Britain, Italy and West Germany', in A. Walther, B. Stauber, A. Biggart, M. du Bois-Reymond, A. Furlong, A. López Blasco, S. Mørch and J.M. Pais (eds) *Misleading trajectories: Integration policies for young adults in Europe?*, Opladen: Leske+Budrich, pp 44-66.

Böhnisch, L. (1994) *Gespaltene normalität*, Weinheim and München: Juventa.

Böhnisch, L. (1997) *Sozialpädagogile de lebensalter*, Weinheim and München: Juventa.

Böhnisch, L., López Blasco, A., Mørch, M., Mørch, S., Rodrígez, J.E. and Seifert, H. (2002) 'Educational plans in segmented societies: misleading trajectories in Denmark, East Germany and Spain', in A. Walther, B. Stauber, A. Biggart, M. du Bois-Reymond, A. Furlong, A. López Blasco, S. Mørch and J.M. Pais (eds) *Misleading trajectories: Integration policies for young adults in Europe?*, Opladen: Leske+Budrich, pp 66-93.

Bynner, J., Chisholm, L. and Furlong, A. (1997) *Youth, citizenship and social change in European context*, Aldershot: Ashgate.

Cavalli, A. and Galland, O. (1995) *Youth in Europe*, London: Pinter.

Coffield, F. (ed) (2000) *The necessity of informal learning*, Bristol: The Policy Press.

Commissariat Général du Plan (2001) *Jeunesse, le devoir d'avenir*, Report from the committee chaired by Dominique Charvet, March, Paris.

Coté, J. (2002) 'The role of identity capital in the transition to adulthood: the individualisation thesis examined', *Journal of Youth Studies*, vol 5, no 2, pp 117-34.

Council of Europe (2003) *Experts on youth policy indicators: Final report*, Strasbourg: European Youth Centre.

Davies, P. (2000) 'Formalising learning: the impact of accreditation', in F. Coffield (ed) *The necessity of informal learning*, Bristol: The Policy Press, pp 54-63.

du Bois-Reymond, M. (1998) '"I don't want to commit myself yet": young people's life concepts', *Journal of Youth Studies*, vol 1, no 1, pp 63-79.

du Bois-Reymond, M. (2000) 'Trendsetters and other types of lifelong learners', in P. Alheit, J. Becker, E. Kammler, R. Taylor, and H. Salling Olesen (eds) *Lifelong learning inside and outside schools*, Collected Papers, Vol 2, Roskilde: Roskilde University, Universität Bremen, Leeds University, pp 360-75.

du Bois-Reymond, M. and Stauber, B. (2004: forthcoming) 'Biographical turning points in young people's transitions to work across Europe', in H. Helve and G. Holm (eds) *Contemporary youth research: Local expressions and global connections*, Aldershot: Ashgate.

du Bois-Reymond, M., Stauber, B., Pohl, A., Plug, W. and Walther, A. (2002) *How to avoid cooling out? Experiences of young people in their transitions to work across Europe*, YOYO Programme Working Paper 2 (www.iris-egris.de/yoyo).

EC (European Commission) (2001) *A new impetus for European youth*, White Paper (www.europa.eu.int/comm/dgs/education/youth).

EGRIS (European Group for Integrated Social Research) (2001) 'Misleading trajectories: transition dilemmas of young adults in Europe', *Journal of Youth Studies*, vol 4, no 1, pp 101-18.

Gillis, J.R. (1981) *Youth and history*, New York, NY: Academic Press.

Hurrelmann, K. (1993) *Einführung in die Sozialisationstheorie*, Weinheim: Beltz.

IARD (eds) (2001) *Study on the state of young people and youth policy in Europe* (www.europa.eu.int/comm/education/youth/studies.html).

Mannheim, K. (1970) *Wissenssoziologie*, Neuwied and Berlin: Luchterhand.

Matthijs, K. (ed) (1998) *The family: Contemporary perspectives and challenges*, Leuven: Leuven University Press.

Mørch, S. (1997) 'Youth and activity theory', in J. Bynner, L. Chisholm and A. Furlong (eds) *Youth, citizenship and social change in a European context*, Aldershot: Ashgate, pp 254-61.

Mørch, S. (1999) 'Informal learning and social contexts', in A. Walther and B. Stauber (eds) *Lifelong learning in Europe, Vol II: Differences and divisions*, Tübingen: Neuling, pp 145-71.

OECD (Organisation for Economic Co-operation and Development) (2001) *Knowledge and skills for life: First results from PISA 2000*, Paris: OECD.

Pais, J.M (1996) 'Erwachsenwerden mit Rückfahrkarte? Übergänge, biographische Scheidewege und sozialer Wandel in Portugal', in A. Walther (ed) *Junge Erwachsene in Europa – jenseits der Normalbiographie*, Opladen: Leske+Budrich, pp 75-93.

Pais, J.M. (2002) 'Laberintos de vida: paro juvenil y rutas de salida (jóvenes portugueses)', *Revista de Juventud*, vol 56 (marzo), pp 87-101.

Plug, W., Kiely, E., Hein, K., Ferreira, V.S., Bendit, R., du Bois-Reymond, M. and Pais, J.M. (2002) 'Modernised transitions and disadvantage policies: Netherlands, Portugal, Ireland and migrant youth in Germany', in A. Walther, B. Stauber, A. Biggart, M. du Bois-Reymond, A. Furlong, A. López Blasco, S. Mørch and J.M. Pais (eds) *Misleading trajectories: Integration policies for young adults in Europe?*, Opladen: Leske+Budrich, pp 94-117.

Plug, W., Zeijl, E. and du Bois-Reymond, M. (2003) 'Young people's perceptions on youth and adulthood', *Journal of Youth Studies* (June), vol 6, no 2, pp 127-45.

van de Velde, C. (2001) 'Autonomy construction in a dependence situation. Young unemployed people and family relationships in France and Spain', Paper presented at the International Conference 'Family Forms and the Young Generation in Europe', 20-22 September, University of Milano-Bicocca, Milan.

Vinken, H. (2003) 'Civic socialisation in late modernity', Paper to the workshop of the section youth sociology of the German Sociological Association, 20-22 February, Berlin.

Voß, G.G. (1998) 'Die Entgrenzung von Arbeit und Arbeitskraft. Eine subjektorientierte Interpretation des Wandels der Arbeit', *Mitteilungen aus der Arbeitsmarkt- und Berufsforschung*, vol 3/1998, pp 473-87.

Walther, A., Stauber, B., Bolay, E., du Bois-Reymond, M., Mørch, S., Pais, J.M. and Schröer, A. (1999) 'New trajectories of young adults in Europe: a research outline', in Circle for Youth Research Cooperation in Europe (CYRCE) (eds) *Intercultural Reconstruction*, European Yearbook for Youth Policy and Research, Vol 2, Berlin and New York, NY: Walter de Gruyter, pp 61-89.

Walther, A., Mørch-Hejl, G. and Bechmann Jensen, T. (2002b) *Youth transitions, youth policy and participation: State of art report*, YOYO Project Working Paper 1 (www.iris-egris.de).

Walther, A., Stauber, B., Biggart, A., du Bois-Reymond, M., Furlong, A., López Blasco, A., Mørch, S. and Pais, J.M. (eds) (2002a) *Misleading trajectories: Integration policies for young adults in Europe?*, Opladen: Leske+Budrich.

Young, M. (1998) *The curriculum of the future*, London: Falmer Press.

THREE

Youth unemployment and the risk of social exclusion: comparative analysis of qualitative data

Thomas Kieselbach

Introduction

YUSEDER

The YUSEDER[1] research project – 'Youth Unemployment and Social Exclusion: Objective Dimensions, Subjective Experiences, and Innovative Institutional Responses in Six European Countries' – tries to answer some crucial questions with regard to the risk of social exclusion associated with long-term youth unemployment. It asks for key mechanisms linking the experience of long-term youth unemployment to various dimensions of social disintegration, conceived of within the theoretical framework of social exclusion, to be put in place. In this context, not only the mechanisms exacerbating the stress of unemployment (vulnerability factors) but also the protective mechanisms preventing or reducing the risk of social exclusion have been taken into consideration. These analyses have been undertaken in three Northern European countries (Sweden, Belgium, Germany) and three Southern European countries (Spain, Italy, Greece).

The research project consisted, first, in a secondary analysis of long-term youth unemployment, social exclusion and health patterns; second, in qualitative interviews with 50 long-term unemployed young people in each country with regard to variables leading into long-term unemployment and the main factors contributing to social exclusion or inclusion; and third, in the analysis of innovative institutional responses on a local, regional and national level in various social sectors that aim to counteract the risk of social exclusion as a consequence of long-term unemployment (Kieselbach et al, 2000a, 2000b, 2001). This chapter concentrates on the qualitative part of the study concerned with the key mechanisms linking social exclusion with youth unemployment.

Development of youth unemployment

In the past 25 years, increasing rates of unemployment have been observed in all countries of the EU. This development has been deeply influenced by the worldwide economic crisis of the mid-1970s (the oil crisis) and the early 1980s. During this period, a considerable level of structural unemployment had been reached in most European countries. In the meantime, increasing globalisation, flexibilisation and worldwide economic competition have been important factors influencing the rise of unemployment rates.

In all partner countries, the extent of youth unemployment is significantly higher than the total unemployment rates with the exception of Germany, where, due to the dual education system and associated longer periods of training, the rates of young unemployed are similar to those of the adult unemployed (see Figure 3.1). However, the German labour market is characterised by a large disparity between West and East German youth. Young unemployed people between the ages of 20 and 24 years in East Germany are particularly affected by unemployment.

In Belgium, the development of youth unemployment rates has been similar to the total rates. At present, a stabilisation, or even a small improvement, can be observed. However, the rates are still two to three times higher than the overall rates; female unemployment rates are particularly high. A striking example of this situation can be found in the Wallonia region, where over 40% of all females under 25 years of age are unemployed.

Parallel to the increase in total unemployment during the early 1990s, youth unemployment in Sweden increased rapidly and equally strongly for 16- to 19-year-olds and 20- to 24-year-olds. After a slight decrease in the mid-1990s, both age group rates are currently at about 15% and thus twice as high as the overall unemployment rate. In contrast to the Belgian situation, the gender differences in Sweden are opposite: the rates are higher there among men than among women – 16.6% versus 14% (1995).

Youth unemployment figures in Greece are also considerably higher than those for adults. Well over a third of young people aged 15-19 were unemployed in 1995. Rates among young women are especially high. In 1995 the rate for young women between 15 and 24 years stood at 37.7%, compared to 19.4% for men.

In Italy, the proportion of young unemployed people constitutes two thirds of the total number of unemployed people, with lower numbers for young men (1997, 29%) than young women (1997, 37.7%). The number of Italian young people who have been looking for a job for more than 12 months is exceptionally high (approximately two thirds of the young unemployed).

Among the partner countries, Spain shows the highest rate of youth unemployment. In addition to a continuous rise during the 1970s, unemployment figures rose in the late 1970s and early 1980s to a peak value of nearly 40%. Among 16- to 19-year-olds, the rate sometimes exceeded 50%.

Figure 3.1: Overall unemployment versus youth unemployment rates (>25 years of age) for six European countries (1997) (%)

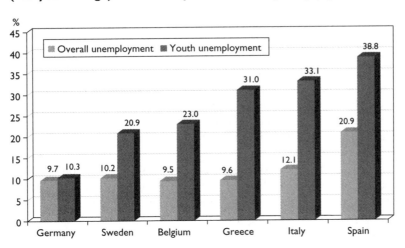

Source: Eurostat (1998)

The concept of social exclusion

In general, the term 'social exclusion' has only recently been introduced in all countries participating in this research project on a public, political and/or scientific level. Despite the increasing number of international experts, and also the interest from the EC in processes of social exclusion (for an overview see Silver, 1994/95, 1998; Starrin et al, 2000), the meaning of this concept is still rather diffuse (see Castel, 1994; Paugam, 1996). Up to now, unemployment and disadvantaged living situations have been tackled mainly by poverty research, which has focused almost exclusively on monetary aspects. Wider social problems, however, do demand a broader focus that takes non-monetary factors and more subjective dimensions into account.

For this research, therefore, the definition of social exclusion developed by Kronauer (1998) has been adopted which meets this requirement of comprehensiveness, at least on a theoretical level. Relating to the use of the term in France and the concept of 'underclass' in the US, Kronauer developed his understanding of social exclusion in light of the current employment crisis, which especially affects low-qualified manufacturing workers. In his opinion, the ever-increasing unemployment rates are becoming a permanent social reality, with the consequence that more and more people cannot lead a life that fits general societal standards for material and social wellbeing. This new quality within the cycle of unemployment and poverty requires a terminology that takes into consideration both monetary and non-monetary aspects of living, and the characteristics of the individual and the society. This broader understanding seems to have also become increasingly important with regard to young people facing unemployment (Kieselbach, 1997). Correspondingly, in this research project social exclusion is understood as a dynamic, multidimensional process that incorporates social and economic aspects of living, subjective experiences and objective situations, and depends on available personal and social resources.

Using the term 'social exclusion' easily evokes the image of a definite result that stands in opposition to social inclusion. However, social exclusion can only be understood when focusing not only on what it means to be excluded versus included, but also on those factors increasing or diminishing the vulnerability of the individual. Figure 3.2 depicts this inclusion–exclusion paradigm. The arrows stand for different hypothetical 'movements' of persons within this continuum.

Kronauer (1998) argues that, on the one side, social exclusion is always linked with unemployment, but that it can only be designated if at least both a marginal economic position and social isolation are experienced at the same time. It must be stressed, however, that this concept can only be understood by considering its multidimensionality. This means that, although unemployment seems to be a central indicator for increasing social exclusion, all possible interactions and sequences between the following six dimensions of social exclusion must be taken into account equally:

1. *Exclusion from the labour market* describes the situation of facing external barriers to (re)enter the labour market combined with a retreat of the affected person leading to resignation regarding their own (re)employment.
2. *Economic exclusion* is usually referred to as poverty and includes financial dependency upon the welfare state or a socially unacceptable income, and the loss of ability financially to support oneself or one's family.

Figure 3.2: The inclusion–exclusion paradigm

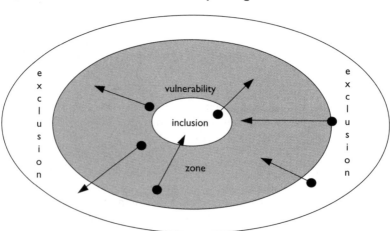

3. *Institutional exclusion* can occur from the side of the educational system (in both schools and further qualification and training institutions), institutions dealing with unemployment and poverty, and public and private service institutions (such as banks and insurance agencies). Besides the lack of support both before and during phases of unemployment, two other factors come into play: the experience of institutional dependency leading to feelings of shame and passivity, and the possible counterproductive effect of state support in the sense of the exclusion of unemployed persons through their inclusion into a stable system.

The fourth and fifth dimensions are closely linked with each other.

4. *Exclusion through social isolation* describes either a retreat of the social network or one's own retreat, which can lead to a reduction of contacts to only one specific group of people or even the general isolation of the affected person.
5. *Cultural exclusion* refers, on a societal level, to the inability to live according to socially accepted norms and values, with the possible consequence of an identification being made with deviance and abnormal behaviours. Stigmatisation and sanctions from the social surroundings are also subsumed within this dimension.
6. *Spatial exclusion* manifests itself in the objective spatial concentration of persons with limited financial possibilities often coming from a similar social and/or cultural background, and in feelings of isolation due to a missing infrastructure within the individual's residential area (such as lack of transportation, shops and cultural events).

Youth unemployment, social exclusion and health

Youth unemployment and social exclusion

In all countries participating in the study, the situation of eight different groups of disadvantaged young persons has been analysed: long-term unemployed young people, unemployed school leavers, dropouts, and young persons with low qualifications, unemployed and marginally employed young people in economically or structurally weak regions, young unemployed single mothers, (juvenile) unemployed immigrants, young unemployed persons with physical disabilities, young unemployed people facing homelessness and poverty and young unemployed criminals (Kieselbach et al, 2000a).

From the analysis of the material presented in the six national reports, it becomes obvious that the main focus regarding a specifically high risk for social exclusion among young people has been on unemployment and its economic effects. This result supports the thesis that work is one of the main mechanisms for an overall societal integration. An inability to enter the labour market in the first place must be understood as a central factor for deciding about the further development of young people. It might even be justified to say that, in the long run, 'having work versus not having work' sets the agenda for the integration into – or exclusion from – society.

One of the main reasons for exclusion from the labour market is derived from missing job qualifications, generally low job qualifications, or not-matching job qualifications. Without vocational training in line with the (future) requirements of the labour market, a lasting inclusion into work seems to be almost impossible. It is not surprising, therefore, that job qualification schemes are understood, on the one hand, to be the most effective measures against unemployment and social exclusion. However, on the other hand, the more or less exclusive focus on this type of institutional answer is slightly irritating when considering other institutions and their possible preventive influence on adolescents. In this regard, it has to be asked what better roles schools and other public and private institutions could play in preparing young persons for their future job situation and in counterbalancing and preventing social exclusion. In Greece, Italy and Spain two factors come into play that are even more important with regard to the prevention of social exclusion: the family and the submerged economy.

The main factors preceding the exclusion of youth from the labour market are increasingly described in terms of spatial processes of exclusion. Young people who have already grown up in a situation of relative poverty often have no or few qualifications, leading to multiple socialisation deficiencies. In this regard, economic exclusion is often also linked with low qualification possibilities through spatial segregation.

In both the Northern and Southern European countries of this study, work plays a central role in the developmental process of young people. The denial of access to the labour market implies foremost financial limitations meaning that for young people a dependency on the family, and because of this, the overall youth to adulthood transition phase becomes prolonged. Although family support is an important buffer, this protection might also hinder the development of the young person to become an independent adult.

This phenomenon is much more important in Southern European countries, where young people are normally not entitled to transfer payments. In Belgium, Germany, Spain and Sweden, different benefit systems exist: some are earnings-related, and apply to those who were once integrated into the labour market. In those cases where young people do not fulfil the requirements to obtain such a transfer payment they have to apply for social assistance that is not earnings-related (which, however, not in all of these countries is universally accessible). In contrast, young people in Southern European countries who have never entered the labour market are in most cases completely excluded from any type of state support. For young people, this means that families have to take on the responsibility to support their children economically.

Youth unemployment and health

Lack of work is linked not only to economic strains but also to limitations in other dimensions of living caused by economic strains. Despite the limited number of available studies and their somewhat limited level of empirical evidence (mainly cross-sectional data), the analysis of the national reports nevertheless produced relatively homogenous results on the link between youth unemployment and ill health (Kieselbach et al, 2000b). In general, it was reported that compared with their employed peers, young unemployed persons have a distinctly higher risk of health-related problems. This is especially true for mental health and psychosocial problems, leading to an increase in depression and a poorer quality of life, but also for objective health indicators especially when considering the higher risk of suicidal behaviour among the unemployed youth. This is also reflected in the health behaviour of young unemployed persons – especially with regard to alcohol and cigarette consumption. Work also has an important intrinsic value, which, when missing, can have detrimental effects on the personality of the unemployed young person. Feelings of general vulnerability, inferiority, worthlessness, uselessness and depression are common among this group, which can lead in the long run to a decrease in self-esteem and a greater dissatisfaction with life in general. Stigmatisation processes from the social environment add to this situation. This interaction between financial and social conditions is reflected specifically in the Swedish research dealing with financial hardship and 'shaming' experiences. Unemployed persons who felt devalued and belittled exhibited more ill health than their employed peers.

Due to the higher expectations on men to fulfil the role of the breadwinner in the family, young men seem to be under more pressure than women when unemployed. Although women seem to adapt more easily to their situation, this has to be seen rather critically because it gives way to further discrimination of women in the labour market and a retraditionalisation of gender roles. In addition, the length of unemployment is an important mediator for the health effects of unemployment, at least in the Northern European countries. With the increasing length of time, the unemployed person suffers more from his or her situation – an aspect that implies that both the possible positive and negative influence of other factors diminishes over time.

Preventive aspects were also highlighted within the country-specific reports. Social support especially, from both family and friends, is an important social resource for unemployed young people. In addition, a very powerful personal resource is the level of education of young people. Not only is employability increased with better qualifications, but also individuals with higher educational levels are more capable in dealing with institutions and their own financial situation.

Consequently, the strong and complex interlinkage between youth unemployment and different health-related aspects calls for innovative and multifaceted answers to the emerging problems of today (see also Viney, 1983;

Jackson and Warr, 1984; Warr, 1984; Olafsson and Svensson, 1986; Spruit and Svensson, 1987; Kieselbach, 1988; Winefield et al, 1993).

As can be seen from the six national reports, the question of key mechanisms linking unemployment and social exclusion has not been dealt with, either on a scientific or on a public or political level. When excluding mechanisms are named, reference is primarily made to aspects fostering exclusion from the labour market, in other words, an in-depth examination of the excluding dimensions that lead to youth unemployment. Processes linking labour market exclusion with social exclusion have not been given priority until now.

It can be assumed that the systematic incorporation of both monetary and non-monetary, objective and subjective factors in further research on this matter will allow for insights into the more subtle processes of societal inclusion and exclusion of the young unemployed in European societies.

Empirical analysis of long-term youth unemployment and social exclusion

Sample

To gain a broad perspective on the specific situation of young unemployed persons, 300 interviews with the target group were conducted (50 interviews in each country). The comparability of the sample – taking into account different schooling, qualification and welfare support systems within the six countries participating in the project – was ensured through the definition of the following common selection criteria: the interview partners should be between 20 and 24 years of age and officially registered as unemployed for at least 12 months[2]. The gender distribution of the national sample was designed to accord with the proportion of men versus women among long-term unemployed persons within each country. The last selection criterion was the qualification level attained. In this regard, a distribution according to the proportion of low- versus higher-qualified persons among long-term unemployed persons within the country was agreed upon. The category 'lower qualification' refers to dropouts, early school leavers and persons without further (vocational) training, whereas 'higher qualification' describes persons with high-school education and/or full vocational training qualifications.

It was decided not to include immigrants in the study, as this would have heightened the diversity of the sample. In addition, language barriers might have made it too difficult to conduct the interviews. Due to strong regional disparities in the unemployment rates of young persons within most countries, national studies contained two regions according to either low versus high unemployment rates, urban versus semi-urban structures, or other structural discrepancies such as those that exist between Southern and Northern Italy or East and West Germany (Sweden being the sole exception).

It should be stressed that, even though each national study group had a similar distribution regarding gender and qualification as exists in the overall

Table 3.1: National study populations in the YUSEDER project according to gender and region

	Region A		Region B		Total	
	Male	**Female**	**Male**	**Female**	**Male**	**Female**
Sweden	Interviews conducted only in one region				20	29
Belgium	11	14	9	16	20	30
Germany	14	12	9	15	23	27
Greece	10	22	7	11	17	33
Italy	7	13	14	16	21	29
Spain	13	21	6	10	19	31
All					120	179

number of long-term unemployed within respective countries, the study group should not be regarded as a representative of a larger population of long-term unemployed young people.

In all the study populations, women are more likely to be unemployed than men. This distribution largely coincides with the statistics concerning long-term unemployed young people. The study populations also largely coincide with the statistics concerning qualification level of unemployed youths in the respective country: in Belgium, Germany and Sweden, young persons with lower qualification levels primarily have difficulties in accessing the labour market, while in Greece, Italy and Spain, the same holds true for young persons with a higher educational background[3].

Qualitative method

The method chosen for carrying out the qualitative interviews with long-term unemployed youth was the problem-focused interview, a method which was developed at the University of Bremen in the 1980s and which contains both standardised and narrative elements (Witzel, 1996). The interview schedule

Table 3.2: National study populations in the YUSEDER project according to qualification and region

	Region A		Region B		Total	
	Higher	**Lower**	**Higher**	**Lower**	**Higher**	**Lower**
Sweden	Interviews conducted only in one region				38	11
Belgium	11	14	10	15	21	29
Germany	10	16	15	9	25	25
Greece	26	6	17	1	43	7
Italy	15	5	25	5	40	10
Spain	24	10	10	6	33	17
All					200	99

consisted of seven thematic fields, based on Kronauer's six dimensions of social exclusion, and on psychosocial strains due to unemployment.

The first thematic field focused on the labour market situation of the young person. It dealt with all aspects related to the concrete experience of (long-term) unemployment, but more specifically the inability to enter the labour market after school (structural barriers to getting a job; forms of self-exclusion/ resignation). The second thematic field covered all aspects related to the economic situation of the interview respondents, and the resulting constraints, but also solutions the affected person found – for example, through work in the submerged economy. In the case of irregular work, the positive effects of such a job were of interest. For the Southern European countries, additional questions on this subject were included to assess the situation in more depth. The third thematic field concentrated on positive/negative experiences with institutions such as schools, further qualification and training institutions, unemployment and social security offices, and public and private service institutions (lack of support, institutional dependency leading to 'shame' and passivity, and so on). The fourth thematic field tackled both the scope and the quality of social relations between the interviewees and their families, partners and friends. The fifth thematic field focused on cultural norms and the socio-political experiences of the interviewees. The sixth thematic field dealt with the spatial environment the interviewees were living in, both on a structural level (housing situation, residential area) and from personal experience (for example, feelings of being at home, security). This field also covered a variety of questions relating to the psychosocial strains arising from unemployment, such as feelings of stigmatisation, victimisation and shame.

Interviewees were clustered in three groups according to whether they faced a high risk of social exclusion, an increased risk of social exclusion, or only a low risk of social exclusion. To give account to the process character inherent in the overall concept of social exclusion, the terminology has been changed to 'risk of social exclusion' instead of 'social exclusion' per se (as a final state).

After a first analysis of all interviews in each country and a preliminary classification of the cases into meaningful groups, each country determined three of the six dimensions that put unemployed young people predominantly at risk of social exclusion. Finally, the following three were laid down as central dimensions for all countries:

- labour market exclusion;
- economic exclusion;
- social isolation.

Based on the result, formal definitions of the ideal types of risk constellations were developed for each country. The group of long-term unemployed young people at high risk of social exclusion is made up of cases that show at least three aspects of social exclusion. Among them, at least two of the three dimensions listed above were defined as central. The group of long-term unemployed young people at increased risk of social exclusion is defined according to the following criteria. First, an increased risk of social exclusion can be assumed if two central categories but no other criteria apply. Second, this type includes cases that show not more than one of the central dimensions and any number of non-central aspects. The group of long-term unemployed young people showing a low risk of social exclusion is made up of cases that show exclusion tendencies in no more than one area, and this area may not be defined as one of the central dimensions. On the one hand, such operationalisation meets the requirement for a common basis in a comparative study. On the other hand, due to the formal typology (two central and one country-specific dimension), it is nevertheless ensured that each country may set up its own priorities for the formation of the different types.

Typology

The three groups are distributed as follows. In the Belgian and German studies the cases at high risk of social exclusion prevail. In contrast, most of the young people of the sample in the Swedish and Spanish study are part of the group at increased risk of social exclusion. In the Greek and Italian study, young people at a low risk of social exclusion make up the biggest group, although in the Greek sample the group at increased risk also plays a significant role. In the Italian study, too, low-risk cases predominate.

Figure 3.3: Types of social exclusion in six EU countries (each country n=50, %)

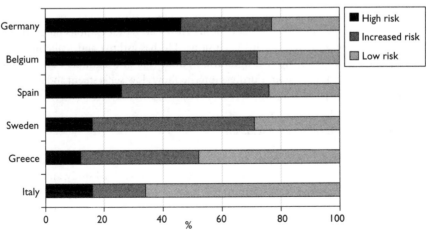

Note: The rank order of national studies is given according to the weighted types (high risk=3, increased risk=2, low risk=1)

High risk of social exclusion

In most of the national studies, a high risk of social exclusion arises for long-term unemployed youth if they experience simultaneously a high risk of labour market exclusion, economic exclusion and social isolation. In the Belgian, German and Swedish studies, individuals in this group also experience cultural exclusion, whereas in the Greek and Italian studies the risk of spatial exclusion is an additional characteristic of this group. Due to financial and other problems in their family of origin, these young unemployed are at a disadvantage from childhood onwards. Their qualification level and self-esteem are low, they are not sufficiently supported by their social environment and governmental institutions, and they tend to be passive, or, in some countries, even tend toward problematic behaviour such as drug dependency and deviance. The main factor that increases the risk of social exclusion is the *low level of qualification* of the persons affected. Lack of qualification becomes an obstacle in building a professional career, and to overcoming the situation of unemployment. The young persons involved have access only to poor and precarious jobs. These young people also exhibit high passivity toward the labour market. It was observed in all countries that *personality-related factors* such as low self-esteem and poor mental health can increase the risk of social exclusion.

Andi is an example of those in the high-risk group. Twenty years old, he comes from East Germany and has been without work since he left school at the age of 14. He lives alone in a one-room flat and his girlfriend is expecting his child. Problems with his family and socialisation deficits led to failure in school and, in turn, impeded his integration into the labour market. Other circumstances make him vulnerable to the various dimensions of functional exclusion that can lead to social exclusion. Alcohol and drug consumption and increased propensity for violence, for example, make it all the more likely he will be socially excluded. The only countervailing forces are a circle of friends and the emotional support of his girlfriend. Andi exhibits illness that is both a cause and effect of his exclusion. He has asthma and hallucinations, which mainly result from drug consumption. He also exhibits nervousness, restlessness and aggression. Furthermore, he shows low self-esteem and expresses high insecurity towards his personal future.

Increased risk of social exclusion

The group of young people at increased risk of social exclusion seems to be a relatively heterogeneous one in all studies. In each national study, an increased risk of social exclusion is coterminus with the risk of labour market exclusion. Further relevant exclusion dimensions of this type vary in each country: institutional exclusion, spatial exclusion (Greece) and economic exclusion (Sweden, Spain). With regard to qualifications, a lack of educational resources could be found across all countries. The risk of social exclusion for this group is mainly counteracted by the high degree of family support (Greece, Italy,

Figure 3.4: Case chart type 'High risk of social exclusion'

Figure 3.4: Case chart type 'High risk of social exclusion'

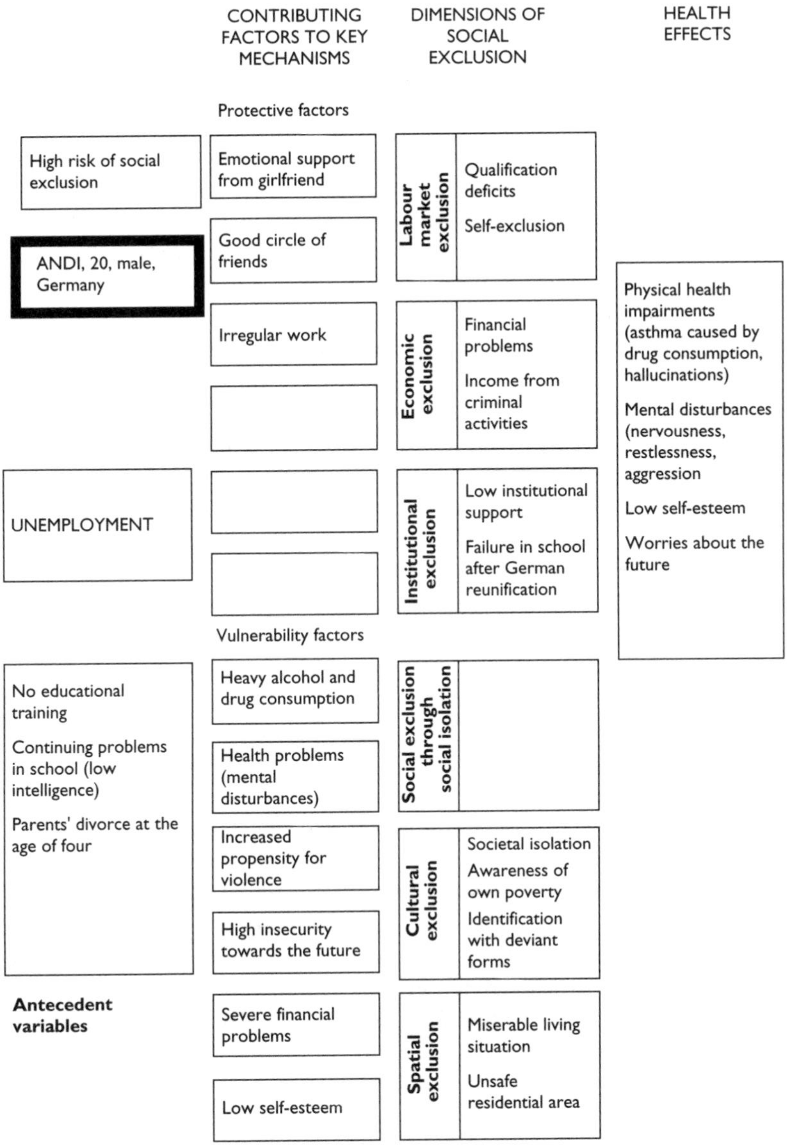

Sweden, Spain) or support from the social environment (Belgium, Germany). Furthermore, general level of life activity is high, which must also be regarded as a protective factor.

A strong link to the social surrounding (friends and family) counteracts the risk of social exclusion. Social isolation is the dimension that makes the difference between high and increased risk of social exclusion. The strong link to the family described in the Italian, Greek and Spanish studies, however, is often not only regarded as positive: although the existence of good social networks (especially family, but also friends) reduces exclusion, the resulting economic dependence of these young people on the family can add to their exclusion. The youth of this group are not as much affected by problems as youth at high risk of exclusion – a small number of exclusion dimensions apply – but nevertheless the situation is vulnerable from the perspective of exclusion.

Olga is an example of the type at increased risk of social exclusion. She lives in West Germany, is 23 years old, lives without a partner and has been unemployed for two years. Problems before being unemployed are deficits in education and a three-time failure in vocational training. A balance between protective factors and vulnerability factors marks her situation during her period of unemployment. By living with her parents, her financial as well as spatial situation is secured. She feels that she does not receive sufficient institutional support. However, she can count on the help of her circle of friends. Besides her continuing failure in vocational training schemes, which has resulted in demotivation, there are other factors that are an obstacle to integration into the labour market. One is her low mobility. Furthermore, the security of the family means at the same time a withdrawal into family dependence. In addition, feelings of 'shame' play an important role for her. Altogether, however, only the dimension of labour market exclusion is proved (although this is a central dimension). Psychological consequences of the unemployment experience are feelings of shame, irritability and boredom.

Low risk of social exclusion

Long-term unemployed youth in this group are at maximum affected by only one (but not a central) dimension of social exclusion. The risk of labour market exclusion for this group is low because individuals within it regard unemployment as a temporary moratorium, and also as a time for personal development and planning. In the Belgian and Italian studies, this group also includes young persons who are not primarily aiming for integration into the working world. People at low risk of social exclusion feel neither socially isolated nor economically excluded. In Southern Europe, they receive sufficient financial support from their families and in Northern Europe from state institutions. Compared with the other groups, youth at low risk of social exclusion have higher qualifications, are more actively seeking a job, are in a financially relatively secure situation and are supported by their social environment. Besides that, they are satisfied with the support they receive from governmental institutions. Many of those in this group are socio-culturally active and have a high self-esteem.

Ingo is 22 years old and has been without work for one year. He comes from West Germany. He has completed vocational training and lives with his parents. He was not taken on after his apprenticeship, possibly because he lost

Figure 3.5: Case chart type 'Increased risk of social exclusion'

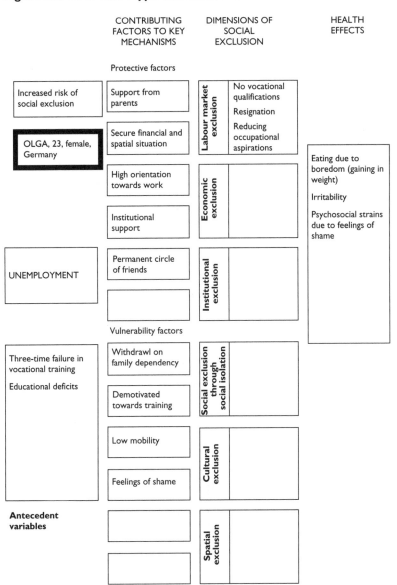

many working hours through absenteeism. The situation in his time of unemployment is marked by a number of protective factors. Due to his educational and vocational training, he is relatively highly qualified. He has clear objectives concerning his career and receives adequate support from the unemployment office. He is emotionally and financially supported by his family and has good secondary income possibilities. However, his unrealistically

Figure 3.6: Case chart type 'Low risk of social exclusion'

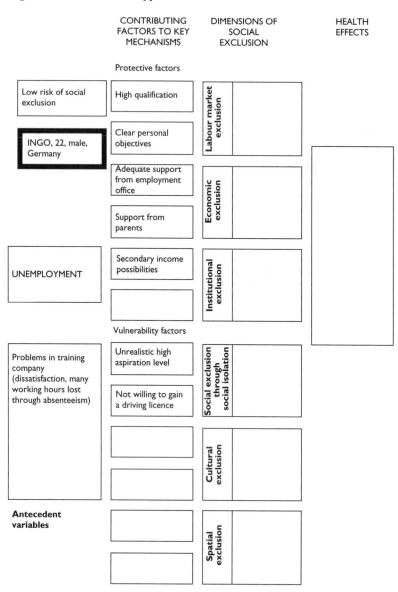

high levels of aspiration and his unwillingness to gain a driving licence are barriers to a quick integration into the labour market. Nevertheless, none of the six dimensions of social exclusion are proved in his case, and his circumstances have not had an adverse effect on his health.

Sociodemographic data

Although all the studies show a high level of congruence regarding school education, duration of unemployment and partly social origin, there are marked differences regarding the regional origin of the young persons and the gender distribution for the different types. The following similarities were found:

- for the group at high risk of social exclusion, the duration of unemployment is longer in all countries compared to the other groups; the qualifications of those in the high risk group are quite low. Furthermore, they come from lower social classes or from families with major social and financial problems;
- a higher level of qualification can be observed in the group at increased risk of social exclusion in all studies except in Greece; the duration of unemployment is the same (Germany) or somewhat lower than for the group at high risk (Sweden);
- compared with the other two groups, the young people at low risk of social exclusion in all studies are younger, are more highly qualified and have been unemployed for a shorter period of time.

Vulnerability factors and protective factors

For young unemployed people at high risk of social exclusion, the main vulnerability factor is the *low level of qualification*. In addition, these young people exhibit high levels of passivity toward the labour market. These persons affected see few or no chances of finding regular work. Often they are no longer actively seeking work or, if they are, they are doing so only to a low degree. Moreover, their endeavours to enhance their qualifications are also significantly reduced or limited. Furthermore, cases of this type distinguish themselves by a *precarious financial situation*. In the Southern European studies, poverty and other social problems in the family of origin play decisive roles in the financial dependency and the lack of social support young unemployed people have. In all the studies, *low social support* contributes to increasing the risk of social exclusion. In the Italian, Greek and Spanish studies, the emphasis lies on lack of support by the family, whereas in the Belgian, German and Swedish studies a lack of or decrease in social contacts is of prevailing importance. *Low institutional support* is a central vulnerability factor for all study populations except Sweden. In the Swedish study, some members of this group receive a relatively high amount of institutional, as well as social, support. Finally, it was observed in all countries that *personality-related factors* such as low self-esteem and poor mental health can increase the risk of social exclusion. A few people within this group display problematic behaviour, such as drug dependency and deviant behaviour (Germany, Spain, Sweden).

Contrary to that, for those at low risk of social exclusion, the following *protective factors* reduce that risk of social exclusion:

- high qualifications;
- active behaviour at the labour market;
- secure financial situation;
- social and institutional support;
- high self-esteem;
- high level of socio-cultural activities.

All the studies point out that an important protective key mechanism for this group is a high level of school qualifications and vocational training. Moreover, the interviewees are not only actively looking for a job but are also more committed to socio-cultural activities than those in the other risk groups. Most of them are continuously occupied with activities of personal interest. They also participate actively in associations and organised groups.

Different kinds of support (financial, social and institutional) are of major importance for this group. Some interviewees subordinate the search for a job to the maintenance of their current lifestyle, which is characterised by temporary jobs and personal interests, such as music (Italy). For some others, unemployment is rather a free choice enabled by social support, be it the family (Italy) or the state (Belgium). Youth at low risk of exclusion usually show protective personality features. All have a high level of self-esteem and good communication skills. They are able to make decisions, to plan and implement positive changes in their lives and to cope with new requirements. Some of the young people at low risk of social exclusion depend to only a limited extent on institutional support due to their high ability to help themselves (Sweden).

While the key mechanisms for the two extreme types high and low risk of social exclusion are similar in all studies of the YUSEDER project, the intermediate type at increased risk of exclusion shows – similar to the sociodemographic data – different key mechanisms for social exclusion and inclusion, varying over countries and consisting of a combination of vulnerability and protective factors. The level of social support, however, is a protective factor that determines this type in all the studies.

Conclusions

In conclusion, the findings of the YUSEDER study suggest that the relation between long-term youth unemployment and the risks, processes and mechanisms of social exclusion is far more complex and dynamic than has been considered up to now. Analysis and support of young people needs to be informed by a consideration of the vulnerability and protective factors affecting individual transition processes. The YUSEDER contribution towards a model of Integrated Transition Policies, as suggested by du Bois-Reymond and López Blasco (Chapter Two of this volume), can be summarised as follows:

- Unemployment is a central risk factor for young people. In the long term, it threatens the overall integration of young people into society.
- The most important vulnerability factors that contribute to an increase of the risk of social exclusion for young unemployed people in the long term are, in all countries, low qualifications, passivity in the labour market, a precarious financial situation, low or missing social support, and insufficient or non-existent institutional support.
- The most important protective factor for unemployed youth is social support. While integration into social networks is of great importance for youth from Northern Europe, in Southern Europe the family is more important. Due to high levels of family support in Southern Europe, the number of youth at high risk of social exclusion in general is lower here than in Northern Europe.
- Individualisation processes in Southern Europe might weaken this buffer effect of family support. In these countries, institutional support should be improved to counterbalance the effects of modernisation.
- The normalisation of youth unemployment and the prolongation of the youth phase, although not meeting central developmental demands of maturing young people, as well as the fact that working in the submerged economy is widely accepted, strongly influence the individual experience. Predominantly in Southern European countries, these factors moderate tendencies to 'blame oneself', considerably lower the risk of social exclusion, and concomitantly reduce ill-health effects associated with long-term unemployment and social exclusion.
- Social origin can be a protective factor for young people as well as a decisive vulnerability factor: poverty and other social problems in the family can increase the risk of social exclusion. This can be interpreted in the sense that the effects of social origin are reinforced by the experience of long-term unemployment for young people.
- The higher involvement of young people in the Southern European countries in irregular work (81% versus 24%) acts as a buffer as well as a trap (Borghi and Kieselbach, 2000). Bridges out of irregular work into the labour market should be sought that reduce the stigmatising impact of the submerged economy.
- Training and qualification approaches have to be based on concrete career development plans in which the individual's wishes for career and life goals are prioritised. Realistic career perspectives have to be developed together with the young people concerned and require the introduction of intermediate qualification steps that are documented and certificated, for example by conducting real work projects that combine direct benefits with possibilities for subjective identification.
- Networking and cooperation between different social actors is needed to address the multifaceted structure of social exclusion processes. This means especially cooperation between enterprises and counsellors *to close the wide gap between supply and demand for job training places for young people*. Such a

step requires regular meetings of all cooperating partners, mutual trust and enthusiasm and the appeal for social responsibility on the part of the enterprises without whose active cooperation such concepts would otherwise be condemned to failure.

- Psychosocial stabilisation and personal development before integration into training or education is often necessary for young people in critical social and financial situations. Outreach programmes may *improve access* to young people who refuse contact with labour institutions; young people's creativity may be stimulated in order to help them to discover and formulate their own interests (for example, by theatre and role-play); or, for youth with low qualifications, *new forms of learning* need to be made available, such as short-term qualifications, practical work experience and jobs that do not require specific qualifications.
- To reduce the risk of social exclusion and to help young unemployed people regain control of their futures, programmes such as the Swedish '100-days guarantee' need to be considered. This includes the offer of employment or training from the side of institutions at the latest after 100 days of being out of work.

Notes

[1] The YUSEDER project has been funded within the Targeted Socioeconomic Research Programme (TSER) of the Fourth Framework Programme between 1998 and 2000. It has been coordinated at the University of Bremen (Germany) by Professor Dr Thomas Kieselbach, Gert Beelmann, Andrea Stitzel, Ute Traiser, and has included the following national partners: University of Gent (Belgium) with Professor Dr Kees van Heeringen, Wouter Vanderplasschen, Tine Willems, Gwendolyn Portzky; University of Bologna (Italy) with Professor Dr Michele La Rosa, Dr Vando Borghi, Federico Chicchi, Roberto Rizza; Autonomous University of Barcelona (Spain) with Professor Dr Louis Lemkow, Dr Josep Espluga, Josep Baltierrez; Greek Network of Health Promoting Schools and Institute for Child Health, Athens (Greece) with Katerina Sokou, Demetra Bayetakou, Valentine Papantoniou, Katerina Christofi; University of Karlstad (Sweden) with Professor Dr Bengt Starrin, Erik Forsberg, Marina Kalander Blomqvist, Dr Ulla Rantakeisu.

[2] This selection criterion could not be achieved from all countries. In four national studies (Greece, Italy, Sweden and Belgium), persons aged 25 have also been included.

[3] In the Swedish study, 49 instead of 50 are included in the analysis: one individual dropped out at a fairly late stage of the analysis when closer inspection showed that a central selection criterion had not been filled.

References

Borghi, V. and Kieselbach, T. (2000) *The submerged economy as a trap and a buffer: Comparative evidence on long-term youth unemployment and the risk of social exclusion in Southern and Northern Europe*, Paper presented at the EU Workshop on 'Unemployment, Work and Welfare', European Commission (DG Research), Brussels, 9-11 November.

Castel, R. (1994) 'De l'indigence à l'exclusion: la désaffiliation', in J. Donzelot (ed) *Face à l'exclusion: Le Modèle Francais*, Paris: Edition Esprit, pp 137-68.

Eurostat (1998) *Basic statistics of the Community*, Brussels: Office of the Official Publications of the European Communities.

Jackson, P.R. and Warr, P.B. (1984) 'Unemployment and psychological ill health: the moderating role of duration and age', *Psychological Medicine*, vol 14, pp 605-14.

Kieselbach, T. (1988) 'Youth unemployment and health effects', *The International Journal of Psychiatry*, vol 34, no 2, pp 83-96.

Kieselbach, T. (1997) 'Individuelle und gesellschaftliche Bewältigung von Arbeitslosigkeit – Perspektiven eines zukünftigen Umganges mit beruflichen Transitionen', in H. Holzhüter, R. Hickel and T. Kieselbach (eds) *Arbeit und Arbeitslosigkeit: Die gesellschaftliche Herausforderung unserer Zeit*, Bremen: Kooperation Universität–Arbeiterkammer–Bremen, pp 39-64.

Kieselbach, T., van Heeringen, K., La Rosa, M., Lemkow, L., Sokou, K. and Starrin, B. (eds) (2000a) *Youth unemployment and health: A comparison of six European countries*, Psychology of social inequality, Vol 9, Opladen: Leske+Budrich.

Kieselbach, T., van Heeringen, K., La Rosa, M., Lemkow, L., Sokou, K. and Starrin, B. (eds) (2000b) *Youth unemployment and social exclusion: A comparison of six European countries*, Psychology of social inequality, Vol 10, Opladen: Leske+Budrich.

Kieselbach, T., van Heeringen, K., Lemkow, L., Sokou, K. and Starrin, B. (eds) (2001) *Living on the edge: A comparative study on long-term youth unemployment and social exclusion in Europe*, Psychology of social inequality, Vol 11, Opladen: Leske+Budrich.

Kronauer, M. (1998) '"Social exclusion" and "underclass" – new concepts for the analysis of poverty', in H.-J. Andreß (ed) *Empirical poverty research in a comparative perspective*, Aldershot: Ashgate, pp 51-75.

Olafsson, O. and Svensson, P.-G. (1986) 'Unemployment-related lifestyle changes and health disturbances in adolescents and children in the Western countries', *Social Science and Medicine*, vol 22, no 11, pp 1105-13.

Paugam, S. (1996) *A new social contract? Poverty and social exclusion: A sociological view*, EUI Working Papers, European University Institute, no 96/37.

Silver, H. (1994/95) 'Social exclusion and social solidarity: three paradigms', *International Labour Review*, vol 5-6, pp 531-77.

Silver, H. (1998) 'Policies to reinforce social cohesion in Europe', in A. De Haan and J.B. Figueiredo (eds) *Social exclusion: An ILO perspective*, Geneva: International Institute for Labour, pp 2-41.

Spruit, I.P. and Svensson, P.-G. (1987) 'Young and unemployed: special problems', in D. Schwefel and P.-G. Svensson (eds) *Unemployment, social vulnerability, and health in Europe*, Berlin: Springer, pp 196-210.

Starrin, B., Rantakeisu, U., Forsberg, E. and Kalander-Blomqvist, M. (2000) 'International debate on social exclusion', in T. Kieselbach, K. van Heeringen, M. La Rosa, L. Lemkow, K, Sokou and B. Starrin (eds) *Youth unemployment and social exclusion: A comparison of six European countries*, Psychology of social inequality, Vol 10, Opladen: Leske+Budrich, pp 15-25.

Viney, L. (1983) 'Psychological reactions of young people to unemployment', *Youth and Society*, vol 14, no 4, pp 457-74.

Warr, P.B. (1984) 'Job loss, unemployment and psychological well-being', in V.L. Allen and E. van de Vliert (eds) *Role transitions*, New York, NY: Plenum, pp 263-86.

Winefield, A.H., Tiggeman, M., Winefield, H.R. and Goldney, R.D. (1993) *Growing up with unemployment: A longitudinal study of its psychological impact*, London: Routledge.

Witzel, A. (1996) 'Auswertung problemzentrierter Interviews. Grundlagen und Erfahrungen', in R. Strobl and A. Böttger (eds) *Wahre Geschichten? Zur Theorie und Praxis qualitativer Interviews*, Baden-Baden: Nomos, pp 49-76.

Part Two:
Young people and transition policies in Europe

Transition policies: strategy of actors and employment policies for young people in Europe

Lorenzo Cachón Rodríguez

Introduction

The analysis of the transformation of contemporary modes of socio-economic regulation leads to a consideration of the subject of young people's professional transitions as the means of entry to regular paid employment. This chapter reflects on the changes in the national arrangements that affect young people's professional transitions, the policies implemented in this regard, and the respective effects of young people's insertion into the labour market. The first section draws on a European research project entitled 'European comparisons about the mechanisms of young people's professional insertion: strategies of actors, production of regulations, devices, genesis', which examined the employment policies of six countries (France, Germany, Italy, Spain, Sweden, the UK) aiming at adjusting young people's trajectories to changed social and economic constellations[1]. The focus here lies on the norms that inspire such different measures and the relationships between key actors involved. The second section deals with the question of how recent policy changes are reflected in new forms of professional transitions with a specific focus on the case of Spain. The final section concludes by drawing the two perspectives together.

A comparative approach to analysing the professional transitions of young people

International comparison is the privileged tool that can be used to confront different patterns of access to paid employment in different national contexts. Consequently, comparative research has been articulated around two axes: on one hand, the detection of the cross-sectional trends leading to a transformation in the professional transition processes of young people in the reported countries; and, on the other hand, the identification of national specificities that arise from historical patterns of policy development and from the institutional dynamics typical of each of the countries involved in the comparison.

The following four factors have played a decisive role in determining young people's access to employment in the countries under consideration:

- Technical and organisational change has led to a radical change in the structure of employment and the qualifications required by young people to enter the labour market. This development does not only affect qualifications *stricto sensu* (knowledge and skills), but also a set of wider and more imprecise skills: initiative, adaptability, mobility and professional flexibility. However, this tendency coexists with the maintenance of neo-Taylorist management and organisation that has been adapted to the new technologies. In all the cases, the recruitment procedures used by employers to assess young people's employability have been transformed. For example, the traditional probationary period tends to be longer and more diversified.
- Under the combined effects of a strong social demand and of growing requirements of the productive system, initial training has been strongly extended to work as something of a refuge against the chances of unemployment, while at the same time increasing the chances of finding subsequent employment. However, this development has led neither to a global improvement nor to an equalisation of the conditions of insertion.
- The increase in unemployment figures over the past two decades has coincided with enhanced competition for jobs among the active population. The contraction of labour markets has led companies to adjust their recruitment strategies, especially with regard to young people. New selection rules have been established that are increasingly concerned with the statutory body of employment policies. Young people who have left initial training, together with women, immigrants and the long-term unemployed, have been the main recruitment sources in those secondary labour market sectors.
- And finally, in order to alleviate the growing difficulties of entering the labour market, the public authorities have intervened in an increasingly active way through the implementation of professional 'transition measures'. This generic term designates a set of measures, frequently heterogeneous in each country (regarding the goals and targets, the modes of intervention, the funding mechanisms and the status provided to young people, and so on), that operates between the time of exit from the initial training system and the time of access to employment according to the rules of the common labour laws. Thus, a new space between training and employment has been institutionalised and amplified, providing young people with a very diversified status, and building a new order in the systems of professional transition.

The first hypothesis of the international comparison was based on the fact that these four trends were common to all six countries covered by the research project (Germany, Spain, France, Italy, the UK and Sweden), although their articulation, as well as the degrees and modalities of intervention, were distinctive.

Hence, a number of factors were selected to identify the historical inheritance of the professional transition system in each country.

On the one hand, the way in which initial training and first employment has been implemented in the different countries allowed us to distinguish, as a first stage of comparison, between the countries where education and training have maintained a central role since the 1970s as a distinctive phase of institutionalised trajectories, and the countries that have suffered a disruption between education and productive systems. Following on from this comparison, the question arises as to why, in some countries (such as Sweden), the training system was flexible enough to be adapted to the drastic changes of the past two decades, while in others (the UK, for example) it has crumbled. Similarly, the question emerges as to why the responsibility of the education system in Sweden was enlarged and extended, while in other countries it was considered as possessing insufficient transformation power (France, Italy, Spain), thus producing the establishment of alternative specific training-insertion measures outside the school system.

On the other hand, reference to a typology of professional, internal and external labour markets should allow us to describe young people's access to employment and the management of the measures on the part of the companies involved:

- In *professional labour markets*, the measures allow the attainment of a qualification that is recognised at the national level and is transferable in a space between companies, and sometimes between different sectors. The transmission of the know-how, which follows concrete rules, and access to the labour market for a concrete wage are controlled by the unions according to institutionalised professional logic. Professional labour markets tend to find more difficulties when strong professional institutions do not assure their administration in the long run (such as the adaptation of training to the technical changes, regulation of the flows to make them depend to a lesser extent on the immediate necessities of the companies, and commitment on the part of the companies to avoid a logic of piracy).
- In the *internal labour markets* of such companies, access to employment accords with recruitment criteria defined by the employer. The initial training level is usually an indicator of potential competition for selection at the entrance point – something that is completed by other less objective criteria such as adaptability to a workplace. The experience in a company subsequently allows the recognition of qualifications within the system of professional accreditations. Consequently, the space for mobility is internal to the company through the attainment of specific qualifications. This is an explanation for the disqualification processes that force young graduates to accept low-skilled or even unskilled jobs for transitional periods of varying length. The company can transfer the role of selection or adaptation to the measures of public insertion according to its needs.

- *External labour markets* fulfil the requirements of flexibility in the management of manpower, provided that the company does not demand specific qualifications. In the past 20 years, companies have increasingly reverted to the external market in the case of categories of workers who do not play a strategic role. In this context, young people may follow a durable but precarious path, with an alternation of unemployment, unstable employment and training courses under different policy initiatives that lead to misleading trajectories (see Chapter Two of this volume; Walther et al, 2002).

A key question is to what extent these devices serve employers/companies, either as a means of access to precarious and cheap labour, or as a filter to entering the internal market (both functions not excluding each other).

The second premise is based on the absence of determined national specificities. The diachronic dimension that forms part of the comparative approach must not be used to reduce societal effects to a frequently simplifying culturalist perspective. Recognition of the changes produced under the effects of the four common patterns described earlier lead to a measure of the malleability of each national system. Here, the main question has been focused on the explanatory factors of this malleability (or its absence) as the different systems experience ongoing change.

It was necessary to place geographical limitations on the research, as well as limits upon the period in time and the age group to be studied. Only six countries were analysed in order to avoid an excessive degree of heterogeneity: Germany, Spain, France, Italy, the UK and Sweden. The period considered was from the mid-1970s until the early 1990s, and the selected age group was that of 15- to 24-year-olds. However, neither the notion of 'young people' nor that of 'measures' has identical meaning in the six countries involved. With regard to the notion of 'young people', the age categories applied by the measures varied from one country to another and reflected the social dimension and the prolongation of youth. The terms 'insertion' or 'professional transition' were generally used to represent a fragmented process in time that consists of a succession of different statuses. Agreement upon the terminology used, however, was difficult to establish among the research teams, since very often the words did not have a satisfactory translation in German and Swedish[2].

Strategy of actors and rules of professional transition

The central assumption of this chapter is based on the idea that the professional transition, as the way of entering into regular paid employment, becomes a privileged site of production and experimentation in new employment standards, of vocational training and of young people's unemployment, especially through insertion measures.

The status given to the 'beneficiary' (participant in a training course or employee), the nature and duration of the work contract (specific or general), the different modalities and definitions of training (placements, standardisation, and so on), its organisational framework (private or public), the underlying notion of insertion (recognition of a right or only an incentive), and the selection or not of the beneficiaries are the different – yet interrelated – possible approaches for the definition of these rules and regulations. These standards are not reduced so that they are no more than a set of legal modalities; rather they are the result of negotiation processes, agreements or conflicts produced by the complex and changing strategies of the social actors. In consequence, their content reflects not only the state's diagnosis of the nature of the obstacles that young people may find in their insertion trajectories, but also the relationships that the public authorities maintain with other social actors. The latter intervene on various levels and can be understood in different ways.

We can distinguish the level of the definition of rules which involves the actors, such as representatives of social groups with specific interests: to simplify, on the one hand one may find instances of representation of the workers and employers' organisations, each one of them adopting heterogeneous strategies, on the other hand there is the state also showing a number of different logics regarding the measures (young people's employability, decrease of unemployment, social equality, training of the workers). In this way, the reflection concerns the degree and the types of relationships between the actors in defining the rules of professional transition. The possible situations are located on a continuum between two extremes: the centralised and unilateral production of insertion rules on the part of the state, and the existence of stable commitments starting from a balanced division of responsibilities among the social actors. The six countries illustrate – with variations over time – a range of possible situations between both poles.

Those rules make sense of the concrete way in which the measures are used. Thus, the social actors turn into those of the labour market and of their margins: employers, public institutions, workers, young people 'benefiting' from the measures, public employment services, local networks, training organisations, and so on. An insertion measure does not have mechanical effects; rather, its use merely translates the strategy of its promoters. The users, however, whose behaviour is not the same from one company to another, from one sector to another, or from one local labour market to another, are those who decide about the sense of its use. Both levels are strongly interconnected, since the behaviour of the actors, interpreted in their second meaning, are largely conditioned by the rules implemented at the first level, while the specific use of the measures can be an obstacle for the (future) transformation of these rules and standards.

Stages of the professional transition path

Transformation of the final phases of initial training

Although the insertion measures have been separated, by agreement, from the initial training system, it seemed necessary to address the radical changes in secondary education that have been usually concomitant with the establishment of insertion measures and whose content has been partially inspired in the experience of the latter. Obviously, the border between initial training and the labour market does not make the same sense if vocational training is incorporated in the education system (as in Sweden, France, Italy and Spain) or not (Germany or the UK). Nevertheless, according to different institutional modalities, a number of common trends may be underlined.

- In each of the six countries, a prolongation of the initial schooling process has been observed beyond the legal age of compulsory education. The most paradoxical case is that of Italy, where the legal leaving age for a long time had remained at 14 years (recently changed to 15), while the schooling rates show a massive retention of young people in the educational system. Even the UK, where entry into the labour market used to be early, there has recently been an increase in school participation rates beyond the age of 16 years. The causes of this prolongation are varied: they depend at the same time on strategies to increase human capital as well as on effects produced by the contraction of labour markets. In the countries with higher rates of youth unemployment, the prolongation of initial training is an authentic escape into higher education, considering the scarce recognition given to vocational training diplomas.
- Germany is something of an exception, because the social recognition of education and technical and professional knowledge is a social fact. Each of the countries involved in the study, however, have experimented with a valorisation of vocational training.
- Alternation between theoretical instruction and practical experience, as set out in school statutes under different modalities, has been extended in the four countries with a more school-based training system (Spain, France, Italy and Sweden).

The first three processes have coincided with a search for ways of cooperation between the education system and other 'actors' (such as companies, unions, local authorities). Also, the education system has proved in most of the countries a certain capacity to adapt to the social demand for education, as well as to the transformations of the productive system. However, it seems that these patterns are very divergent between the six countries, and the strategies of adaptation have not led immediately to a better matching between the system of initial training and the labour market.

Creation of specific measures and emergence of a new status for young people

What is the status of young people between their exit from initial training systems and their access to standard employment? In this perspective, status should not be reduced to a statistical category defined by national and international surveys on employment. The very broad definition of employment applied by such surveys tends to hide the border situations that contribute to creating and extending measures of insertion; that is, between employment and unemployment; between inactivity and employment; and finally inside employment itself, since it is a category that includes a variety of legal statuses (such as standard employment according to collective regulation, particular contracts, low-skilled work without contract).

Taking into account the risk of simplification, we can construct three ideal types from the measures that enable the definition of the status of young people:

1. The *social treatment of unemployment* illustrates the boundary situations. In this category young people experience a status that is frequently very devalued and is materialised in the lack of a job contract excluding the individual from the guarantees of labour rights, the shortage or even non-existence of the contents of eventual training, or precariousness due to low income. The perfect image is that of 'parking' a certain number of young people outside of the unemployment statistics and limiting, yet in a very relative way, the social risks created by this. After completing the measure the employability of the young people is still very low. This does not exclude the possibility that, in an individual case, the young person may succeed in associating this status to more positive forms of integration in a professional manner, socialising activity or in training, due to the measures, hence avoiding rupture of the social bond (see Chapter Two of this volume).

2. The *continuation of initial training* shows that training is the dominant pole in some measures. Young people can be defined as 'active' (for example, by means of training or learning contracts) or as 'inactive' (as in the case of the pre-vocational measures in Germany). In the first hypothesis, the training dimension of the measure prevails on the legal status of employment as in the German dual system of regular vocational training.

3. *Particular employment situations* are configurations in which the employment dimension prevails. However, there are frequently 'atypical' modes of employment that confer upon the young person a specific contractual status or the status of a mere participant on a training course within the company. Hence, the individual is subjected to particular rules as regards labour rights as well as social benefits. This kind of measure is mainly considered to be a way of avoiding the 'rigidities' of the labour market or of reducing the salary costs of young people; they turn into an experiment of new ways of managing the labour force, of new employment statuses that may eventually be extended beyond young people.

This typology concerning the status of young people related to measures of insertion not include that of the legal statutes nor that of the measures, since the same measure can involve something from all three dimensions. For example, a contract in alternation (employment training) can put a young person into a prolonged situation of initial training and at the same time into one of particular employment, and even in some cases into a situation of social treatment of unemployment. In a comparative perspective, this may help to identify the choices and solutions of each country among each one of the three components. The choices are very conditioned by the hypothesis or by the justification on which the measures in each country are based and by the nature of the relationships existing between the different actors of those measures.

Professional qualification and/or flexibility of salary costs

The assessment of employment and training measures shows that the (explicit) justification is frequently based on a double argument: the obstacles to young people's professional transition exist either because of the inadequacy of their training level or because of the inadequacy of the latter to the characteristics of the employment on offer. The obstacles for young people's professional transitions result from the fact that their productivity level at the moment of recruitment is lower than the current salary cost which is determined by the labour market and the system of social deductions. These difficulties increase because of the uncertainty that the employer feels in relation to the productivity and the behaviour of young people who lack professional experience.

Most of the measures show, in this way, a combination of improvement of training (working, therefore, as compensation for the initial training system, which calls into question its validity) and a reduction in salary costs. These factors and the way in which they are set up also vary in time and space, and depend on the type of measures involved.

Relationships between the actors of the measures

As a first step, the question of the effectivity of the measures can be analysed from the point of view of the relationships that each one of the three actors (state, employers, unions) maintains with the others, considering them as global institutions. Next, one must recognise the relative internal heterogeneity of the goals and strategies adopted in relation to the measures.

In Germany and Sweden, under very different modalities, the measures have acquired a wide sense of relatively stable commitment regarding the qualifications of the labour force and the rejection of widespread and prolonged unemployment of young people. The established measures stand for a strategy of adaptation combining long-term progressive transformation with exceptional measures during phases of recession. The relationship between employers and unions excludes the possibility of radical ruptures in the management of the labour force. The state is not neutral, but tries to find solutions that can lead to a tripartite agreement. The Southern European countries reflect a complex articulation between the law and collective negotiation through a large number of measures and programmes depending on a chronology of events that are often influenced by political fluctuations.

The actors have to manage heterogeneous strategies. In the case of public authorities, the division of competencies between the national, regional and local levels usually leads to a deepening complexity and may produce some conflicts in the management of some of the measures. However, the key tendency observed in the six countries of our study is one towards a stronger degree of decentralisation: structural in Germany, with a four-policy-parties model at both national and regional level and including the social partners as well; reinforced in Sweden, with the confirmation of the growing responsibility of the local administrations, combined with privatisation in the British framework of the Training Enterprise Councils; impelled in France by the law on decentralisation from 1983 and concretised by the five-year law of 1993 transferring the responsibility for vocational training to the regions. Similar transfer processes are carried out in Spain and Italy. This development of decentralisation is articulated through regionalised EU policies.

Besides a discourse among employers, who have been relatively unified by a virulent criticism of the education system – especially in the Southern European countries – considered inadequate to satisfy the 'needs of companies', we may find a great variety of strategies on the management of the human resources located between two extreme clusters: either the system will engender the creation, in the long run, of a qualified workforce adapted to the productive logic of the company by filtering and adjusting the labour force to the logic of the internal market, or it will allow avoidance of effective labour market rules, especially the salary-related ones, meeting the companies' needs for a cheap and flexible workforce through the external market. Yet, the same measure can be applied in very different ways. However, there are also other logics to be found: the 'civic logic' in the case of companies recognising their social responsibility in relation to young people's unemployment; and the 'domestic logic', where the measures and the recruitment of young people start from proximity networks such as the family enterprise.

As regards trades unions, although the general objectives (fight against youth unemployment, elevation of vocational training to a socially recognised level, fight against precarious employment) do not tend to produce disagreement, the positions of the different unions are often the result of difficult choices – for example, between young people's interests and those of older salaried members; between the guarantee of qualifications and the need of work experience for young people with a low qualification level. The attitudes oscillate (sometimes inside the organisation itself) between the recognition of the dangerous precariousness of the labour force and the necessity of accepting some degree of flexibility, in order to promote insertion by means of social commitments offering some forms of compensation through training.

While these reflections on the relationships between actors primarily referred to institutions and companies, the following section, focusing on Spain, deals with the effects of such constellations and processes on young people's professional transitions.

Trajectories of young people in their transition to the labour market: the case of Spain

Over the past few years in Spain, a number of regional studies have been carried out focusing on the professional transitions of young people in the regions of Catalonia, Asturias and Valencia. Some of these works have developed typologies allowing classification and better understanding of the different ways of entering active working life after leaving the school system and the role played by policies addressing professional transitions in the constitution of different trajectories (see also Chapter Two of this volume).

The first study to be pointed to is that of Casal (1999). It outlines six different types of trajectories among young people in their professional transition processes in Spain:

1. *Trajectories with immediate success* (young people with high expectations regarding their vocational careers, assuming positive results in the case of continuation of academic instruction, or the option of a professional transition with a high probability of gradual improvements starting from training and/ or a quick internal promotion). A significant proportion of young people who have attained an impeccable university trajectory have achieved stability and a solid projection of their vocational career in the first three years of their working lives. Most of the university students from the leaving cohorts of some years ago have followed similar trajectories. Postgraduate education is not an indispensable requirement to attaining this status, although many of those holding lower degrees have opted for this kind of trajectory.

2. *Worker trajectories* (young people who are socially guided toward a culture of manual, low-skilled work). Here, there is the implication of a limited social horizon concerning education and training and 'learning on-the-job', something that depends largely on the employment offers available rather than on personal vocational options. The basic vocational qualification shapes the limits of their 'career' and makes such trajectories particularly vulnerable to changes in the labour market. The expansion of the construction sector, for example, is the most clear recent example of the development of such trajectories that at present are followed by large numbers of Spanish young people.

3. *Trajectories ascribed to family.* This type of trajectory, not so important in quantitative terms, is related to family enterprises.

4. *Trajectories of successive approach.* This form of trajectory is characterised by high expectations of social improvement and professional careers in a context where the choices available are complicated. It is a transition type dominated by a 'rough calculation' that necessarily leads to a significant delay in achieving professional success and independence from the family. These trajectories imply longer periods within education, previous work experiences before final insertion, partial failure in the transition from school to active life, precariousness and unstable jobs, and so on. Such trajectories are dominated

by the continuous adjustment of expectations (generally not improving) and the gradual achievement of partial success. This form has always existed, but at the moment it has become the dominant pathway of the professional route for Spanish youth, and therefore can be seen as close to the yo-yo pattern (see Chapter Two of this volume; Walther et al, 2002).

5. *Precarious trajectories* (itineraries of scarcely constructive results in the labour market; intermittent unemployment situations, strong work rotation and insecurity are three dominant characteristics). The particularity of this type in relation to the previous one resides in the fact that it is not constructive from the point of view of professional transition. This trajectory can end up in some degree of professional stabilisation, but the analysis of the insertion of young adults has shown that a proportion of the generation in their thirties remains stuck in this pathway.

6. *Unstructured trajectories* (insertion itineraries characterised by blockages regarding the construction of the professional transition and family emancipation, as well as by aspects of social exclusion). In general, expectations of social position are low from the beginning, and school trajectories are characterised by early leaving, failure and negative certification. The specific feature of this type is the systematic blocking of labour market insertion, such as situations of chronic unemployment and incidental entrances in the secondary labour market, most of which are developed in the marginal or informal economy.

While the first two types of trajectory were the most typical until the oil crisis in the mid-1970s (while the third was decreasing), in the past two decades the latter three types have gained in importance. According to Casal, at present the *successive approach* is the dominant modality; the *precarious trajectory* has increased in significance since the mid-1980s; and the *unstructured trajectory* is a phenomenon that, although not being very important in quantitative terms, is beginning to become a major social problem. Results of a study on Asturian young people (García Espejo et al, 1999) point to the general preponderance of the 'precarious' pattern in that region and the impact of education levels and gender in explaining significant differences in the labour market successes or failures of young people.

The second study highlighted here (Masjoan et al, 1999) deals with the analysis of the professional transitions of young people from different disciplines in higher education in Catalonia over a period of three years after having finished their studies between 1986 and 1989. Masjoan et al (1999) suggest that distinctions should be made between the following professional routes:

- *liberal:* starting a professional career as self-employed and staying in this situation three years after having finished studying (7%);
- *moving towards liberal:* starting mainly with a temporary contract but ending up as self-employed (6%);

- *permanent contracts:* starting and staying in a job with a permanent contract (28%);
- *mobility toward permanent contracts:* passing from a temporary job or from self-employment to a stable employment situation (18%);
- *temporary jobs:* starting and continuing with temporary work (33%);
- *unemployment:* failing to achieve labour market insertion (9%).

The third study outlined here (García Montalvo et al, 1997) is a research project on a sample of 1,920 young people (16- to 29-year-olds) from the region of Valencia who had been in the labour market during 1995 and 1996 for up to four years. García Montalvo and Peiró (1999) define the following seven patterns of professional transition as the most comprehensive ones (according to the methodology of clustering) in the region of Valencia:

- *precarious* transition at an early age (52%);
- transition at an *early age* and *progressive development* (11%);
- transition at an intermediate age with *labour instability* (19%);
- transition *forced* at an intermediate age (3%);
- transition at an *early or intermediate age* and *later exit* from the labour market (7%);
- transition at a *late age* and *progressive development* (4%);
- transition at a *late age* and *irregular development* (3%).

The results of these studies, especially the first two, may be interpreted by taking into account two dimensions of segmentation – the qualification level of young people and the different types of labour market (professional, internal and external) – as well as the different mechanisms implemented by existing employment policies. The ideal types proposed by Casal could thus be read from this triple point of view: the first two models ('immediate success' and 'worker') would correspond to professional markets of university or vocational training graduates who are able to attain permanent contracts in a relatively short period. Neither of these two types seems to represent the prevalent situation at present among Spanish young people. The category 'successive approach' could be also be partly related to university and vocational training graduates, but in this case insertion is produced by means of apprenticeship contracting (and in some cases training contracts) and other temporary forms until they reach, after a few years, a stable job that allows entry to professional markets or promotion into the internal markets of the companies. At the moment, therefore, it has to be considered an important model of insertion. The 'precarious' type affects mainly young people with no or few qualifications who follow unskilled pathways with temporary contracts, acceding only to secondary labour markets. The other two models ('family ascription' and 'unstructured') have a minority character and follow particular logics.

Were we to revise the typology established by Casal, taking into account the results of Masjoan et al for university graduates, we could say that, more or less, one third follows successful trajectories (the liberal and those permanently hired); one third follows trajectories of successive approach (mobility towards liberal or permanent contracts, together with some of the temporary); and one third takes precarious trajectories. The first group are self-employed or have stable jobs; the second may achieve apprentice contracts or placements; and the last would be typically in other temporary contracts (or in unemployment).

Conclusions

From the comparative perspective ...

When analysing the transformation of the institutions that regulate the access of young people to the labour market in the countries involved in the study, the impact of four factors is observed within each of them:

1. The set of technical and organisational changes that have produced a significant transformation in the structure of employment and in the nature of the qualifications required by young people.
2. The considerable prolongation of the period of initial training on the part of the young people.
3. The transformation of the strategies of companies in their selection of their workforces (this is linked to the hardening of the competition conditions within the labour market).
4. The intervention of public authorities to establish special mechanisms to promote the labour insertion of young people. Hence, a new space has emerged between training and employment, which shapes different modes of insertion into active life.

These four patterns are common to all the national contexts under analysis. Although their modes of articulation and their modalities vary in each context, they do not do so to such an extent as to be able to speak of nationally determined specificities.

Different models of transition policies have been observed in the countries involved in the study:

- The German 'dual system', built upon the 'logic of proficiency', with active participation from the state and the social partners (unions, employers and institutions), historically consolidated and socially stable.
- The French system, governed by its 'logic of diversity', where the state institutionalises diverse forms of selecting the workforce for different employment institutions, and where modifications are introduced depending on the tendency of the government, the political priorities, or the need to pass 'messages' to civil society. The Spanish and Italian systems may gradually move towards assimilation of this model. However, due to the stability of

respective normative and institutional devices this will require a considerable period of time.

- The British model, with its 'logic of professional exchange', operates against a background that is very politically marked (against the unions), and that regulates the 'delabourisation' of young people, a model inspired by the Thatcherist neoliberal model.
- The Swedish model, with its 'logic of professionality', is built upwards from the educational system with an active employment policy conceived of as an attempting to promote the permanent adjustment of the labour market in the search for full employment.

The main differences between the six countries involved in the study may be described as follows.

In Germany and Sweden, there is a strong social commitment, which is manifested in the stability of the principles to facilitate the transition from education to stable employment that underpin the policies as well as in the flexibility of their structures and their contents to be adapted to the changing conditions of the labour market (also, in the case Germany, when this model seems experience a period of crisis). On the other hand, in France, the UK, Spain and Italy, it seems that there is no social commitment in this regard and this is manifested by the permanent mutability of the principles (which are frequently subjected to discussion) and by the rigid resistance to change shown by institutions and the contents of their measures.

... to the Spanish situation

In the past 20 years, there have been significant changes in the labour market, the educational system and government policies towards both sectors in Spain. These changes have had a strong impact on young people and their position in the labour market.

The decline in the number of 16- to 24-year-olds in the labour market is the result of the decreasing size of the cohorts acceding to the labour market since 1992 and especially of the increase of schooling rates, a highly relevant phenomenon in these years, especially since the mid-1980s. This increase, having significantly favoured the incorporation of women into employment after completing their studies, has in turn produced a radical change in the educational attainment level of the active population, from the prevalence of low educational levels in the mid-1970s, to the opposite situation in only two decades. The contribution of young people (and of young adults aged between 25 and 29) has been the key ingredient in bringing about this change.

Research, however, has highlighted a significant phenomenon of 'over-qualification' with regard to the first employment destinations of labour market entrants – something that tends to diminish in later positions, which, over time, become increasingly appropriate to the educational level of the individuals concerned. The conclusions highlighted by the authors of the research on

Asturian young people in this regard can be extended to the rest of the country. A certain prevalence of the 'logic of the waiting line' takes place, being concretised in a number of phenomena, for example, in the important role played by educational credentials in the time required to enter employment and in the progression to more highly qualified positions; in the replacement of young people with lower educational levels by university and second-level vocational training graduates in their competition for the less qualified jobs; in the huge difficulties of young women in entering stable jobs and being promoted; and in the fact that the labour experience accumulated in the low-skilled labour market segments is almost the only factor with a positive influence on young people's careers (García Espejo et al, 1999).

Young people concentrate and have a bigger relative presence in five branches of activity (manufacturing industries, construction, trade, catering and hotel business and community services), and in agriculture in the case of those aged less than 20 years. These branches have been classified as a 'secondary' segment (Álvarez, 1996) and as 'less desirable' due to their working conditions (Cachón, 2002). A similar concentration is revealed if the distribution of young people in the labour market according to occupations is considered. This supports the existence of an effect of 'polarisation' (sectoral as well as occupational) that does not, however, exclude the existence of another effect of 'differential management', carried out mainly through different managerial applications. Temporary recruitment is a key component in companies' strategies and practices of managing the labour force that is differentiated by a diversity of approaches (on the supply side as well as the demand side).

The extension of temporary work is a manifestation, perhaps the most significant, of the transformation of the traditional Fordist model of employment in Spain. Although it is not a phenomenon that exclusively affects young people, its impact upon young people is considerably more extensive than on older people. Nevertheless, it seems that temporary work is not a trap in which the young people will be permanently caught but, according to Malo and Toharia (1999, pp 310-11), "there is an integration pattern into permanent employment similar to that of previous generations, although it may be slower", which can be interpreted as possible steps from the 'precarious' aspects of temporary work towards progressive 'stabilisation'. However, such integration implies a longer, more complex and more precarious professional transition period than that of their predecessors.

This professional transition occurs in very diverse ways. Different typologies of professional trajectories have been described, showing that the pathways followed by young people in their insertion into active life are very different, and that social origin, educational level, gender, ethnicity and national origin – among other factors – contribute to these trajectories or transition patterns. Also, the different trajectories are related to different labour market segments.

Drawing together the comparative perspective on the commonalities and differences of transition policies and the changes in young people's transitions to the labour market, as illustrated for the example of Spain, we get a diversified picture of the ongoing transformation of professional transitions. If one applies the typology of trajectories presented for Spain to other countries, one will see how the different models of professional transitions emerging from both public devices and the practices of social actors in different markets contribute to the appearance of certain trajectories being dominant in the insertion processes of a considerable proportion of the younger generation. Although all countries are confronted with the same challenges with regard to their labour markets, the different institutional approaches in general and transition policies in particular, together with 'societal differences' (Maurice et al, 1982), lead to different models of professional transitions.

Notes

[1] The project included researchers from Germany (Beate Krais), France (Jacques Freyssinet and Florence Lefresne from IRES, and Annie Bouder, Michèle Mansuy and Patrick Werquin from CEREQ), Italy (Lea Batistoni), the UK (David Ashton, Alison Balchin and Alan Felstead), Sweden (Yves Bourdet and Inga Persson) and Spain (Lorenzo Cachón). The findings have been published (Lefresne, 1995; La Revue de l'IRES, 1995, 1999; Cachón and Lefresne, 1999; Cachón, 2000).

[2] Editors' note: to respect this diversity, which is not only cultural, we have decided not to match the terminology used by the authors from Northern European countries in terms of 'youth transitions' or 'school-to-work transitions'.

References

Álvaraz, C. (1996) *El impacto de la contratación en el sistema productivo español*, Madrid: CES.

Cachón, L. (2000) 'Los jóvenes en el mercado de trabajo en España', in L. Cachón (ed) *Juventudes y empleos: Perspectivas comparadas*, Madrid: INJUVE, pp 133-76.

Cachón, L. (2002) 'La formación de la "España inmigrante": mercado y ciudadanía', *Revista Española de Investigaciones Sociológicas*, no 97, january-marz, pp 95-126.

Cachón, L. and Lefresne, F. (1999) 'Estrategia de los actores, lógicas y políticas de empleo juvenil en Europa', in L. Cachón (ed) *Juventudes, mercados de trabajo y políticas de empleo*, Valencia: Ed 7 i mig, pp 65-96.

Casal, J. (1999) 'Modalidades de transición profesional y precarización del empleo', in L. Cachón (ed) *Juventudes, mercados de trabajo y políticas de empleo*, Valencia: Ed 7 i mig, pp 151-80.

García Espejo, I., Gutierrez, E. and Ibáñez, M. (1999) 'Inserción laboral y movilidad en el mercado de trabajo', in L. Cachón (ed) *Juventudes, mercados de trabajo y políticas de empleo*, Valencia: Ed 7 i mig, pp 181-202.

García Montalvo, J., Palafox, J., Peiró, J.M. and Prieto, F. (1997) *Capital humano: La inserción laboral de los jóvenes en la Comunidad Valenciana*, Valencia: Fundación Bancaja.

García Montalvo J. and Peiró, J.M. (1999) 'La inserción laboral de los jóvenes en la Comunidad Valenciana', in L. Cachón (ed) *Juventudes, mercados de trabajo y políticas de empleo*, Valencia: Ed 7 i mig, pp 203-20.

La Revue de l'IRES (1995) 'Comparaison européenne des dispositifs d'insertion professionnelle des jeunes', *La Revue de l'IRES*, special edition no 17.

La Revue de l'IRES (1999) 'Jeunes et marché du travail: comparaison européenne', *La Revue de l'IRES*, special edition no 31.

Lefresne, F. (1995) 'Comparaison européenne des dispositifs d'insertion professionnelle des jeunes: presentation et synthèse', *La Revue de l'IRES*, no 17, hiver, pp 3-26.

Malo, J.L. and Toharia, L. (1999) 'Costes de despido y creación de empleo en España', *Economistas*, no 80, marz, pp 308-16.

Masjoan, J.M., Toiano, H. and Vivas, J. (1999) 'La inserción profesional de los universitarios en Cataluña', in L. Cachón (ed) *Juventudes, mercados de trabajo y políticas de empleo*, Valencia: Ed 7 i mig, pp 223-50.

Maurice, M., Sellier, F. and Silvestre, J.-J. (1982) *Politique d'education et organisations industrielle en France et en Allemagne: Essai d'analyse sociétale*, Paris: PUF.

Walther, A., Stauber, B., Biggart, A., du Bois-Reymond, M., Furlong, A., López Blasco, A., Mørch, S. and Pais, J.M. (eds) (2002) *Misleading trajectories: Integration policies for young adults in Europe?*, Opladen: Leske+Budrich.

FIVE

The European strategy for youth employment: a discursive analysis

Amparo Serrano Pascual

Introduction

There is an abundant literature that highlights and discusses the ongoing process of economic internationalisation and globalisation, as well as the increasing use of new information and communication technologies in the production of goods and products. A very specific example of this discussion is the study of the economic and, to a lesser extent, social processes of 'Europeanisation' that have arisen due to the increasing intervention of the EU and the emergence of a supranational dimension of regulation in the social and economic spheres. As result of the process of Economic and Monetary Union (EMU), with concrete convergence criteria, the national states' space for manoeuvre at the economic level has been redefined. In this framework, reinforcement of the EU's social dimension – in order to secure the operation of solidarity at the supra-national level – becomes a crucial element.

This chapter draws on the conclusions reached in earlier work aimed at deconstructing the key principles of the European Employment Strategy (EES) (see Serrano Pascual, 2000a; Crespo and Serrano, 2002; Serrano Pascual, 2003: forthcoming). The focus will centre on the concept of activation with regard to young people, since it is considered that this concept is central to the paradigm of intervention proposed by European institutions. The aim is the analysis of the role of this European strategy to combat youth unemployment, developed on the basis of the notion of activation, in the 'reconstruction' or 'invention' of youth unemployment. Although it is far from evident that this European strategy directed at young people has had significant repercussions in terms of reducing youth unemployment figures, it seems to have had a certain impact on the institutional management of the social consequences of youth unemployment. Therefore, the regulatory nature of the European institutions, as well as their potential role in the socialisation processes, is discussed, with the aim of answering the question of whether or not the EES constitutes a relevant approach to the problems to be solved, and whether or not it has an impact at the national level.

Special attention will be paid to the implications of the change that has taken place at the heart of the analysis of unemployment, now that the discussion, formerly expressed in terms of 'lack of employment', has come to focus on the 'lack of employability'. This kind of analysis is necessary for the assessment of employment policies, as the dominant understanding of unemployment will play a central role in the redistribution of the social responsibilities generated by this situation of unemployment (Salais et al, 1986), as well as in the mobilisation and collective intervention against the exclusion of young people from the labour market. The construction of social categories, such as that of a person being 'unemployed', has a central function not only as an instrument for describing reality, but also for changing and transforming it. The dominant notion of youth unemployment shapes the experience of unemployment, contributing to the way in which the difficulty encountered by young people seeking to enter the labour market comes to be viewed as normal.

The open method of coordinating the European Employment Strategy

The 1997 Luxembourg Summit, at which the EES was institutionalised, represented a major step forward in the shaping of a social dimension for the process of European unification. The so-called 'Luxembourg process' has endeavoured to coordinate national employment policies at the European level. It is not a matter of creating uniform regulations or directives at the European level nor of putting in place uniform labour market institutions; rather, it aims to achieve coordination between the European and the national levels.

Why is it necessary to coordinate European social policies?

This 'Europeanisation' of the social question may be justified on a number of grounds. In the first place, in the wake of the EMU, a major asymmetry is observed between economic and monetary policies, both of which are highly integrated at the European level, and policies for the promotion of social protection, which remain under the control of each individual state (Scharpf, 2002). This could lead to a situation in which the rules of European economic integration (internal market, monetary union, stability pact) are accorded precedence over and above issues of justice and social cohesion.

Second, in a situation of economic integration, member states have a reduced capacity to set their levels of public expenditure, as well as reduced possibilities for economic policy intervention for social policy purposes, by, for example, adjusting exchange rates between different currencies, or with monetary policies, potentially inflationary policies, fiscal policies, and so on. In the presence of a common monetary policy and restrictions of a fiscal order, another kind of instrument is required (Begg et al, 2001).

Finally, there is the risk of falling wages as well as taxes as a result of social dumping. The free movement of persons and products within the EU allows companies to move their production locations quite easily, enabling them to exploit differences in tax levels and non-wage labour costs as factors of competition.

In such a situation it appears urgent to strengthen the social dimension of European integration. However, this is no easy task given the considerable diversity of welfare states within the different European countries. This diversity leads not only to very different capacities of countries to invest in social dimensions, but also to a considerable variation in values and social and historical compromises (Scharpf, 2002). Labour markets are also very dissimilar, as are the models of young people's transition to the labour market predominant in each country (Serrano Pascual, 2000b).

Given this high level of disparity among the countries, and the reluctance of the national governments to lose their sovereignty on such a highly sensitive issue, it is extremely difficult to put in place a social dimension. Coordination such as is carried out in the economic and monetary area, characterised by detailed sanctions and strict rules, is hardly feasible and, from a political point of view, is probably unacceptable. Coordination based on strict regulations, such as European directives or legislation, also faces major obstacles, since it is not easy to reach agreement on common European solutions, and it would be very hard to achieve progress in this direction, beyond the (relatively minimal) standards acceptable for all member states.

Regulation in diversity

In the face of this need to regulate diversity, and taking into account the need to legitimise this European dimension, what kind of regulation would then be feasible on the part of the EU? The 'open method of coordination', inaugurated by the 2000 Lisbon Summit, represents an attempt to answer to this question. This method basically consists of four stages. First, the European institutions propose some guidelines consisting of general measures and goals, structured around four pillars; namely, the promotion of employability, adaptability, entrepreneurship and equal opportunities. Second, these guidelines are translated by the member states into their national and regional policies. The third stage of the process is the establishment of indicators (benchmarking) to enable comparison between countries and identify best practices. Finally, there is a process of evaluation of the National Action Plans (NAPs), based on these indicators, by the European institutions and peer reviewers.

This open method of coordination (OMC) allows political choices to be carried out at the national level, their results being nonetheless subject to comparative evaluation and a process of ongoing revision. The aim of such an approach is the promotion of political learning (Scharpf, 2002). Although responsibility for the adoption of specific solutions still lies with the national governments, the latter are also encouraged to focus jointly on common problems and political goals. Therefore, this allows for efforts in the direction of shared objectives, while respecting different underlying values (de la Porte, 2002).

What is meant by 'open' in the open coordination method?

This concept refers primarily to three dimensions. First, 'open' is understood here in the sense of 'flexible', in contrast to other stricter types of regulation, such as those deriving from the establishment of legislation or from sanctions such as those introduced in Maastricht for the purposes of economic convergence. Unlike other types of regulatory mechanism, whether legal or economic, the EES does not introduce formal sanctions. Non-fulfilment of the goals outlined in the guidelines would imply no more than public admonishment on the part of the European institutions. The non-compulsory nature of the exercise allows member states to adopt political choices at the national level (principle of subsidiarity), enabling adaptation to a great diversity of situations. The aims or principles (such as employability or activation) set in the context of this strategy display a general and ambiguous character that facilitates adaptation to a wide range of labour and economic situations.

Second, the 'open' concept designates a dynamic process of mutual policy learning. The objectives outlined by the European institutions are submitted to public scrutiny and collective monitoring, facilitating adjustment in the wake of evaluation and/or in order to adapt to fluctuating and uncertain situations. Subjecting the national results to comparative and jointly agreed indicators, to the peer group and to public evaluation, provides the ideal conditions for learning. Third, 'open' is also understood in the sense of 'inclusive'. In so far as it encourages participation by different players (multi-level governance), this process allows the cooperation of actors working at different levels (various segments of civil society, such as the social partners, geographical level, or administrative department).

This openness is the key element in the regulation of this strategy, so that the European institutions have to coordinate the social policies by use of comparison and evaluation, benchmarking and the pressure of peer reviewers, rather than by economic or legal sanction (Jacobsson and Schmid, 2002). The lack of specific sanctions, the vagueness of the concepts, the fact of aiming at the achievement of uniform practices, yet without being able to intervene at the level of instruments, is explanation enough of the way in which the drafting of the NAPs can be understood as a mere rhetorical exercise consisting of the use by the member states of the EU 'vocabulary' (for example, employability, activation, partnership, gender mainstreaming employability, and so on) and translation, into the concepts proposed by the EU institutions, of previously existing practices that would have been implemented anyway, even without this EES. Furthermore, this exercise seems to be restricted to a small number of people, without being part of the general process of policy design in a range of ministries (Jacobsson and Schmid, 2002) and, as such, the process is not reflected in a national debate.

Finally, there is a risk of imposing specific modes of intervention that seem to be particularly popular and identified as 'good practices'. This supranational dimension of the regulation of social policies can make it easier for governments to push through unpopular reforms in delicate areas that in other circumstances would have no chance of being accepted by civil society (see, for example, the activation approach). On the other hand, it is not easy to identify 'good practices', since often a practice is 'good' on account not so much of content as of the institutional setting surrounding this practice and which explains its effectiveness (Serrano Pascual, 2001). The difficulty in making these models transferable derives from the fact that a certain policy can be reproduced in a different context, while it is not possible to export the institutional model that gives a framework and meaning to this practice.

In spite of the potential weaknesses of such a regulation method, it is also possible to set the above arguments in perspective and to conclude that this employment strategy may not be devoid of significant impact. The first factor to be taken into account is the strong influence able to be exerted by the European institutions at the level of knowledge. The very fact of using the concepts proposed in the EES and popularising them at the level of the public debate can entail an important effect at the cognitive and ideological level. This exercise of establishing a framework for reflection and discussion implies that the NAPs have to be communicated in the language proposed by the European institutions. The concepts are not neutral, and the fact of having adopted them as the basis for explaining and justifying national policies has significantly affected the definition of the terms of the debate. It is not the same thing to discuss the problem of unemployment in terms of lack of employment as to treat it as a lack of employability, as will be shown later in this chapter. In this sense, the EC may be seen as an 'ideational entrepreneur' for the diffusion of strategic concepts and its fundamental role, regarded from such a standpoint, would be regulation by persuasion (Kohler-Koch, 2002). These key concepts lead to operational norms around which different national actors may converge.

Thus, the mere exercise of reclassifying existing policies within the cognitive framework proposed by employment guidelines has an important symbolic impact and effects a rapprochement between national policies and the social representations of the European institutions' discourse. The essence of its regulatory nature thus becomes its socialising capacity, its power to intervene in the construction of the terms used to refer to the problem of labour market exclusion, and in this sense, it affects the general framework of reflection and construction of public intervention (Behning and Serrano, 2001; Palier, 2001; Goetschy, 2002; Serrano Pascual, 2003: forthcoming).

The comparative exercise, furthermore, forces member states to justify their policies with reference to a public policy framework proposed by the European institutions (Barbier and Sylla, 2001). It is thus possible to argue that the main goal of this regulatory method is to influence national conceptions and intervene in the general approach adopted by the policy-making authorities. In this case, the emerging question is to what extent a change in the ideas and conceptions relating to the problem of unemployment would necessarily lead to a change in government behaviour (Kohler-Koch, 2002).

The polysemy of these concepts (Serrano Pascual, 2000a, 2003: forthcoming) is simultaneously a weakness and strength, since it allows work within different contexts and thus respect of national traditions. Some kind of 'convergence' is possible within the 'plurality' that is the hallmark of the principle of subsidiarity forged by the European institutions for their regulation model.

And finally, in some countries at least, it has facilitated participation (which does not necessarily mean integration) of actors traditionally excluded from policy making in this sphere, such as social partners (Barbier and Sylla, 2001) or local authorities (Goetschy, 2002). However, the excessively hierarchical character of the partnerships promoted in the EU, with a dominant top-down structure, has received criticism from many quarters (Serrano Pascual, 2001).

These problems will be discussed and highlighted in relation to activation, a concept and practice central to the European 'social model'. One of the most important trends that can be highlighted in relation to the evolution of the EES is the paradigmatic change that has been produced:

> The Strategy has brought a shift in national policy formulation and focus – away from managing unemployment, towards managing employment growth. (EC, 2002, p 5)

Corresponding to this shift, the employment rate is one of the scarce indicators defined in the strategy:

> The Stockholm European Council agreed to complement the Lisbon targets for 2010 with intermediate targets for 2005 for the overall employment rate (67%) and the employment rate for women (57%), as well as a target of 50% for the employment rate of older persons (55-64) to be reached in 2010. (EC, 2001a, pp 2-3)

The aim of the following section of this chapter is to exemplify the limitations and the dangers of this process, and of the activation model proposed by these institutions. It hopes to show the deeply contradictory character inherent in the understanding of the concept of activation by considering two levels of this discourse: the promotion of the economic and productive 'activation', on one hand, and the way in which, at the same time, it encourages political 'passivity', revealing the ideological character of the institutional discourse on activation.

The activation concept in the discourse of the European institutions

The contradictory nature of the EU discourse on activation

The EU has had an important influence on the directing of employment policies towards more coercive activation programmes and on the reshaping of social protection systems (Lødemel and Trickey, 2001). Even though the notion of activation existed prior to its use in the EES, it is a concept that has become popularised as a result of the European institutions' discourse. This highly ambiguous concept proposes nothing less than a transformation of the conceptual framework governing public policy action. The dominant form of public intervention, mainly directed under a Keynesian political perspective, to increasing the demand for labour, is about to be transformed by focusing government intervention more strongly on the factors of labour. The institutions outline two different (and contradictory) sets of values in order to justify the need for this transformation: on the one hand, the aspiration to self-sufficiency and autonomy (self-regulated moral actors), implying a conception of an internally motivated individual and a policy drive to promote such agency, on the part of 'active individuals'; and on the other, the appeal to pragmatism, to the need for adaptation, in which case the individual should be externally motivated, hence promoting passivity ('activated individuals').

These two conceptions reflect two ways of understanding 'responsibility': the first in terms of an individual being morally autonomous and self-determined, and the second in terms of an individual being economically motivated by positive or negative sanctions (D'Arcy, 1998). Autonomy and responsibility thus become 'nuclear' concepts in the vocabulary of the European institutions.

Activation as promotion of self-sufficiency

Regarding the first type of values – the aspiration to self-sufficiency – the European institutions start from a definition of the economic situation that is undergoing a process of profound change:

> The delivery of lifelong learning ... lay the foundations for productive human resources equipped with core and specific skills and enable people to adapt positively to social and economic change. The development of an employable labour force involves providing people with the capacity to access and reap the benefits of the knowledge-based society. (EC, 2001a, p 12)

This discourse contains plenty of metaphors linked to fight and combat (fight against unemployment, combat against poverty, and so on), in order to reinforce the dynamism on which the discourse about activation is based. This discourse is about *change* and, more specifically, about the need for individuals to be proactively involved in this change. In order to ease the transition toward this new knowledge society, the role of the public institutions should be to provide the means for this adaptation.

> Preparing the transition to a knowledge-based economy, reaping the benefits of the information and communication technologies, modernising the European social model by investing in people and combating social exclusion and promoting equal opportunities are key challenges for the Luxembourg process. (EC, 2001a, p 8)

In this sense, 'activation' comes to mean more than mere 'activation of the economy' (provision of new technologies, facilitation of the exchanges, and so on); it also means activating the labour power (to promote its adaptation to new technologies). This activation of citizens will lead to a revision of previous intervention strategies, which, it is claimed, have a tendency to increase or promote passivity and self-indulgence on the part of workers (the so-called 'modernisation of the European social model'). Dependency is an outcome of a pathological psychological and moral condition that is generated by the social protection system and may lead to erosion of the work ethic (Levitas, 1998). This dependence on the welfare state may, in this case, have important moral consequences, functioning as a brake against initiative. Social protection systems, it is then argued, adversely affect the behaviour of workers and companies.

On the other side, the European institutions point out that the aim of social protection should not be merely the provision of financial resources to fight unemployment but rather the provision of 'employability' in terms of personal adaptability. But what does 'employability' mean? This relatively new concept exhibits a blurred and confused character that is illustrated by the diverse meanings given in the documents of the European institutions. Although it has been used in very different ways, it appears to have three main meanings, which are based, in turn, on three ways of understanding the problem of unemployment (or of lack of employability): lack of technical and general competencies; lack of social competencies; and lack of 'moral' competencies. Each one of them calls for different intervention strategies.

> Every unemployed person is offered a new start before reaching six months of unemployment in the case of young people, and twelve months of unemployment in the case of adults in the form of training, retraining, work practice, a job, or other employability measure, including, more generally, accompanying individual vocational guidance and counselling with a view to effective integration into the labour market. (EC, 2001a, p 11)

In spite of these different connotations of the concept of employability, both share two features, the first of which regards the problem from an individual dimension, according to which, unemployment is produced by some personal shortcoming. This representation of the unemployed person as a 'deficit' makes the individual in some way responsible for this situation. The second feature is to share the concept of 'competencies' that goes further than that of 'qualification', for example. The difference lies in the individual's control over assessment of the value of the work performed. In contrast to the concept of qualification, which is something objective, certified by a diploma, recognised and made official by the educational and labour institutions, the notion of 'competencies' is much more subjective, so that its assessment may be much more arbitrary. Although we need to recognise the crucial value of these informal competencies, there is no way of certifying the 'competencies' of an unemployed person. Furthermore, it is too easy to excuse the social exclusion of certain groups on grounds of the lack of various kinds of competencies, leaving few possibilities of providing a collective answer on the part of the young unemployed. Whereas under previous productive paradigms workers were expected to place their mental or manual skills at the disposal of their employer, demands currently and increasingly seek to call into play the worker's 'spirit and readiness'. This leads to an evaluation and interpretation of unemployment as being the result of 'defects of personality or character', thereby legitimising the social division between workers that results from the focusing of measures on the concept of employability, namely a nucleus of stable labour power (supposedly in possession of capacities that make them employable) and another more peripheral group (Alaluf and Stroobants, 1994). In this case, the selection criteria for labour market inclusion would seem to be less the result of objective features, such as age or possession or lack of a diploma, as of subjective and moral dimensions, such as the manifestation of an appropriate work ethic (willingness, positive trend towards insertion, and so on) that leaves broad scope for arbitrariness and subjectivity. Factors evaluated include motivation, attitude to employment, fidelity, initiative, loyalty and perseverance. Since the employer subjectively conducts the evaluation, employees lose all control over the criteria by which their work is evaluated. This situation favours the appearance of individualised escape strategies, and the 'capacity' to adapt to the new demands defined by capital is becoming the nuclear dimension of evaluation in relation to the employability of most young people (see also Chapter Eleven of this volume).

In this framework, employability means not only possession of the requisite knowledge but also having the appropriate competencies (at the psychological and moral levels), for example, flexibility, permanent availability and personal autonomy. Social protection would consist of the promotion of self-help: individuals become responsible for seeking their own paths to self-sufficiency. The argument regarding personal autonomy is, accordingly, a discourse about personal involvement and responsibility. The individual required by this discourse is an analytical person able to choose the best alternative in a creative and interdependent context, with a high degree of control over his/her personal project and who acts following his/her own convictions, values and ethical principles. The role of the welfare state is redefined, in this case, according to the redistribution of the opportunities rather than of wealth, to provide the tools for 'self-help', and to make individuals responsible for seeking their personal trajectories towards self-sufficiency (Begg et al, 2001).

Activation as supervision of behaviour and instrument of social discipline

The change towards a knowledge society that frames the argument of the European institutions' discourse is defined as a global reality transcending the frontiers of the EU. This concept becomes an unquestionable fact, presented in absolute terms as an objective reality:

> The rapid changes in information technology, communication and life sciences make it necessary for each Member State … to be at the cutting edge of the knowledge-based and innovatory economy and society, the wellspring today of growth and development. (European Council 2000, Nice Summit, Presidency Conclusions, p 14)

This way of presenting a given situation as 'natural' is an ideological process, whereby social processes and explanations are turned into natural facts. The main function of this process is to avoid any political questioning of this definition of the situation. Something natural is not something that may be called into question, the only possibility being to seek to understand it and adapt to it. Therefore, the baseline of this discourse is its definition of what an information-based society is: it is a reality that has to be accepted, there being no choice in the matter. The only political response would thus be to seek to derive the highest possible benefit from this situation.

> Social policy is not simply the outcome of good economic performance and policies but are at the same time an input and a framework. In this context, the modernisation of the social model means developing and adapting to take account of the rapidly changing economy and society and to ensure the positive mutually supportive role of economic and social policies. (EC, 2001b, p 5)

Were political conflict to arise, it would be of a technological rather than an ideological nature. It is a question of 'passive adaptation', implying a predominantly reactive capacity. The type of person required by the reactive discourse is one who acts and thinks in a manner that is adaptive rather than analytical. Such individuals would choose the most gratifying (and the least unpleasant) course of action. They would be motivated by external factors and would adjust their action to the circumstances. Employability (personal adaptability, total readiness) may, accordingly, be understood as adaptation to a naturally arising, externally imposed and unavoidable situation.

The clients of the activation process are viewed as objects of activation, rather than as active agents of their own activation process (van Berkel, 2000). As such, the discourse about autonomy, mobility and quality of work is in stark contrast to the coercive nature of the instruments put in place to increase the activity rate and compel individuals to work. In this context, it is necessary to understand the methods used to create this employability, focused on disciplinary incentives for the labour market integration of individuals. We encounter a discourse that legitimates the use of coercive instruments to increase the activity rate and in which work is presented as the panacea. Measures devised to motivate – or better, to persuade – people to join the labour market consist in revision of the unconditional right to unemployment benefits, thus entailing a system of sanctions for those individuals who might not wish to cooperate.

Activation should be understood, therefore, as an instrument for the promotion of appropriate forms of behaviour, with the role of the welfare state becoming mainly to ensure social discipline. Individuals thus come to be regarded as thinking and acting in a reactive and adaptive – rather than an analytical and autonomous – manner, and as being motivated by external factors. The behaviour promoted in this case is the ability to react within an environment structured in terms of rewards and sanctions: to be prepared to accept authority, and to respond to financial incentives. Activation comes to be an exercise in supervision of individual behaviour conducted through strict controls on the behaviour of young unemployed people. Unemployment and social exclusion thus come to be understood not as a (social) condition but as the answer to this condition in terms of behaviour (D'Arcy, 1998). The question to be tackled by social intervention comes to be the fight less against poverty than against social exclusion. This concept, particularly favoured in the discourse of the European institutions, involves an important paradigmatic change in the treatment of the social question. In so far as it is an approach that deals with the problem as if it were a division between an included majority and an excluded minority, the point is no longer to undertake a structural analysis of poverty, which might call into question inequality and demand a policy of social distribution of power and wealth.

> Exclusion appears as an essentially peripheral problem, existing at the boundary of society, rather than a feature of a society which characteristically delivers massive inequalities across the board and chronic deprivation for a large minority. The solution implied by a discourse of social exclusion is a minimalist one: a transition across the boundary to become an insider rather than an outsider, in a society whose structural inequalities remain largely uninterrogated. (Levitas, 1998, p 7)

The EU's discourse displays a limited notion of social inclusion that is reduced to no more than economic inclusion. The aim of public policy in this discourse is not so much to facilitate the distribution of wealth as to inculcate appropriate behaviour patterns. Social protection may no longer be considered an unconditional right; it depends on whether or not the individual displays a positive attitude concerning a series of norms. If the notion of citizenship has been understood, in the past, as a status (that is a source of social rights), a new concept has been brought into being – that of citizenship as a contract (conditionality of rights).

In this sense, the notion of activation shows the attitude that people should adopt in the face of the current changes, contrasting with the way these changes are observed as natural and unavoidable, as well as with the methods used to discipline the potential labour power in order to meet the demands of this new productive paradigm.

Social policies are then conceived not so much as an instrument for the distribution of wealth, but as tools in the service of indoctrination in order to inculcate the appropriate behaviour norms (D'Arcy, 1998). The primacy of the distinction between the 'deserving' and the 'underserving' poor is rehabilitated as a starting point in the conception of public policies. Social benefits are then considered as rights conditional upon the (positive or negative) attitude of the individuals concerning a series of norms (of work, discipline and aspiration for self-sufficiency), or, in other words, as a way of governing the behaviour of the unemployed young people (D'Arcy, 1998). Under this perspective, the angle for intervention becomes the promotion of changes in behaviour through strict controls of those individuals who are able to benefit from such treatment.

The contradictory nature of this discourse is dissolved when we consider that it is part of a two-level structure. The first level comprises the economic dimension and the operation of the productive model. The second level refers to a social dimension or a political answer. The discourse about activation would seem to be directed to promoting the requisite economic dynamic, while simultaneously producing political resignation and passivity. In other words, individuals have a high degree of autonomy to adapt to changing rules, but this autonomy will not allow them to call the rules into question.

Are activating social policies so 'social'? Individualisation of unemployment

One of the difficulties with intervention models of this kind is that they attempt to deal with structural issues as if they were personal problems. With the intervention paradigm based on activation, the focus of intervention changes from a structural analysis of the causes of poverty to an analysis of the individual and moral character of social exclusion. Social differences are made to appear as technical differences on the one hand and as individual and moral differences on the other (attitude in relation to changes and orientation towards work). The uncertainty and instability of the economy thus becomes a personal problem.

The digital metaphor is extended, changing its use from the definition of the information society to the description of the social and labour relationships within it. The term 'digital divide' is used to designate the polarisation in the labour market between those with a high level of training in the use of information and communication technologies, and those who are not at all used to them, thereby naturalising the differences and dualities raised by the crisis of the labour market. The differences among individuals are ascribed to the way in which each copes with his or her employability, and to the ability to adapt to a changing world. The socio-political analysis of the information society thus becomes a technical analysis of the most suitable ways of adjusting demand and supply. This individualised form of intervention rejects any perspective that would seek to integrate the necessary structural changes to solve the most global aspects – exclusion being part of them. In other words, the most global context of the problem – in this case, the socioeconomic ground of unemployment – is ignored. The problem is treated in psychological and individual terms, concentrating on measures aimed at changing people's attitudes towards employment. Social differences are presented as differences of personality, differences in people's attitudes and abilities to be adapted to the demands of the labour market. This kind of intervention implies the transfer of conflicts from the social macro level to the individual level.

Most of these activation policies directed at enhancing young people's transition to employment are promoting a new social construction of the experience of unemployment. Public schemes based on this concept of employability start out from a representation of unemployment as a 'personal lack' (of training, culture, personality, and so on), instead of a social risk, and this has important consequences in making young people responsible for their dependent situation. What is, in reality, nothing more than a shortage of work is turned into the absence of a personal project – of motivation, of training (Crespo et al, 1999). This angle of presentation may account to a considerable degree for the lack of proclivity for collective action observed among young people. The attribution of individual responsibility and loss of legitimacy of a fighting attitude operate as mechanisms for avoiding potential conflicts. This reconstruction of the problem will have important consequences in the distribution of social responsibilities and, therefore, in the role that social institutions are called upon by society to play in order to solve it. This analysis, based as it is on an analysis in terms of personal shortcomings rather than social organisations, comes very close to a moral diagnosis.

Moralisation of social support

One of the main assumptions of activation policies is that participation in a paid job signifies inclusion, whereas unemployment is synonymous with exclusion. Accordingly, programmes inspired by the paradigm of activation are focused almost exclusively on labour market participation. Alternative forms of participation, such as voluntary or otherwise non-remunerated work, are not considered and in some cases are even impeded (Levitas, 1998; van Berkel, 2000). This paradigm of activation serves essentially to stress the integrationist and socialising role of paid work that is regarded as supplying not only economic but also social and moral functions. Exclusion thus comes to be understood in terms of the impossibility of incorporation into paid work, not as the impossibility of participation in society, in such a way that the concepts of social exclusion and exclusion from paid work come to be used synonymously (Levitas, 1998). This discourse, focused on social integration through waged or salaried work, tends to reduce the social and political issues to the merely economic. The potential for achieving social inclusion by means of paid work is overstated, while the potential of other types of work or contribution is rejected (van Berkel, 2000). Paid work is treated as a homogeneous category and it is assumed that any kind of paid job leads to social inclusion. There is no incentive for any other sort of labour market participation, since it could reduce availability for this market. Paid work is considered as the only way of coming by appropriate income, social contacts and personal development. However, this pressure on workers to be integrated into the formal labour market may have exactly the opposite effect, namely, a strong increase in the number of working poor, limitation of other possible forms of social network and restricted possibilities for workers' personal expression, since a high proportion of the available jobs are of doubtful quality. As such, the aim of this activation is not always integration of workers, but their socialisation and control.

Clients' refusal of activation offers is interpreted in terms of a lack of willingness to work, rather than in relation to the poor quality of the jobs available. The legitimacy of forcing an unemployed person to accept insecure and low-skilled work is never called into question.

In actual fact, this discourse is not only asking for higher levels of qualification on the part of workers; it seeks also to shape workers' attitudes in relation to work. As such, its main goal is the inculcation of a work ethic and an attitude of constant availability. Under such conditions, the role of the government comes to be the 'regulation of morality', with a view to influencing the behaviour of the beneficiaries of help.

Are activation policies so active?

The construction of the active–passive dichotomy is one of the starting points of the discourse on activation developed by European institutions. According to its premises, the fight against youth unemployment should consist mainly of the mobilisation of young unemployed people, promoting their participation in one programme or another until they cease being unemployed, thus avoiding the fate of becoming long-term unemployed. The aim, thus, is to provide young people with an alternative status to that of unemployed before they become ensconced in such a social position (before six months) and fall into the stigmatised category of 'long-term unemployed'. Mobility between these alternative positions (training, retraining, job experience, voluntary work or guidance) becomes a categorical imperative, coming to form, in the end, an intermediate space between employment and unemployment. A discontinuous, gradual and diversified transition is therefore stimulated. While in previous times the path rituals between youth and adulthood – or between school and work – were highly explicit, young people currently live in a diversified, suspended period somewhere between youth and adulthood (see Chapter Two of this volume). A lot of policy measures are devoted to this period, such as reductions in labour costs, dual training, and so on, operating in the statistical frontiers between categories and producing transitory, alternative and hybrid situations somewhere between the status of worker and that of student. This transitional space contains different conditions produced by the proliferation of 'atypical' situations (in terms of the lack of collectively agreed rights and guarantees such as a minimum wage, protection against redundancy, and access to social security) such as those resulting from youth employment schemes, voluntary work, distribution (courier, press or pizza service riders, and so on), and dual systems. Differences within the same group of workers are then exacerbated, leading to a proliferation of contractual statuses depending on a wide range of criteria, producing different levels of classification in the hierarchy and internal inequalities within the same group of workers (see Chapter Four of this volume).

This situation of hybridisation of categories becomes much more obvious when looking at the difficulty of establishing a borderline between training and employment (following courses), for example, employment/non-employment (voluntary work), market/non-market economy (social economy). The creation of alternative spaces (and status) between work and unemployment, as well as bridges between inactivity, unemployment, informal economy, training and employment, aim at getting people out of unemployment (to avoid a situation where the long-term unemployed become inactive and discouraged, or to avoid the degradations resulting from unemployment). This circumstance has transformed these programmes into hives of exclusion and has extended them to other social areas. In fact, the employment measures geared to young people have contributed to the growing precariousness and diversification of conditions whereby these youngsters accede to the world of work (see Chapter Two of this volume). This situation ensures that the first contact gained by most young people with the world of work is very different from that of the adults.

The construction of this twilight zone has contributed to the deterioration of work and to a growing diversification of young people's conditions of access to the labour market. This situation is not the result of the European strategy alone, in so far as it derives also from previous traditions, but the activation notion provides it with institutionalisation and legitimacy. Insertion programmes designed for young people thus show a lower degree of stabilisation in the labour market. In most cases the employment status offered to young people is temporary, leading to a high level of mobility between different occupational and contractual situations. This diversification and fragmentation of labour status has enabled adaptation of the labour force to a varied, fluctuating and unpredictable market demand. In turn, however, this excessive rotation is also hindering the profitability of investment in training and reduces the possibility of reaching certain professional standards.

Accordingly, we might ask to what extent the so-called active measures are in fact active, since they are directed at promoting the worker's mobility among categories, rather than at achieving stable incorporation into the labour market? This shows the false character of the established active–passive dichotomy that forms the basis of most policies of this kind. At the same time, for a policy to be genuinely 'active', in the sense previously discussed (providing the individual with the means to be able to deal with his personal project in an autonomous way), 'passive' measures become increasingly necessary. These can be used to promote a better and more rational 'active' management of the personal project (see Chapter Thirteen of this volume). Simultaneously, to obtain a real 'active' effect of a measure, the level of public expenditure has to increase; and yet the argument for most of these measures is the financial crisis of the social security system.

Conclusion: the normalisation of non-standard situations

Although the activation-based principle of intervention has inspired very different political models, there is a general trend in the NAPs of several European countries to change the rules concerning the incentives to work. This process of revision has led to limitations in the levels and duration periods of social benefits, as well as in the eligibility conditions. However, very important differences can be observed between the different countries in the coercion mechanisms adopted as well as in the balance that is set between rights and obligations (see Chapter Six of this volume), the options on offer (stability and quality), public expenditure in support of these measures, and the individualisation or otherwise of these programmes (Serrano Pascual, 2003: forthcoming). The political model has thus changed from highly coercive programmes and/or with poor quality and individualisation of the offers to mechanisms more focused on induction procedures and/or with a higher quality of the options available.

While in the Nordic countries there is a mixture of positive and negative incentives, in the UK we may find highly coercive strategies. Alongside the question of the extent to which the 'offer' is coercive, it is important to highlight the differences in the quality of the options, as well as the nature of work offered. Coercive mechanisms directed at providing incentives and motivation for the unemployed young people, together with low-quality options, have more negative consequences for the social integration of these young people. Anyway, it is observed that these activation devices, and their obsession with increasing the activity rate, might lead to a multiplication of atypical jobs as an option against unemployment. When the development of these atypical jobs combines with a low level of employment regulation, the consequences can be drastic for the workers. In this sense, new problems are emerging, such as that of the working poor.

The model of labour market regulation, as well as the welfare institutions prevailing in each country, helps to explain the different political developments in each country as well as their highly variable consequences. This shows what is, in my opinion, one of the most important weaknesses of the OMC. This method aims essentially to achieve a standardisation of ideas, visions and political conceptions, rather than of institutions and laws. Thus, although this kind of regulation can work in the diffusion of political perspectives or ideological models, it has, on the other hand, very little power to achieve convergence of the available means or instruments in each country (institutions and rules). Indeed, the same intervention model can have very different consequences depending on the dominant system of regulation. In other words, an appropriate social policy requires not only the adoption of the right political perspectives (if possible), but also the implementation of the requisite instruments.

In terms of content, the question arises regarding the extent to which the emphasis of these policies focused on workers' motivation, on a basis of positive and/or negative incentives, is necessary and useful; and alternatively, of whether or not it would be advisable to focus these policies on the quality of the activation process and of the activation offer.

References

Alaluf, M. and Stroobants, M. (1994) 'Do skills mobilise the worker?', *CEDEFOP Vocational education and training*, no 1.

Behning, U. and Serrano, A. (eds) (2001) *Gender mainstreaming in the European employment strategy*, Brussels: ETUI.

Barbier, J.C. and Sylla, N.S. (2001) 'Stratégie européenne pour l'emploi: les représentations des acteurs en France', Rapport pour la DARES et la Délégation à l'emploi du ministère du travail et de l'emploi, December.

Begg, I., Berghman, J., Chassard, Y., Kosonen, P., Kongshoj, P., Matsaganis, M., Mayes, D., Muffels, R., Salais, R. and Tsakloglou, P. (2001) 'Social exclusion and social protection in the European Union: policy issues and proposals for the future role of the EU', EXSPRO Research Project, financed by the EC under the Targeted Socioeconomic Research Programme.

Crespo, E., Moreno, F., Serrano, A., Fernández, P. and Sánchez, C. (1999) 'El significado del trabajo y la ciudadanía social para los estudiantes de secundaria', Research Report for the Ministry of Education and Science, Complutense University, Madrid.

Crespo, E. and Serrano, A. (2002) 'The EU's concept of activation for young people: toward a new social contract?', in E. Gabaglio and R. Hoffmann (eds) *European Trade Union Yearbook*, Brussels: ETUI, pp 295-323.

D'Arcy, S. (1998) 'Personal responsibility and the subjection of the poor: a critique of Charles Murray', *Papers presented at Strategies of Critique XII: Justiced subjects*, 25 April, York University (www.yorku.ca/jspot/1/steved.htm).

de la Porte, C. (2002) 'Is the open method of coordination appropriate for organising activities at European level in sensitive policy areas?', *European Law Journal*, vol 8, no 1, pp 38-58.

EC (European Commission) (2001a) *Proposal for a council decision on guidelines for member states' employment policies for the year 2002*, Brussels, 12 September, COM(2001) 511 final.

EC (2001b) *Communication from the Commission to the Council, the European Parliament, the Economic and Social Committee and the Committee of the Regions*, 20 June.

EC (2002) *Taking stock of five years of the European employment strategy. Communication from the Commission to the Council, the European Parliament, the Economic and Social Committee and the Committee of the Regions*, Brussels, 17 July, COM (2002) 416 final.

European Council (2000) Nice Summit, Presidencey conclusions, available at http://ue.eu.int/en/info/eurocouncil/index.htm

Goetschy, J. (2002) 'The European Employment Strategy and the open method of coordination: lessons and perspectives', Report prepared for the ETUC's Florence seminar on the future of industrial relations, 4-6 November.

Jacobsson, K. and Schmid, H. (2002) 'Real integration or just formal adaptation? On the implementation of the national action plans for employment', in C. de la Porte and P. Pochet (eds) *Building social Europe through the open method of coordination*, Brussels: PIE Peter Lang, pp 69-97.

Kohler-Koch, B. (2002) 'European networks and ideas: changing social policies?', *European Integration Online Papers* (EioP), vol 6, no 6 (eiop.or.at/eiop/texte/2002-006a.htm).

Levitas, R. (1998) *The inclusive society? Social exclusion and New Labour*, Basingstoke: Macmillan Press.

Lødemel, I. and H. Trickey (2001) *'An offer you can't refuse': Workfare in international perspective*, Bristol: The Policy Press.

Palier, B. (2001) 'Europeanising welfare states: from the failure of legislative and institutional harmonisation of the systems to the cognitive and normative harmonisation of the reforms', Paper presented at the conference 'Ideas, Discourse and European Integration', Center for European Studies, Harvard University, 11-12 May.

Salais, R., Baverez, N. and Reynaud-Cressent, B. (1986) *L'invention du chômage. Histoire et transformation d'une catégorie en France des années 1890 aux années 1980*, Paris: Presses Universitaires de France.

Scharpf, F.W. (2002) 'Legitimate diversity. The new challenge of European integration', *Cahiers Européens des Sciences*, no 1.

Serrano Pascual, A. (2000a) 'The concept of employability: a critical assessment of the fight against youth unemployment', in E. Gabaglio and R. Hoffmann (eds) *European Trade Union Yearbook*, Brussels: ETUI, pp 253-71.

Serrano Pascual, A. (ed) (2000b) *Tackling youth unemployment in Europe*, Brussels: ETUI.

Serrano Pascual, A. (ed) (2001) *Enhancing youth employability through social and civil partnership*, Brussels: ETUI.

Serrano Pascual, A. (2003: forthcoming) 'Towards convergence of the European activation policies?', in A. Serrano Pascual (ed) *Activation policies for young people in international perspective*, Brussels: ETUI.

van Berkel, R. (2000) 'Activation programmes as an alternative?', Presentation of results of the TSER project 'Inclusion through participation', UWWCLUS workshop Brussels, 9-11 November.

SIX

State policy and youth unemployment in the EU: rights, responsibilities and lifelong learning

Wallace McNeish and Patricia Loncle

Introduction

The aim of this chapter is to develop a critical perspective on unemployment policies for young people. Our framework consists both of questioning the existence of processes of convergence in the ways European countries currently attempt to tackle youth unemployment, and of evaluating the successes and failures of present national arrangements. To achieve these aims, we draw together and summarise key findings, criticisms and policy recommendations made by the research partnership grouping involved in the EU-funded Leonardo da Vinci programme project, 'Integration through training?'[1]. Where appropriate, interview extracts and typologies will be used to illustrate key points made. The Leonardo da Vinci project was a two-year, collaborative, cross-national study that was carried out by researchers working in eight EU countries (Germany, Spain, Netherlands, Sweden, Denmark, Italy, France and the UK) between 1999 and 2001. The final report was entitled *Integration through training? Comparing the effectiveness of strategies to promote the integration of unemployed young people in the aftermath of the 1997 Luxembourg Summit* (Furlong and McNeish, 2001).

Aims, objectives and research process

The starting point for the project was the 1997 Luxembourg Summit on employment, and more specifically the common policy measures and foundational guiding principles agreed by EU member states that aim to promote the social and economic integration of unemployed young people (18-25 age group). As drafted in the official statement that emerged from the summit, the various principles agreed by the EU governments are generally quite vague. Nevertheless, one specific and pivotal commitment does stand out around which the other guidelines revolve; that is, to offer all young people, by the end of

2002, what is termed 'a new start' before they have been unemployed for six months or more (see EC, 1999). Despite its ambiguity, this commitment gave the research project a focus whereby the range of ongoing and developing training programmes, educational initiatives and labour market schemes in each of the eight partner countries could not only be contrasted and compared in terms of best practice, but could also be evaluated in terms of their likelihood of meeting this target.

Hence, the central aims of the project were:

- to highlight differences and similarities of approach to the problem of the socioeconomic integration of unemployed young people;
- to exchange knowledge of the effectiveness of policies aimed at reducing the risk of marginalisation and exclusion;
- to evaluate the progress made in each partner country towards the fulfilment of the commitment to give new training, education or work experience opportunities to each young person after they have been unemployed for six months.

The research process combined a series of in-depth, semi-structured interviews with policy makers, officials and practitioners in each partner country, with the extensive secondary analysis of official statistics and policy documents[2].

Modelling trends in education and training policies

The research reveals that the key trend in underlying perspectives on integration is a shift from a work-oriented perspective towards an 'integration = education', or 'integration through education', perspective. Education, and especially recurring education (lifelong learning), is increasingly considered to be *the* solution to the more general process of restructuring taking place in economic and labour market situations for young people. This trend can be seen most clearly in Sweden and Denmark, countries that are leading the way in putting this perspective into practice. In both countries, reforms within the educational system itself (where vocational education is getting less practical, more general, more theoretical, and so on, and is strongly integrated with the 'general' education system; see Lasonen and Young, 1998), and within the labour market programmes for young people, reflect this development. The following response from a Danish government official clearly illustrates the meaning of this type of thinking about future of educational provision:

> I believe that the labour market of the future will demand the young people who are creative and independent and who think a bit differently .... I very much believe that this will be the type of qualification which the future demands. (Danish government official, 2000, quoted in Furlong and McNeish, 2001, p 60)

As obtaining a longer education becomes more and more important, it is essential that labour market programmes support this shift. In Sweden, the Municipal Youth Programmes (which offer work experience, training and social education to unemployed 18- to 20-year-olds) and the Development Guarantee (which offers equally 'meaningful developmental activity' to unemployed 20- to 24-year-olds) collaborate closely with educational institutions as part of the wider youth policy approach. Hence in the Swedish case:

> The programmes for young people who lack basic education have more and more been designed to make it easier ... to return to school rather than functioning as an alternative to school. Often the school works together with the employment centres in encouraging young people to attain or retain studies in upper secondary school. (Swedish government official, 2000, quoted in Furlong and McNeish, 2001, p 145)

In Denmark, the Youth Effort Programme is even more focused on solving youth unemployment through education. Typically then, instead of simply developing new labour market programmes, a large number of new education-oriented programmes have been established (for example, through the Open Youth Education scheme, Production Schools and Folk High Schools)[3]. In both Sweden and Denmark, then, the aim would appear to be to facilitate individual biographical construction through increased educational opportunity; that is, something that in turn will facilitate social and economic integration.

In contrast, Spain and Italy are countries where in general the issue of integration is still perceived as, above all, a labour market or employment problem. Although educational participation is quickly catching up in relation to other European countries (especially in Spain), the majority of the labour force in both countries is not highly qualified, a problem that is related to the continuing centrality of 'traditional' socioeconomic structures. Therefore, much policy energy is spent in trying to make the conditions for young people in the labour market more secure while at the same time attempting to ensure that competitiveness is maintained. According to the Spanish Report:

> The excessive precariousness of the labour market, mostly due to its high turnover and temporary nature, means that young people are not able to make plans for their future. (Spanish National Report, quoted in Furlong and McNeish, 2001, p 146)

Furthermore, as the final report goes on to point out:

> Among young people those on temporary contracts are approximately 75% for both women and men. Thus a largest proportion of the young population are employed in insecure jobs and young people very often find themselves drifting in and out of different forms of employment over a number of years – this does nothing for gaining professional competency in a particular

occupation and detracts from any form of occupational loyalty as work experiences are short and often discontinuous with one another. (Spanish Final Report, quoted in Furlong and McNeish, 2001, p 146)

In this situation, education and training are mostly sought in labour market-related practical training, and vocational education is geared more towards the labour market demand for professional skills instead of educational ones.

Both the Italian and Spanish governments are currently undertaking large-scale programmes of structural reform across labour markets, welfare, education and training systems, whose aims would appear to be closer integration with the other systems operating across the EU. Hence in Spain, a National Action Plan (NAP) has been pursued over the past few years with the aim of comprehensive reforms across education and training systems to engender a new coherence, and to address the issue of the precarious nature of young people's employment through the introduction of new employment contracts and subsidies[4]. In Italy, similar comprehensive reforms are underway with, for example, the prolongation of compulsory secondary education, attempts to bring together general education and vocational training, and the devolution of labour market policy making. The following quotations from the Italian National Report indicate the sheer scale of reform that is currently being undertaken:

> There are at least three aspects [to the current reforms] .... Firstly, for the first time we are going out from a monopoly of public employment office towards a mixed employment service to improve the supply .... Secondly, now we can talk about active labour policy without separating training from the employment service .... Thirdly, the labour market, training and educational system will be linked up to one another. (Trade union representative, Emilia-Romagna, 2000, quoted in Furlong and McNeish, 2001, p 69)

The main purposes of reform are:

1. eliminating bureaucratic obstacles to entering the labour market;
2. making labour contracts more flexible;
3. enriching the range of labour policies underlying the role of training;
4. letting local bodies have new powers for those actions where the state has failed;
5. giving more management power to local services, allowing private agencies to act as intermediaries.

The German system of integration is similar to that which operates in Spain and Italy in the sense that it also concentrates on integration through vocational training that is specifically oriented towards the labour market. The latest programme for unemployed young people, which is embodied in the Immediate

Action Programme (IAP), epitomises this approach with its stress upon the enhancement of vocational qualifications as the pathway to employment. The dual system in Germany has been highly institutionalised for many years and movement through it for all young people is considered to be an important prerequisite for successful integration and the assignment of social positions in German society. At the same time, however, the dual system is in crisis because of a rigid inflexible structure that is difficult to change while the economy and the labour market are increasingly put under global pressures to restructure. Therefore, since the mid-1990s, increasing numbers of young people have failed to enter regular training and have been placed in pre-vocational schemes as an alternative.

Finally, the UK, the Netherlands and France represent positions somewhere between Sweden and Denmark on the one hand, and Spain and Italy on the other. In the Netherlands, attention is given to reforms of the educational system (introducing more theoretically orientated vocational programmes) and promoting the attainment of (lifelong) learning skills via the 'Study-house' construction in secondary education and the 'primary starting qualification'. Conversely, however, the focus of unemployment programmes such as the contemporary WIW programme (the Act on the Mobilisation of Job-seekers), which targets those aged under 23 years for options such as subsidised employment and schooling or work experience, is still primarily to get young unemployed people into a job as soon possible. Those unemployed young people who flow back into the education system are not, however, considered clients anymore.

The latter situation is equally the case in the UK. As with the Dutch WIW, the New Deal for Young People (18- to 24-year-olds) offers participation in options in return for benefits: in this case subsidised employment, further education or work experience in the voluntary and community/environmental sectors. Its primary aim is to facilitate entry or re-entry into the labour market. In this conception, according to the UK report, 'paid employment = social inclusion = full citizenship'. The British educational system seems largely to be left alone with regard to contemporary reforms except as regards the increasing involvement of the further education sector (largely vocational) in delivery of options within the New Deal programme.

In France, the latest programmes for unemployed young people also tend to be focused on work-based learning, apprenticeships and vocational traineeships. The NSNE (Nouveaux services – Nouveaux emplois) programme actively creates jobs for young people in various forms of social service. In doing so, however, it 'bucks' the 'supply-side' trend of other European programmes. Emploi-Jeunes, which operates through coalitions of social partners organised in 'mission locales', takes on the responsibility of support at the individual level once a young person has been unemployed for six months. Trajet d'accès à l'emploi (TRACE) is a new kind of 'ways-to-work' programme, which offers 18 months of subsidised integrated measures that are especially aimed at young people who suffer from multiple disadvantages.

Table 6.1 gives a typological overview of the policies designed to tackle unemployment among young people and their objectives in the researched countries.

Youth unemployment and state policy: progress evaluation

Since different countries have different starting points due to uneven political, economic and cultural development, some countries are a lot closer than others to meeting the core commitment of the Luxembourg Summit's guidelines. Only two of the countries – the UK and Sweden – can be considered to have fulfilled the pledge to give all young people unemployed for six months or more 'a new start' (through the New Deal and Municipal Youth Programmes, respectively). Most other countries are close though to fulfilling this pledge, but at least one (Italy) – and perhaps another (Spain) – are unlikely to have met this target by the agreed date of the end of 2002.

Similarities of approach: employability and the supply-side orientation

While there is clear variation in policies and programmes due to uneven development, there are also significant similarities that can be highlighted.

Table 6.1: Main objectives of policies against youth unemployment in eight EU member states

Country/policy	Key policy areas	Objectives of policies
DENMARK *Youth Effort*	Education	Education for individualisation through an activation policy
FRANCE *Emploi-Jeunes, NSNE and TRACE*	Employment	State provides employment for social integration
GERMANY *Immediate Action Programme*	Training	State and social partners provide training and pre-vocational measures for skilled jobs (normal biography)
ITALY *Extensive reforms*	Education/ training (+ employment)	Comprehensive reform of school, vocational training and employment policies
NETHERLANDS *WIW*	Employment	Labour market programmes for labour market integration
SPAIN *National Action Plan*	Education/ training (+ employment)	Reform of education system plus labour market programmes
SWEDEN *Municipal Youth Programme and Developmental Guarantee*	Youth/education	Reform of education system plus labour market programme (part of youth policy)
UK *New Deal*	Employment	Reform of welfare, vocational training, further education and labour market programmes

Perhaps most important on a practical level is the fact that each country has adopted, to varying degrees, an active supply-side orientation to labour market policy where the primary objective is to increase the employability of the unemployed (see Chapter Five of this volume). What 'employability' means exactly within the policies and programmes again varies from country to country, but in a very general sense it can be defined simply as the ability to attain and retain paid employment. This policy is commonly implemented through a combination of inculcating soft skills by processes of individualised motivational counselling, and hard skills, through access to educational opportunities and/ or work experience and vocational training. Some countries have adopted this strategy fairly recently (Italy, Spain); others are entering new phases of it (UK, France, Germany), while others have much longer established programmes (Sweden, Denmark, Netherlands).

Closely related to the focus upon employability is a common acceptance by European governments, to greater (for example, UK and Denmark) or lesser extents (for example, France and Germany), that reforms pertaining to labour market deregulation and flexibility are needed to make it easier for employers to hire (and fire) workers (for example, on a part-time, temporary contract or casual basis) and, hence, enhance competitiveness[5]. Here it would appear that, over the past couple of decades, the Anglo-Saxon American model of liberal free-market capitalism has increasingly assumed a hegemonic status over indigenous European models – Rhineland, Scandinavian and Mediterranean (see Hutton, 2002). The effects of this shift in policy orientation upon both those in work and those without work has been the creation of a heightened sense of insecurity and fear regarding the future as traditional social protections and safety nets are eroded, and resistance from the trade unions, as in the recent general strikes in Italy (April 2002), Spain (June 2002) and Austria (May 2003). Employment, education and training programmes for the young unemployed and the new opportunities for lifelong learning operate within this framework, where there is an implicit assumption that for young people entering the labour market today, their experience of paid employment will no longer be either continuous or lifelong. Instead, individuals need to be prepared for a fractured, destandardised life biography, where the experience of what have been called 'yo-yo' school-to-work transitions (see Chapter Two of this volume; EGRIS, 2001) is in fact extended over the period of an individual's working life. Thus, while individuals may have a life that is predominantly in work, that life will be punctuated by periods of unemployment, education and retraining in order to acquire the requisite employability skills required by the labour market.

Similarities of problem: weaknesses of the supply-side approach

Due to the commonality of the active supply-side approach across the EU, the problems encountered in relation to the effectiveness of policies and programmes targeted at unemployed young people are also very similar. From the research, six key types of interrelated problem can be identified:

1. There is the problem generated by the *uneven geography of unemployment*, which means that unemployment tends to be concentrated in areas of deprivation (usually inner cities or peripheral estates) where there is little business and hence no demand for labour (see Turok and Webster, 1998). Such areas are inhabited by the poor working class and ethnic minorities and it is these young people, the most vulnerable and marginalised, who are increasingly left behind by national or regional labour market programmes, while those living in enterprise-friendly environments benefit the most. This problem of the uneven geography of unemployment also pertains to regional socioeconomic divisions where, for example, Italy and the UK are affected by North/South divisions, while Germany is affected by the East/West split.

2. There is the problem that centres on the fact that the *most disadvantaged group of young people grows proportionately in relation to the total unemployed* as education and training programmes develop over time. This is due to a 'creaming off' effect, which means that those unemployed young people who are most 'work ready' are advantaged very quickly by policy and programme interventions, while it takes much more concerted effort and time to benefit those who are least 'work ready' (see Chapter Fourteen of this volume). The Danish example is instructive here because, despite youth unemployment having fallen to frictional levels in recent years, there continues to be a problem with what is referred to in the Danish National report as the 'Remainder Group':

> Our most important task is to ensure that this group doesn't increase, but there are signs of it doing just that. We see an increase in this group. It probably has to do with marginalisation, this development makes it more difficult to participate and it will probably call for a different kind of effort. (Municipal official, Herlev, Denmark, 2000, quoted in Furlong and McNeish, 2001, p 61)

This point is also made quite pointedly in the following interview extract concerning the New Deal for Young People in the UK:

> There is a bottom percentage that I used to think was around 20% – that maybe was true at the start of New Deal but I think that percentage is now getting bigger because you are left with the difficult group .... What you are left with is people who are going to have to come back for New Deal Two. It hasn't failed them but it hasn't got them to the level of job readiness that you would like them to be at. But you live in the real world, everybody ain't going to go through this process within the first year and New Deal resolves everything for them – all I'm saying is that it is probably greater

now than 20% at the bottom of the whole cake, and something different needs to be done for them. (Employment Service district manager, UK, quoted in Furlong and McNeish, 2001, pp 113-14)

Equally the French Report makes this point clear in relation to the TRACE programme:

> Young people who benefit ... tend to be more and more qualified. This element introduces two pernicious effects: the exclusion of the low-qualified young people who should be the targeted population of employment policies; and the overall disqualification of the system as long as qualification contracts are seen as a perquisite for accessing the job market. (French National Report, quoted in Furlong and McNeish, 2001, p 64)

In essence, the very grouping the policies and programmes are meant to reach often benefits the least, and in fact current approaches may even serve to reinforce marginalisation and social exclusion. This is especially so in national contexts such as the UK, where the reasons for labour market success and failure are strongly individualised.

3. There is the problem that there is often a *mismatch of labour supply to demand* when demand is high. Labour market programmes for young people across Europe often fail to supply employers with the type of skills they require. The research reveals that this tends to be due to the lack of local flexibility, and not enough partnership with employers, in the design and delivery of education and training programmes. Here, as the French National Report indicates, the multi-agency NSNE programme is designed to solve this problem:

> Far from only aiming at matching a supposedly well known supply and demand of jobs resulting from the market's invisible hand, at the core of the programme lies the assumption that complex/professional services (engineering the contents of new jobs, training, new qualifications etc) need to be built under decisive PES [Public Employment System] direction, but in cooperation with a wide array of social actors: private firms, non-profit organisations, local authorities, training and education agencies. (French National Report, quoted in Furlong and McNeish, 2001, p 65)

4. There is the problem of *sustainability and retention* whereby young people move through employment and training programmes finally to secure employment, only then either to be made redundant very quickly again or leave voluntarily. These young people will return once again to the benefits system or may indeed be lost to the system altogether. This problem of the 'revolving' door in countries such as the UK accounts for up to 25% of all young people passing through education and training programmes.

5. There is the problem of the *type of 'employability' skills* offered (that is, the content of training and education programmes) and the way in which programmes tend to lock young people in to one particular transition pathway or maybe even into what might be called a 'misleading trajectory' (see Chapter Two of this volume; Walther et al, 2002). European labour societies appear to be moving towards a hollowed-out labour market where there is an increasingly sharp demarcation between primary and secondary sectors, and multiple segmentation existing within each. Employment in the primary sector is increasingly based upon high degrees of educational capital and highly specialised types of competency and knowledge. However, the training and education programmes on offer to unemployed young people across Europe are, in the main, of the low-skilled generic variety that categorises those participating as failures, while locking participants into a biographic pathway that is almost always characterised by insecurity and low pay in secondary sector-type jobs, or indeed into a trajectory that furnishes them with outdated skills.

6. There is the problem of the way in which *occupational segregation by gender* is built into the fabric of the education and training programmes on offer to young people. Young women in particular suffer from this institutionalised sexism where the emphasis is upon the reproduction of traditional female roles in the labour market, such as services, caring and so on. Moreover, there is reluctance among governments to take seriously the problem of the reconciliation of the desire to take paid employment while at the same time fulfilling family commitments (this problem is dealt with in more detail next in this chapter).

Gender issues and the transition to work

In consideration of the issue of gender in relation to issues of unemployment and employment, the following points – identified by research in the field of gender studies – apply as a general critical starting point across the eight European countries where the Leonardo da Vinci research project was conducted:

- the persistence of distinctive trends of segregation (both horizontal and vertical segregation). European women at work are concentrated in four main sectors of activity (health, teaching, distribution and catering); women at work continue to occupy positions of less responsibility and autonomy than their male counterparts (this is especially the case in the private sector);
- the precariousness of the forms of paid employment engaged in by women (although women currently occupy two out of five jobs in Europe, they also occupy four out five part-time jobs and are much more likely to be employed on a temporary or casual basis);

- women are usually the first victims of unemployment (rates of women's and young women's unemployment are systematically higher than men's unemployment except in the UK and Sweden);
- women generally occupy less well-paid jobs (across Europe, the average pay gap between male and female wages varies between 20% and 30%).

When *young* women's transitions to work are focused upon, the following elements can be highlighted. Generally speaking, even if the process of convergence appears to be very slow, the gap between young women and young men is narrowing in relation both to numbers in paid employment and to pay rates. Young women are staying in education longer, and therefore are increasingly obtaining better and better qualifications. Nevertheless, young women do have to cope with more complex and difficult transitions to work. The period of transition is longer for them and the risk of long-term unemployment is higher – this is especially so in Southern Europe.

The case of Germany illustrates this issue well. In Germany, female unemployment rates are only slightly higher than male rates, except in East Germany where women have been particularly affected by labour market restructuring after reunification. Nevertheless, the political will to reduce the gap in unemployment rates has been expressed in the framework of the IAP. However, two current trends are impeding success. First, there is evidence of an increase in gender-specific segmentation in the dual system. For instance, the percentage of young women in the dual system in 1997 stood at 40.5% in West Germany and 37.9% in East Germany; this is despite higher grade school qualifications of young women (Furlong and McNeish, 2001). Statistics of the national employment service reveal that this is a matter of structural determination and not a matter of 'female choice', since 50% of the applicants in 1997-98 were female. The employment service argues that this problem arises because young women are concentrating their interests on training for only a few selected professions. Second, gender segmentation can be identified as operating within school-based vocational training. This means that vocational guidance pushes young women into the 'typically female' professions associated with care, health and social services, thus reproducing the dominant ideologies of femininity that permeate wider society. In this sector, young women in 1997 accounted for 80% of trainees. However, because they do not involve 'productive labour', these transition routes lead to employment positions with lower wages and less opportunity for mobility and further training (Krüger, 1991, see also for a more general account, Rees, 1992). As research interview respondents indicated, several negative effects of the normative conception of women's work could be identified:

- The orientation towards regular vocational training is by far the highest priority, which tends to form a hegemonic tunnel perspective. This is the main reason for the disadvantages young women face and that are most often dealt with institutionally by either 'cooling out' their occupational choices or placing them in schemes related to home economics.

- The gender segmentation of the dual system is not tackled seriously. Campaigns such as 'girls in male professions' can be considered as token gestures that reduce equal opportunities to the formal aspects of the employment service; for example, informing young women that technical professions could be an option for them, or employers agreeing in principle to take on female apprentices without any substantial changes regarding the reality of training in these sectors.

- When employers accept young women as apprentices, they hesitate to employ them after their apprenticeship finishes. Equal opportunities still have to be promoted with regard to working conditions that facilitate the reconciliation of work and family.

The research evidence points to the fact that the issue of young women's transitions to work is still strongly related to two strong contextual determining factors. First, the dominant conception of the place of women in society; and second, the opportunity for young women to have their children cared for when they are at work. Beyond policies that promote equality, it is only when these two factors are addressed seriously by policy makers and politicians that the difficulties faced by young women in the transition to work will be ameliorated. As demonstrated by Ostner and Lewis (1995), in most societies questions relating to women's employment are closely linked to the way in which the state supports families. National policies that aim to promote female employment often have to reconcile contradictory principles – the right for women to choose a professional career, and the needs of children. Simple and straightforward solutions, therefore, are hard to find and the consensus on which they can be built is often precarious. Consequently, policies towards women tend to lack coherence and direction.

Divergences in approach: the meaning of integration and citizenship

At the level of ideology, a key research finding was the pervasive extent to which the discourse of 'rights and responsibilities', with the emphasis firmly on the latter, has permeated the European political landscape and has impacted on policy making in relation to employment and unemployment (see also Chapter Five of this volume). This political discourse – essentially one of communitarian citizenship (see Etzioni, 1993) – and associated discourses such as 'inclusion/exclusion', 'the underclass', 'dependency culture', 'deserving and undeserving poor' and so on (all in fact resonant of US workfare, which individualises the causes of unemployment and hides the structural causes) have come to challenge the classic liberal conception of citizenship (see, for example, Marshall, 1950), which framed postwar welfare policy making in the core EU countries. In the UK, this communitarian discourse has become very familiar due to its constant articulation by New Labour politicians and various related think tanks over the past few years and is reflected in interview responses from senior policy makers as well as practitioners working at the front line of New Deal delivery:

> I think it is part of a broader framework of rights and responsibilities. I think that is the right framework to have. It is basically saying that those who can work should work and those who can't work, unlike the United States, need to have a system of support and security. The question is how far are we going to go on who should work. (Senior Official, New Deal Task Force, UK, quoted in McNeish, 2000, p 7)

> For once it is maybe going to break this cycle if you hit 16, you leave school, you go and sign on – the attitude that you are owed money: "you owe me" .... It is going to take something like this to stay for six or seven years to catch the generations and then maybe change the whole culture – "No, this isn't an entitlement! This comes with responsibilities and as long as you fulfil your side of the bargain, your responsibilities – you will get your benefit". We want to get rid of that whole 80s, early 90s kind of 'You owe me my giro' mentality. We're quite hopeful and we see it happening already – clients do now realise. (New Deal adviser, Glasgow, UK, quoted in McNeish, 2000, p 8)

However, it is surprising to see just how influential this discourse is in the countries of the EU where varieties of Christian and social democracy have traditionally been in the political ascendancy. Outside the UK, evidence for the institutional penetration of the rights and responsibilities discourses is especially strong in Germany and Netherlands where it can be linked to moves towards 'weak' or 'indirect' forms of workfare (see discussion later in this chapter). For example, the German report points to the fact that a number of social work officials who were interviewed criticised what was perceived to be an "increasingly repressive climate induced by the [IAP] programme". This was because:

> due to its size and variety of measures, the programme has been allowed to 'flush' all the young unemployed through the employment service and thus to distinguish the 'deserving' from the 'undeserving'; those to be supported from those to be 'punished' (by cutting benefits or rejecting applications for further support). (Social worker, Germany, quoted in Furlong and McNeish, 2001, p 68)

Equally in the Dutch report, the WIW programme was held to be operating in a paternalistic manner due to its implicit adherence to the notion of 'rights and duties', which is held to be applied less stringently to those over 23 who take part in adult programmes. Another piece of evidence that points to the strength of the responsibilities discourse is the reality that in each of the researched countries where benefits of some form or another are granted to young people (all except Spain and Italy), benefits sanctions (of varying degrees of severity) are used to ensure compliance among the unemployed young with their education and training programmes (Lødemel and Trickey, 2001). The notion of communitarian citizenship and the associated discourse of rights and responsibilities is set to gain in strength as the general political climate in Europe moves increasingly to the Right and the EU moves towards enlargement.

Citizenship rights of the classic liberal welfare variety are thus being challenged by the communitarian responsibilities discourse. Hence, in countries where the latter discourse informs policy making, welfare becomes conditional and dependent upon the willingness to engage in activities that will either directly or indirectly lead to productive labour (van Berkel and Hornemann Møller, 2002). Underpinning this discourse is the valorisation of productive labour and the social, moral and increasingly legal imperative to engage in what is held up as the ultimate standard of all human behaviour. Ruth Levitas (1996, 1998) has described this European-wide moralising about paid employment as a key aspect of what she calls the 'new Durkheimianism'. Although it is important to recognise that its impact and form varies depending upon the national context – and indeed that its final victory is far from assured – this discourse of an employment-based communitarian citizenship can be characterised as increasingly acting as a kind of European ideological master-frame for policy making in relation to young people, employment and welfare. As part and parcel of 'the third way' (Giddens 1998), this version of citizenship is bound up with 'modernisation' and all that is 'new' about post-ideological pragmatism, while it also paradoxically appeals to conservatives because of its authoritarianism and strong moral paternalism. Unless there is a fundamental political shift across Europe, it is likely that those young people growing up today will make the transition to full adulthood in a societies where citizenship does not simply mean belonging to a given community but rather means engaging in paid employment in return for being allowed to belong to that community. This, of course, raises fundamental questions about the citizenship of those who are excluded from the labour market due to lack of demand for their skills, disability, illness, age or indeed for any other reason.

Integration through training?

Using Gallie and Paugam's (2000) adaptation of Esping-Andersen's (1990) model of comparative welfare regimes as a starting point, and drawing upon the findings of the Leonardo project, a typology of 'transition regimes' (Walther, 2000) pertaining to the eight researched countries can be constructed that is useful for the purposes of critical comparison.

It can be seen from Table 6.2 that 'training' is indeed central to the policies of the researched states in attempting to facilitate the socioeconomic integration of unemployed young people. However, the 'training' on offer is wide-ranging

Table 6.2: Transition regimes in Europe

Welfare system	Countries	Concept of youth	Concept of youth unemployment	Concept of disadvantage	Transition policy aims
Universalistic	Denmark, Sweden	Personal development	'Not foreseen' (education)	Individualised and structure related	Education and youth policy
Employment-centred	Germany, France, Netherlands	Allocation to social positions	Qualifications Individual deficit	Individualised	Vocational qualifications
Liberal-minimal	UK	Economic independence	Dependency/ exclusion	Individualised	Employability
Sub-protective	Spain, Italy	No clearly defined status	Segmented labour market, no formal trajectories	Structure-related	Comprehensive reforms for recognised status (employment, training or education)

and varies from country to country, where some favour theoretical/abstract education, others favour vocational qualifications and apprenticeships related to industry, and still others favour the fostering of basic soft skills that allow employability in low-status services. This variance arises from different traditions of welfare, dominant discourses vis-à-vis the objectives of youth, concepts of unemployment and disadvantage, and is reflected in the different aims of transition policies.

Different historical constellations of social, political and cultural development have given rise to different welfare systems, which range from universalistic in Denmark and Sweden, where coverage is comprehensive and high; employment-centred in Germany, France and the Netherlands, where coverage is variable and dependent upon contributions; liberal-minimal as in the UK (and US), where coverage is incomplete and weak; to sub-protective in Spain and Italy, where the family acts as complementary social support to a very incomplete and very weak welfare system.

Differences in welfare system feed into differences that exist from country to country regarding the socially and institutionally defined prime objectives of young people. The following ideal types can be constructed which help to illustrate this difference:

- economic independence: UK;
- adaptation to social position: Germany;
- construction of individual biographies: Denmark, Sweden;
- adaptation and biographic construction: France, Netherlands;
- the struggle to introduce a distinct and independent youth status: Italy and Spain.

These ideal types help to give some clarity to the shifting picture across the researched countries with regards to the prime developmental/societal objectives of the youth phase of an individual's development. It should be recognised, however, that these objectives are generally interlinked and operate alongside each other in the researched countries – the emphasis here is on primary objectives.

Connections can be made between the interpretations and explanations of youth unemployment and disadvantage that are given primary status in different transition systems, and respective assumptions regarding the development/societal tasks of youth. In Denmark and Sweden, it is mainly the shift towards high-qualified jobs in the IT sector that is seen as the cause of youth unemployment. Widening the pathways to higher education and the widespread provision of short IT-oriented courses reflect this assumption. Due to the strong emphasis upon individual choice, lack of qualification is broadly interpreted as lack of motivation due to failures in the educational system or labour market institutions as opposed to failures on the part of the individual. Hence, the transition policy that is in operation should be viewed as one whose aim is to activate the individual through youth policies (Sweden) and the provision of educational opportunity (both Denmark and Sweden) that will enable personal development and 'integration through education'.

In Germany, the main concept explaining youth unemployment is 'disadvantage'. This is related to the notion of individual deficits regarding learning capabilities, social behaviour or language skills. This concept is institutionalised through the combination of a selective school system, a standardised vocational training system and a paternalistic welfare state that has the aspiration to 'care' for all young people. Disadvantage thus serves as a criterion of eligibility (or selection) for pre-vocational measures and training schemes provided by social youth work/vocational youth assistance agencies. Disadvantage at the same time smoothes the process of social allocation. In Germany, the aim of transition policies is the generation of vocational qualifications that will allow entry into the dual system.

There is some overlap with the explanations prevailing in the Netherlands, France and Denmark. France is the context in which policies conceive of youth unemployment most clearly as the result of a straightforward lack of jobs. For example, the objective of NSNE is to promote the shift towards the service economy by creating jobs in those sectors where market dynamics are less developed (social services). In France and the Netherlands, however, the emphasis of the transition policies is upon vocational qualifications as opposed to education (like Germany).

The ascription of youth unemployment as resulting from individual behaviour prevails primarily in the UK. In the context of a dynamic low-wage service economy and the expansion of the New Deal programme for 18- to 24-year-olds (to other social groupings of the unemployed), those remaining unemployed are considered to be reluctant to engage in education, training or employment due their being mired in a 'culture of dependency' on welfare benefits. Similar interpretations have begun to gain prominence in the Netherlands, where unemployment is increasingly restricted to young people from minority ethnic groups who are seen as 'not willing'. In Britain, however, the overall objective of transition policies is simply employability of any form – something that ties into the dominant notion of the objective of the youth transition as being economic independence.

Young people in Italy and Spain are vulnerable to risks of unemployment and exclusion for two key reasons. The first is labour market segmentation according to age, which keeps young people broadly out of regular work places (for example, by temporary contracts). This problem is even more acute for young women or in regions with a mainly rural economic structure. The second problem is a considerable qualification mismatch between supply and demand. The mainly school-based education and training system increasingly fails to meet employers' needs. This does not only concern young people with low qualifications but also those with post-compulsory and higher education certificates. Due though to recent reforms leading to a differentiation of education and training systems, 'problem' groups are increasingly being identified and subjected to specific programmes. The aim of the transition policies in these countries is some form of recognised status for young people, whether it be through education, training or employment.

Policy recommendations

The 'Integration through Training?' report makes the following recommendations to policy makers dealing with the problem of youth unemployment in Europe. Those recommendations that are not feasible in the short term due to the nature of the current socioeconomic framework should be viewed as long-term goals:

1. In order to address the problem of the uneven geography of unemployment, some form of government-backed *demand creation* is required in areas where there is little or no demand for labour.
2. Particular attention needs to be given to the development of *programmes that deal specifically with the most disadvantaged, marginalised and excluded young people*. This will require something very different and innovative from what is on offer in the current mainstream of education and training, as well as the allocation of substantial resources (see Chapter Fourteen of this volume). This might involve the funding of projects that facilitate empowerment, build confidence and advance soft skills and competencies (see Chapter Nine of this volume). Such projects may not be resource-effective in the short term; they may not lead straight to employment and, therefore, they require that progressive policy makers in this area take a lead against those who view all policy making in terms of short-term cost-effectiveness.
3. In order to tackle the problems of mismatch of supply and demand and of misleading trajectories, education and training schemes need to be tailored more effectively to the demands of local labour markets – in essence, greater local *flexibility* within national or regional programmes for the young unemployed is needed (see Chapter Thirteen of this volume).
4. Stronger measures need to be introduced on the *retention* side of the equation in order to encourage employers to retain young employees who have come through training programmes and to encourage those same employees to stay with employers. Here, changes in employment law and increased tax breaks might be useful, as would substantial increases in minimum wages and opportunities for both young workers' career advancement and personal development.
5. In order to engender at least a modicum of security in individual life trajectories, it is suggested that there should be a shift from employment-oriented models of integration to educational-oriented models that are backed up by strong welfare provision (that is, the Scandinavian model). With this should come the development of skill bases and the enhancement of competencies that enable adaptability to the demands of lifelong learning.
6. It should be recognised by policy makers that, should governments allow work to become increasingly casual, deregulated, flexible and insecure, then

individuals and especially young people will inevitably spend periods, perhaps even long periods, of their lives unemployed and hence in forms of training or education acquiring the skills and competencies demanded by an ever-changing labour market. If individuals are not to become demotivated (and hence at risk of exclusion) and the socio-political system is not to lose its legitimation, then both material security – possibly in the form of a living citizens wage or basic income – and other non-employment-based opportunities to construct satisfying biographic pathways must be made available, to ensure that society does not continue to suffer the growth of multiple dysfunctions, social pathologies and social polarisation.

7. Equal opportunities policies need to be taken seriously at the levels of advisory agencies, education and training, and at the level of resources provided for childcare. Moreover, education and training agencies and employers need to facilitate the fulfilment of family commitments, whether it be females or males engaged in them.

8. In order to promote harmonisation and even out the most damaging aspects of uneven development, an equalisation of the proportion of GNP (at the high end of the scale) that countries commit to education and social welfare is required (OECD, 2002).

Conclusion: the challenge for European governments

Across the EU there is a general trend towards an increasingly flexible, deregulated economy, despite its uneven progression and the resistance to it. This economy operates a progressively hollowed-out labour market, where middle-range skilled jobs of the traditional manufacturing variety are being relocated to the developing world or are replaced by technology, while middle managers are culled as lean production methods are imported from the US and Japan. This is part of a process of change towards an uncertain post-Fordist order (see Amin, 1997), where the protections, rights and certainties of the past are being eroded. At the same time, however, the employment and training schemes on offer to the unemployed young are still operating (despite recent reforms and apart from in the most advanced states, such as Sweden and Denmark) along largely inflexible, rigid, predetermined, preset lines – that is, in a Fordist manner. Hence, there is something of a mismatch.

The challenge facing EU governments in relation to unemployed young people (if they are going to abandon attempts to regulate their economies), therefore, is to equip those young people through an adaptable flexible education system with the competencies required to deal with the training demands of the ever-changing economy (lifelong learning). Equally, those governments must go much further in meeting the material requirements of the young unemployed (by providing a genuine living income) in order to guarantee some form of security in a sea of uncertainty – 'flexibility' must be complimented by 'security' (see Chapter Thirteen of this volume). This should go hand in hand with the recognition that unemployment is a 'normal' by-product of capitalism, and hence the unemployed (both old and young) are a 'normal' facet of capitalist societies. Indeed, if present post-Fordist trends continue within advanced capitalism, then structural reasons for unemployment cannot do anything else but deepen and an alternative framework of development centred on the notion of a 'post-wage' society may have to be contemplated (see Gorz, 1999). Finally, governments must try to ensure that opportunities are given to young people to satisfy their personal aspirations by providing them with the capabilities to construct biographic pathways that they feel they have control over and are therefore meaningful to them, as opposed to being imposed from outside by the rigidities of the system as they are in many cases just now. In other words, the encouragement of secure but flexible lifestyles and biographies should be concomitant to the increasing flexibility in labour markets and economies.

Notes

[1] We are grateful to the Leonardo da Vinci Research Group for their collective input into this chapter. Andreas Walther (IRIS) should be especially singled out for thanks for his advice and constructive criticism on an earlier draft of this chapter, as should Andy Furlong (University of Glasgow) for his coordination of the research group.

[2] The final report is structured around six chapters, entitled: 'Contexts and perspectives'; 'Models and modes of delivery'; 'Evaluating effective delivery and implementation'; 'Theorising youth and models of transition'; 'Integration through training: explaining variation between policy objectives and delivery'; and 'Structural variation in youth unemployment policies'.

[3] The future of these educational programmes, however, was put in doubt by the election of a Conservative government in 2002.

[4] At the same time, however, increasing 'flexibilisation' and 'deregulation' has somewhat undermined this strategy.

[5] In terms of the flexibilisation of young people's employment, Spain could perhaps be viewed as a cutting-edge 'trendsetter'.

References

Amin, A. (1997) *Post-Fordism – A reader*, Oxford: Basil Blackwell.

EC (European Commission) (1999) *The European Employment Strategy and the European Social Fund in 1998*, Luxembourg: OPEC.

EGRIS (European Group for Integrated Social Research) (2001) 'Misleading trajectories: transition dilemmas of young adults in Europe', *Journal of Youth Studies*, vol 4, no 1, pp 101-19.

Esping-Andersen, G. (1990) *The three worlds of welfare capitalism*, Cambridge: Cambridge University Press.

Etzioni, A. (1993) *The spirit of community: The reinvention of American society*, New York, NY: Touchstone.

Furlong, A. and McNeish, W. (eds) (2001) *Integration through training? Comparing the effectiveness of strategies to promote the integration of unemployed young people in the aftermath of the 1997 Luxembourg Summit*, Glasgow: University of Glasgow/ European Commission.

Gallie, D. and Paugam, S. (eds) (2000) *Welfare regimes and the experience of unemployment in Europe*, Oxford: Oxford University Press.

Giddens, A. (1998) *The third way*, Cambridge: Cambridge University Press.

Gorz, A. (1999) *Reclaiming work: Beyond the wage based society*, Cambridge: Polity Press.

Hutton, W. (2002) *The world we're in*, London: Little Brown.

Krüger, H. (1991) 'Doing gender. Geschlecht als Statuszuweisung im Berufsbildungssystem', in D. Brock, B. Hantsche, G. Kühnlein, H. Meulemann and K. Schoser (eds) *Übergange in den Beruf – Zwischenbilanz zum Forschungsstand*, Weinheim and München: Deutsches Jugendinstitut, pp 139-69.

Lasonen, J. and Young, M. (eds) (1998) *Strategies for achieving parity of esteem in European upper secondary education*, University of Jyvaskyla: Institute for Educational Research.

Levitas, R. (1996) 'The concept of social exclusion and the new Durkheimianism hegemony', *Critical Social Policy*, vol 16, no 1, pp 5-20.

Levitas, R. (1998) *The inclusive society? Social exclusion and New Labour*, London: Macmillan.

Lødemel, I. and Trickey, H. (eds) (2001) *'An offer you can't refuse': Workfare in international perspective*, Bristol: The Policy Press.

Marshall, T.H. (1950) *Citizenship and social class*, London: Pluto Press.

McNeish, W. (2000) *New Labour's New Deal for Young People: A critical discussion*, Research Working Paper prepared for the Leonardo project, Glasgow: University of Glasgow.

OECD (Organisation for Economic Co-operation and Development) (2002) *Education at a glance, OECD Indicators 2002*, Paris: OECD.

Ostner, I. and Lewis, J. (1995) 'Gender and the evolution of European Social Policy', in S. Leibfried and P. Pierson (eds) *European social policy: Between integration and fragmentation*, Washington, DC: The Brookings Institution, pp 159-93.

Rees, T. (1992) *Women and the labour market*, London: Routledge.

Sivera, R. (2000) *L'emploi des femmes en Europe*, Lettre CAF, no 100-101.

Turok, I. and Webster, D. (1998) 'The New Deal – jeopardised by the geography of unemployment', *Local Economy*, vol 12, no 4, pp 309-28.

van Berkel, R. and Hornemann Møller, I. (eds) (2002) *Active social policies in the EU: Inclusion through participation?*, Bristol: The Policy Press.

Walther, A. (2000) *Spielräume im Übergang in die Arbeit. Junge Erwachsene im Wandel der Arbeitsgesellschaft in Deutschland, Italien und Großbritannien*, Weinheim and München: Juventa.

Walther, A., Stauber, B., Biggart, A., du Bois-Reymond, M., Furlong, A., López Blasco, A., Mørch, S. and Pais, J.M. (eds) (2002) *Misleading trajectories: Integration policies for young adults in Europe?*, Opladen: Leske+Budrich.

SEVEN

Transitional Labour Markets and training: rebalancing flexibility and security for lifelong learning

Harm van Lieshout and Ton Wilthagen

Introduction

This chapter applies the transitional labour market (TLM) perspective to the (re)institutionalisation of education, training and labour markets in order to facilitate a new perspective on lifelong learning. Following this introduction, this chapter introduces TLM theory, and a related policy paradigm that has developed in the Netherlands over the past few years that operates under the label of 'flexicurity'. Section three applies these general perspectives to the field of education, training and lifelong learning. Section four illustrates how a traditional institutional training model such as apprenticeship functions as a TLM to facilitate the transition from education to employment, and how similar models might serve to facilitate other transitions. Section five shows how the TLM perspective can be applied to an analysis of new developments by focusing on the example of the combination of apprenticeship and work placements for the unemployed in the Netherlands. Section six then discusses the contribution of TLM and flexicurity perspectives to the concept of Integrated Transition Policies (ITPs) that animates this book.

Transitional labour market theory and flexicurity

Transitional labour market theory argues that the borders between the labour market and other social systems have to become, and indeed are becoming, more open to transitory positions between paid work and gainful non-market activities that enhance and preserve future employability (Schmid, 2000, pp 223-34). It is based on three interrelated principles:

- labour markets are inevitably exposed to shocks to which workers or employees have to adjust; hence, chaotic patterns of employment/ unemployment are increasingly becoming a fact of life for everybody;

- labour markets are social institutions, whose adjustment through wage flexibility is limited as status and human dignity forbid wages below a certain level. Therefore, they require effective and socially legitimate institutions of adjustment;
- enforced or unplanned idleness of labour can be used positively, but newly constructed buffers are required. TLMs are the solution in providing functional equivalents to the 'hinterland' of the traditional subsistence economy, or social security through the family network (Schmid, 2000, pp 227-8).

In sum, TLMs can be regarded as institutional responses to critical events in labour markets. Critical transitions can be said to occur when events result in a change in assumptions about oneself and the world, and thus require a corresponding change in one's behaviour and relationships. Events that change important elements of social networks (such as actual or potential job losses) are especially critical. They are like exits through doors that are in fact bolted shut on the other side, while the opening of the doors from the front remains uncertain. Thus, the danger is that they initiate processes of social exclusion (Schmid, 2000, p 228).

As a normative concept, TLMs envision new kinds of institutional arrangements to prevent those transitions from becoming gateways to social exclusion (exclusionary transitions) and to transform them into gateways to a wider range of opportunities for the employed (maintenance transitions) as well as for inactive or unemployed people (integrative transitions) (Schmid, 2002, p xiv). Active labour market policies can help to cope with these difficult situations by providing a supportive institutional environment. Four principles characterise TLMs (Schmid, 1998, p 9):

1. they combine paid employment with other *useful activities*;
2. they combine various *income sources*, such as wages and transfer payments;
3. there are legally enforceable *entitlements* that are related to a choice of transitional employment;
4. *fiscal incentives* operate in such a way as to finance employment rather than unemployment.

Five types of transitional employment can be distinguished:

1. transitions between part-time work and full-time employment, or transitions between dependent work and self-employment, or a combination of both;
2. transitions between unemployment and employment;
3. transitions between education or training and employment;
4. transitions between productive (but unpaid) private work and (paid) market work;
5. transitions from employment to retirement.

Figure 7.1: Education and training in the Transitional Labour Market model

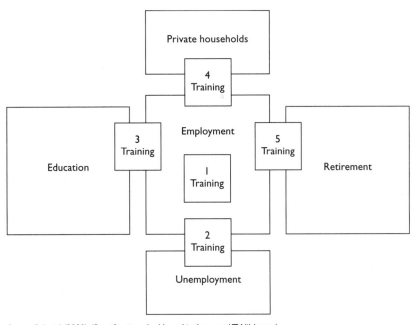

Source: Schmid (2000) (Specifications by H.van Lieshout and T.Wilthagen)

Schömann (2002) has recently developed an elaborate and innovative application of TLM theory in relation to education and training in a volume where it is applied to research of both a quantitative and qualitative kind (Schömann and O'Connell, 2002). He offers a challenging and complex methodological framework (modelling both learning and working processes as an independent process as a pendulum of fixed length and weight, with the addition of an elastic connection between the two), as well as specific hypotheses to be tested in empirical research. The object of this chapter is comparatively modest, and more exclusively policy-oriented. It illustrates how TLM theory can help us to refine our research questions and hypotheses on the agenda of the institutionalisation of lifelong learning.

One general point needs to be emphasised, however, with regards to the particular objectives of this book. While our main emphasis is upon institutions and policy, one of the most appealing characteristics of TLM theory is its explicit multi-level character. Following Coleman (1990), its explanatory approach consists of three basic steps (Schömann, 2002, p 9):

- the explanation of macro influences upon individual-level explanations, which constitutes the macro to micro link;
- the explanation of individual actions through individual characteristics and individual behaviour, as in micro-level theories;

- explanations of how individual actions in their sum, or collective actions, determine macro-level outcomes.

A concept related to TLM theory is 'flexicurity', a compound of flexibility and security (Wilthagen, 1998; also Chapter Thirteen of this volume). While the term flexicurity incorporates the need for flexibilisation, it differs from the neoliberal call for flexibilisation in that it simultaneously underlines the importance of (re)regulation for an adequate operation of the labour market, by providing both workers and firms with the basic security they need. The concept does not oppose (labour market) regulation as such, but points at the existence of mismatches between traditional working practices and modern labour markets. Working practices that may once upon a time have been necessary instruments for the emancipation of workers (and particular weaker groups among them), may sometimes today unintentionally reinforce the exclusion of the 'have-nots' into the secondary segment of (or even outside) the labour market.

The 'flexibility and security nexus' appears as one of the typical paradoxes in modern society and can be considered to reflect the distinct and different codes, logics or rationales of two social subsystems – the economic system, on the one hand, and the legal/labour–law/social security system on the other (Muffels et al, 2002). In less abstract terms, one can speak of a double bind for policy makers. The need to adjust labour market policies and systems of labour law is frequently being advocated by the OECD and others for reasons of competitiveness and employment growth. On the other hand, there is a growing concern in Europe about the socioeconomic positions and prospects of flexible workforces, among other things, in terms of training and education, and a broader fear of bifurcation of the labour market and diminishing social cohesion. The flexicurity paradigm in labour market policy making explicitly deals with this double bind that policy makers are facing by (re)connecting and (re)balancing economic and social goals and rationales. Thus, we contend, the flexicurity paradigm might serve as an implementation strategy for the development of TLMs that address both policy ends by creating transitory states between paid work and other socially productive sub-systems.

Both flexicurity and the TLM perspectives commonly acknowledge the need for flexibility in modern labour markets and simultaneously emphasise the need for security – for both workers and firms. As Schmid (2000, p 233) argues:

> The more dynamism is required or desired, the higher the level of transitional unemployment and the greater the need to build bridges – which means transitional employment – leading back into the regular labour market. The more workers can put their trust in such arrangements, the more they will accept uncertainties.

Both also share the characteristic that they see more than just economic reasons as warranting a certain level of flexibility, for example, caring responsibilities at home.

A TLM perspective on lifelong learning

TLM theory has sometimes tended to lump education and training together in one transition, that between education or training and employment (Schmid, 2000). We prefer to distinguish between education and training, in particular in view of the need for lifelong learning. First, and in the line with the international literature on the school-to-work transition, we specifically speak of the 'transition between education and employment' when referring to the transition of youth from educational systems into employment. Second, this opens up the opportunity to reserve the term 'training' (including, but not exclusively, apprenticeship) as a part of the other TLMs. While school-to-work/education-to-employment transitions continue to have their own problems, it is safe to say that this transition, today, is generally less problematic than the other transitions, in particular that between unemployment and employment. The call for lifelong learning is nothing more than the idea that the (re)institutionalisation of training opportunities as part of the other transitional labour markets would ease transitions there. Equally, the call for lifelong learning is in itself quite 'flexicure' in nature. It is based upon the conviction that, first, labour markets require increased flexibility from workers. Second, it is based on the conviction that education and training (resulting in improved skills) contribute to workers' flexibility. Third, given persistent problems in successfully reintegrating the long-term unemployed in the European labour market, it is based on the conviction that skills (and therefore the education and training for improving them) are, in essence, the best security workers can have. While social security systems still provide a treasured safety net for those falling out of the labour markets, the security they provide is increasingly viewed as a second-best alternative, as long as significant numbers of unemployed find themselves incapable of ever escaping the net (Wilthagen, 2002; Nagelkerke and Wilthagen, 2003: forthcoming). Moreover, social security systems have come under strong fiscal pressure during recent decades, which make it doubtful that past or even current benefit levels will successfully survive.

Fourth and finally, the call for *lifelong* learning points to a mismatch between traditional rules, working practices and modern labour markets that is perceived to be a problem that can be addressed by (re)regulation. Traditionally, institutional supports stimulating education and training have focused on youth and young adults. Government intervention aimed to achieve the goal of each youth having a chance at a decent education, this being a necessary foundation for prosperous citizenship in general and a successful individual career. It is one of the more successful examples of government intervention, as initial education and participation have expanded substantially over the past few decades. However, as the successful growth era of the first post-Second World War period ended with the oil crises of the 1970s, mass unemployment again appeared prominently on the European policy agenda. By then, mass unemployment had taken on a different face than before. Besides the obvious quantitative problem it always posed, its make-up increasingly came to indicate qualitative problems as well. As coal gave way to oil and gas, non-European countries successfully gained market shares in shipbuilding from European ones, and agricultural employment decreased due to technological innovation and imports. Hence, increasing numbers of unemployed came to possess skills that had been rendered obsolete (within their country at least), as the type of employment such skills were targeted towards had disappeared. These types of shifts continue today. Bank telling, for instance, is a waning occupation in the age of digital banking, Automatic Telling Machines and currency integration. No longer can macro-economic improvements alone be thought enough to solve unemployment problems: people have to be retrained for different occupations.

The call for lifelong learning, then, points to the fact that the idea that initial (vocational) education and training for youth can suffice to supply the market with an adequate skills base to last an *entire* occupational career is becoming increasingly obsolete. The life span of occupations themselves seems to have shortened; and even within occupations themselves, the actual skill requirements change much more rapidly. Since the call for lifelong learning was first heard in the 1960s, there has been a growth of adult training, sponsored by firms, social security funds, or general taxation.

What has not changed, however, is the importance of initial (vocational) education and training. It is no secret that current further training investments are substantially higher for those who have already achieved higher education and training levels. Rather than further training diminishing the importance of initial (vocational) education and training for the success of labour market careers, it may very well have increased it. Put bluntly, if you miss out on your first shot, the chances are you will never get a second shot again. And, for those unemployed people who do gain access to (re)training programmes, the simple fact is that, in general, completion rates and subsequent labour market successes are at a level that lies well below those on initial education and training pathways.

This has two key implications. First, the transition from education to employment does not grow less important – quite the contrary, in fact. A successful initial education career followed by a successful transition into (stable) employment often signals the start of a prosperous career that will include (self- or firm-sponsored) further training. Second, the task for the other transitional labour markets (those that aim to [re]integrate those who currently find themselves outside the labour market) grows more difficult when those who enjoy stable employment continuously upgrade their skills. Put simply, if the employed in a particular labour market segment cannot significantly upgrade their skills simultaneously, training in TLMs would only have to provide skills training up to an entry level. However, to the extent that those employed in particular labour market segments also continue to upgrade their skills, (re)entry requirements of firms will rise, and reintegrating people into the labour market will require more significant skills training.

The institutionalisation of training to facilitate transitions: new futures for old models?

The relative ease of school-to-work transitions as compared to others makes it useful to explore the potential of institutional models that have proven to be relatively effective at one transition (from education to employment) to help ease the passage of other transitions. We will illustrate this regarding apprenticeships in this section. The *auctor intellectualis* of TLM theory, the German labour market researcher Günther Schmid, has praised apprenticeship for the 'flexible coordination' it provides (Schmid, 1992), and suggests it as a possible way to implement transitions between work and education or training for adults on a larger scale (Schmid, 2000, p 236). We use the apprenticeship model here as a heuristic example to explore requirements for TLMs that are meant to include and support training to ease the education to employment transition as well as other transitions. In the process, we define apprenticeship in a very broad way as training that includes a noticeable work-based component. In no way, however, do we mean to imply that this type of training could be the answer to everything, would not have problems of its own, or would provide a superior alternative to other possible institutional configurations. Again, we use this model for illustrative purposes.

One other model, that is advocated by economists in particular for future education and training reforms, is the idea of a subsidised voucher system, in which training rights could be used flexibly over time. The idea of a voucher system in itself is not new – in fact, each system with sponsored training rights is, in essence, a voucher system. We welcome this concept to the discussion on lifelong learning, because it explicitly focuses our attention on the following questions:

- To what extent can subsidised training rights in fact be made available to all citizens, and is this particular distribution both effective, efficient and equitable (and under what conditions are they enforceable)?
- To what extent are such rights institutionalised flexibly to ensure that citizens can use them when needed, as opposed to only in a particular life phase where they are *generally* considered most suited within some explicit or implicit notion of a standard biography?

We are sceptical, however, over voucher notions that focus exclusively on the institutionalisation of the (individual's) demand side of the education and training market, and subsequently assume that an invisible hand will automatically lead to the optimal training supply. While much is to be said for strengthening consumer power in education and training markets, and increasing the room for tailor-made solutions, the vision of a completely individualised training market is naïve. For instance, an experiment with a completely modularised supply of the final two years of Dutch university education at the faculty where one of the authors was previously employed showed that (a) only a small minority of students chose truly individualised trajectories, while (b) the large majority asked for suggested standard combinations, and stuck to those, which (c) soon resulted in the reinstitutionalisation of a required choice between a fixed number of standard trajectories, to be complemented by a limited number of freely chosen modules. If this happens to a serious attempt to institutionalise a completely free subject choice for academic students, it is doubtful that weaker social groups would be able to effectively plan their own individual ways out of a skills deficit. So at the very least, they will have to be informed of various relevant options and their expected (labour market) results. Institutionalising this type of service, as well as (to some extent) standardised routes to choose from, remains a necessary component of reform policies in this area.

Confronting an apprenticeship model with the principles characterising TLMs will not only show us that apprenticeship can easily be seen as an example of a TLM facilitating the transition from education to employment, but also help us to pinpoint particular challenges facing the (re)institutionalisation of lifelong learning to facilitate the other transitions.

Combining paid employment and training

Apprenticeship fully complies with the first principle that characterises TLMs; this is because it combines paid employment with another useful activity: training. This element is key. Instead of the sequential institutionalisation of the transition from education to employment as a (instantaneous) transition from full-time school participation to (typically) full-time employment, as implied by general secondary education and school-based vocational education and training (VET), apprenticeship implies a parallel institutionalisation of labour market and school participation (school-based related instruction, usually for one day each week). This way, apprenticeship in itself constitutes a separate transitional labour market.

Transition from education to employment through apprenticeship is a two-step process. First, there is a transition from (general) secondary education into the TLM/apprenticeship ('first threshold'); second, there is a transition from the TLM/apprenticeship into 'regular' employment ('second threshold'). Transitional labour markets should ease the second transition, and apprenticeship is generally found to do so for the education to employment transition. In fact, school-based VET can easily be remodelled in this fashion, as has been the case in the Netherlands, where all school-based upper secondary VET currently has to include a work-based internship component of at least 20%.

Overall evaluations of TLMs have to be based upon both steps, however, and not just the latter. Important disadvantages of otherwise fairly successful apprenticeship systems have in fact been related to the first step. In general, successful apprenticeship systems tend to enforce the labour market exclusion of groups failing to graduate from (or even enter into) them. In particular, disadvantaged groups such as women and ethnic minorities have tended to be overrepresented within this excluded group (see Chapter Fourteen of this volume).

Combining various income sources

Apprentices themselves typically receive direct income from just one source: an apprenticeship wage from their training firm. Closer scrutiny, however, reveals that young people themselves in fact pay a part of the training costs through accepting apprenticeship wages that are lower than what they could have received elsewhere, in exchange for the training they receive. In a typical case, however, the training firm will require that the apprentice stay with the firm for a little while upon completing the training, in order fully to recoup its training investments. The inherent uncertainty about this actually happening might deter an individual firm from such an investment. To circumvent this problem, many sectors have created joint training funds through collective bargaining to finance apprenticeship. By forcing individual firms to contribute to the fund, it subsequently becomes much more attractive for them to train individually, as this is the only way to recoup the levy. Government subsidies and/or tax cuts for training firms achieve a similar effect, albeit throughout the general economy rather than being limited to a specific sector.

It is this pooling of funds that is perhaps the most attractive characteristic of apprenticeship systems as an example to inspire institutionalisation of training to facilitate other transitions. Training costs are high not so much because of the direct costs of training provision, but because there is a simultaneous need to give the trainee an income. To the extent that both trainee and firm agree to bear part of the costs, there is relatively little need for further government funds – meaning government resources can be spared for training investments for other groups.

At the same time, there is a reason why apprenticeship has so far been primarily a factor in facilitating the education to employment transition, rather than other transitions. Young people generally do not have to support a (large) family, meaning that individuals in that life phase can generally afford to contribute to training costs by accepting a relatively small apprentice wage. Once people grow older, their immediate financial needs (children, mortgage/ rent) tend to grow, meaning they will be less and less able to afford an extensive training period at a relatively low income level. On the other hand, the younger people are, the longer the expected period over which they and their training firms can expect to profit from any training investments. Other things being equal, we can therefore expect firms to prefer younger apprentices to older ones. The very success of apprenticeship in easing the education to employment transition may point, therefore, to an important challenge for the institutionalisation of lifelong learning: other things being equal, training investments are more easily made for young persons, both because the cost (of living) is lower, and because the period over which one can benefit from the training is longest.

Legally enforceable entitlements

While apprenticeship is not a legally enforceable entitlement, in the sense that the government guarantees an apprenticeship position, it does include various legal entitlements for those who acquire apprenticeship positions (for example, apprentice wage entitlements, dismissal protection), and often includes a back-up plan (for example, school-based training) for those who do not.

The legally enforceable entitlements that apprenticeship typically brings go a long way towards identifying the main lines of the institutionalisation of training to facilitate other transitions. First and foremost, it is the certification of acquired skills that is of crucial importance. For the trainee, the fact that her skills will be certified in an established and broadly recognised diploma is an important safeguard for her investment (in terms of foregone higher earnings). Collective bargaining agreements generally link apprenticeship graduation to (more) attractive wage scales; and an apprenticeship diploma will ease transfer to another employer (should the current one have either no job openings or unattractive ones upon graduation). For firms, the diploma (typically linked to a set of national or at least regional skills standards, and ideally to some form of independent examination of graduates) eases recruitment of external recruits – and the transaction costs thereof (see Chapter Four of this volume). This way, a set of rules concerning skill standards, examination and certification contributes both to security (diplomas leading to pay raises) and flexibility (subsequent labour mobility eased by reliable skills certification).

Skill standards in formal apprenticeships regulate and certify skills training both in schools and in workplaces. However, skills are not only acquired in formalised training settings but also, in an informal way, as a result of learning 'on the job'. Recognition of previously acquired skills has therefore gained prominence on the policy agenda. Examining and certifying skills that workers already command will clarify and pinpoint the nature of true deficiencies towards other credentials. This will help keep training time (and, hence, costs) as low as possible, and will therefore stimulate demand. It is no coincidence, therefore, that various states have embarked upon the development of national skills standards systems not (or no longer) exclusively linked to formal apprenticeship systems. There is no reason to exclude skills that might have been acquired from access to certification. In practice, apprenticeship systems often already had some possibility of recognition of previously acquired skills, although this was usually the exception rather than the rule. In fact, it is conceivable that the more detailed skill standards are (and they tend to be fairly detailed with apprenticeship systems), the lesser the (relative) extent of credit towards which recognition of prior learning will generally lead. As with TLMs in general, a set of rules (here, skill standards) that is an effective tool in easing the transition to employment for those that achieve them will simultaneously widen the gap for those who do not. Job competition is, after all, a matter of competition.

Fiscal incentives to finance employment and training

We have already discussed the possibility of using tax cuts to finance (apprenticeship) training. Here, we wish to repeat the point made on the declining attractiveness of apprenticeship and training in general as an investment for both firms and citizens as the latter grow older. The need for fiscal incentives seems to be greater for older citizens than for younger ones. At the same time, state investments (tax breaks and subsidies together) are still predominantly focused on youth and young adult training. While there are still good reasons for the latter, it may be opportune to question the current division of state training investments over the life course in the future.

In addition, it may be opportune to question the wisdom of (extensive) general tax cuts to stimulate training. As long as firms are inclined to predominantly select those with already substantial skills for further training, general tax cuts will to some extent subsidise training for more privileged groups that would have occurred anyway in the absence of tax cuts. In addition, the 'extra' training generated by such a general tax cut might predominantly trigger training for somewhat less-privileged groups, but fail to reach those with the highest skills deficiencies. In that case, it might actually unintentionally widen the skills gap between the haves and have-nots.

Apprenticeship as a TLM from unemployment to employment

To illustrate how a TLM perspective can also help us analyse new empirical developments in labour and VET markets, we briefly discuss an example of how existing institutions have historically facilitated one particular type of transition that can be used to ease another type of transition (van Lieshout and van Liempt, 2001)[1].

The combination of apprenticeship and work placements for the unemployed is important because it explicitly aims to use an institutional arrangement (apprenticeship), proven to be effective in easing the transition between education and employment, for simultaneously easing another transition – between unemployment and employment. This is particularly relevant as the costs of extensive (and not just job or skill-specific) training of the unemployed are high enough (because of the necessary income support) to still limit the numbers of unemployed trained – even decades after the OECD started to declare the institutionalisation of lifelong learning vital for future economies – and because many training projects for the unemployed have not reached the levels of effectiveness and efficiency that their architects aspire to.

While most countries have extensive apprenticeship systems, they have generally remained reluctant to encourage substantial numbers of the unemployed from embarking on such proven tracks because they fear a crowding-out effect of youth by the unemployed. This would also correspond to training firms saving expenditures for apprenticeship wages, while the government picks up the bill in terms of unemployment benefits for (the first stages of) apprenticeship training. If, however, the trend towards lifelong learning continues to materialise, apprenticeship-type tracks simultaneously remain theoretically attractive institutions to facilitate its growth (Gelderblom and de Koning, 2001). This is because they would allow the government to phase out welfare subsidies to the unemployed and have training firms pay them apprenticeship wages instead during (the final stages of) the training period itself. In a European review study, Gelderblom et al (1997) find confirmation for the hypothesis that apprenticeship plays a role in enhancing employability and job creation, and that unemployment is low for apprenticeship graduates, even when compared with graduates from comparable other tracks. Specific evaluations of apprenticeship schemes for the unemployed also point to positive (although not large) effects. Gelderblom and de Koning (2001), for example, see the expansion of dual (apprenticeship-type) training as a promising avenue to facilitate employment and training in a TLM.

The first Dutch experiment in this area connected a work experience programme for young people (first JWG, currently WIW) with apprenticeship. The combination of JWG (Jeujdwerkgarantiewet – Youth Employment Guarantee Act) with apprenticeship implied that the work experience placement for the young unemployed sponsored by the JWG simultaneously served as the work-based component towards regular apprenticeship training for the first half of their training duration; at that point, the training firm would have to take over the trainee as a regular apprentice to complete training. To prevent crowding out of regular apprenticeships through this combination, there were additional conditions to be met. For instance, unemployed youth had to be placed in a 'regular' JWG placement for a year before they could enter this combination – the implication being that this combination is preserved for the most disadvantaged group of unemployed youth.

Since that time, apprenticeship has become a regular training option available for all unemployed, nationwide, under a new national act governing unemployment reintegration, the WIW (Wet Inschakeling Werkzoekenden – Act on the Inclusion of Jobseekers). Instead of exclusively being available for young unemployed under the JWG, it may now also be offered to older long-term unemployed, provided they have been unemployed for over a year and their labour market position has been diagnosed as weak. While a negative selection bias can thus be expected to remain a problem for the effectiveness of the combination for this target group, it should no longer be a problem for the category of youth under 23 years of age: municipalities are no longer required to wait one year before they can combine WIW job placements with the apprenticeship training pathway. In addition, there is no longer a national requirement that the training firm has to take over the trainee as a regular apprentice halfway through the training period. Municipalities in principle now have the freedom either to require a firm to take over apprentices from the start of apprenticeship training, or alternatively to keep them on welfare until graduation (firms, on the other hand, would have to meet relevant stipulations in collective labour agreements).

Two municipalities have tried out another way to use apprenticeship to train the unemployed: contract compliance. Contract compliance can be defined as the inclusion of additional, social clauses in contracts concluded in the course of regular or incidental government activities (government assignments and tenders, the granting of subsidies and permits). Both local experiments include a requirement to train (long-term) unemployed as apprentices in local publicly funded building plans, upon which contractors place their bids. The experiments include various supporting facilities, such as preliminary training trajectories to upgrade the skills of the unemployed to a level where they can subsequently start apprenticeship training with a fair chance of completion. Apprentices remain on welfare during preliminary training, but are regular apprentices (subsidised by an apprenticeship training fund in the respective sector) once they start apprenticeship with one or more individual contractors. Here, too, numbers of unemployed trained are still very low.

Dutch examples of contract compliance provide an easy theoretical way out of the financial dilemma regarding the relative expensiveness of substantial training for the unemployed, as here the government can limit itself to just paying welfare benefits for necessary preliminary remedial teaching and occasional additional counselling, while firms pay apprenticeship wages for the entire duration of regular apprenticeship training. The combination of job-seeker schemes and apprenticeship could in principle be conceived in a similar way – and under the new act, the WIW, Dutch municipalities have the freedom to do so. This could work in practice as long as apprenticeship wages are not lower than welfare benefits recipients would otherwise receive; if they are, however, supplementary income support will be necessary. In addition, firms' potential *ceteris paribus* preference for recruiting fresh education graduates rather than unemployed people as apprentices might suggest at least a partial wage subsidy (Schmid, 2000, p 234). The availability of unemployment funds in all Dutch sectors, and training funds in many of them, implies that such wage subsidies will not necessarily have to be covered by the state alone. We currently lack the detailed empirical material necessary to settle these issues more precisely, but the recent emergence of two types of arrangements that make apprenticeship training available to Dutch unemployed guarantees that it is there to gather and explore. This research will evaluate whether or not these arrangements do actually succeed in hosting a subsequent higher outflow to regular employment than other labour market reintegration measures for the unemployed.

Transitional labour markets, flexicurity and Integrated Transition Policies

Integrated Transition Policies are defined as a policy approach with regard to transitions to work that integrates separate policy areas (mainly education and training, labour market, welfare and youth policies) in an individualised and biography-oriented perspective (see Chapter One by Walther and McNeish and Chapter Two by du Bois-Reymond and López Blasco).

The TLM perspective centres on similar assumptions and aims, and provides an adequate foundation for the development of such policies. The combination of paid employment with other useful activities is the first principle defining TLMs, and the combination of various income sources is the second. In addition, the TLM perspective routinely proposes the integration of various types of policy (such as income policy and fiscal policy). Moreover, the idea of legally enforceable entitlements provides a strong legal backbone for the integration of different activities and policies. Without such entitlements, TLM participants are at risk of facing conflicting demands of various agencies they have to relate to. An infamous example is when unemployed people enrolled in a substantial retraining course are suddenly forced to quit in order to accept a certain job opportunity that their social security agency has unexpectedly come up with. The most important difference between the concept of ITPs and TLM theory is that the former is focused on the category of youth, while the latter explicitly offers an integral labour market vision, focusing on all transitions for all age groups.

The flexicurity concept, briefly described in the second part of this chapter and further discussed in Chapter Thirteen of this volume, likewise complements the notion of ITPs. The idea of re-evaluating the pros and cons of current regulation for different groups is a necessary and adequate start for the development of such policies. In addition, the flexicurity concept has the advantage of explicitly focusing on the relation between different groups, and the possibility of reducing the security offered to some in order to enhance that of others. Integrated Transition Policies should not be developed with a blind eye that excludes all but the youth groupings they are immediately concerned with. To the extent that labour market (re)integration is one of the (eventual) goals pursued, an awareness should be retained that employers always have alternative recruitment channels at their disposal. Analysing those alternatives, and the reasons why employers might prefer those to recruiting the current unemployed group, will go a long way towards bolstering policies for that group.

Integrated Transition Policies should be careful not to become, let alone remain, *separated* transition policies. First, separate policies for disadvantaged groups have an unfortunate tendency to become the first casualties of recession-induced budget cuts. Second and more importantly, separated policies have often led to separated credentials (that is, training diplomas from retraining institutions rather than credentials from the initial vocational and education system). And such alternative credentials have had, more often than not, a lesser labour market value than more prevalent counterparts (that is, credentials from initial VET) – in the worst case, even to the extent where the negative signalling of having been in such programmes comes to outweigh the positive signalling of newly acquired skills. The gradual international trend towards the development of national skill standards systems that allow skill credentialisation to become independent of a particular provision structure is promising in this respect. What should matter is the skills portfolio one carries, not where and how it was acquired, and an independent and uniform credentialising system for all skills should prevent or at least mitigate the negative screening of specific training programmes for disadvantaged groups. Third and most ambitiously, ITPs should aim to address some of the weaknesses of current mainstream institutions. Remaining separated from mainstream institutions would limit the chances of helping to change those institutions; and without change to mainstream institutions, the fruits of ITPs will remain smaller than we would hope. In this sense, TLM theory is again a good example, as it is much more than the sum of its parts. Rather than propose isolated policies for disadvantaged groups, it puts forward a labour market model of which other spheres of life, and transitions between those spheres, are an integral part of the model. Structured TLMs and ITPs then become a logical and necessary key component of any modern labour market policy – rather than remaining fringe exceptions created to accommodate one weaker group or another.

As Schmid (2000) has argued, coordination in the form of public partnerships represents a major precondition for TLMs, and the same goes for the development and implementation of ITPs. The traditionally strong role for social partners in the governance of, for instance, Dutch and German VET (further enhanced by recent developments in national-, sector- and firm-level collective bargaining negotiations between the social partners) indicate that such partnerships do indeed provide an apparently congenial environment for the developments of TLMs there. We do have to realise that the role of these associations presents a specific type of partnership. Associations have members that bestow certain capacities within these associations, allowing them to balance their members' interests – the "logic of membership" – with the constraints and opportunities offered to these associations by their environment – the "logic of influence" (Streeck, 1992, p 105). Striking a balance between the two logics is not easy as they may not always be compatible, and in some cases may even contradict each other (Streeck, 1992, p 105). Associations are in principle better equipped to solve this contradiction, either on their own or through binding (collective) agreements between them, than looser partnerships. However, there are distinct national differences in the availability of this specific governance mechanism of associations and partnerships, as well as distinct differences in their specific institutionalisation (for example, unions that focus on the firm level versus those who focus on the sector/national level), that cause differences in the extent to which this model applies to varies nations. At the European level, therefore, much is to be said for an implementation approach to ITPs that adopts this looser partnership perspective. This should prevent countries lacking well-developed associations in some of the relevant fields to adopt such policies (and to strengthen associational governance in their wake), while allowing those that have strongly developed associations to give them more substantial roles than is currently the case.

The latter is an important perspective from which to re-evaluate current European policies. The fact that current European Social Fund regulation, for instance, is interpreted to imply that mutual training funds established by Dutch employers' associations and unions do not count as 'private co-funding', but instead are taken to be 'state support' when the collective bargaining agreement is extended by the Dutch state to cover all employers in a sector (*NRC Handelsblad*, 24 June 1993), entails a fundamental error in mistaking the voluntary private initiative of a majority of employers and unions for state action. It prevents the accumulation of competitive advantages for (continental) European countries, as compared to the US, to contribute towards European growth. Frankly, we are waiting for Dutch and other government leaders to demand their money back in a 'Thatcheresque' way should this Anglo-Saxon fallacy continue.

Finally, ITPs need agents to implement them. The ambition for ITPs to become mainstream routes, rather than a remain a separate pathway for disadvantaged groups, translates into the requirement of having standard agencies in education, training, labour market governance, welfare and youth policy adopt them as such. In addition, it would be wise to keep on open mind towards unconventional agents to carry out such policies. The case of Dutch temporary work agencies and their involvement in labour market transitions and training (see Chapter Thirteen of this volume for further discussion; van Lieshout and van Liempt, 2001) offers an interesting example of the possible and potential role of private-for-profit actors in achieving public policy goals. The case of Dutch temporary employment agencies has shown the emergence of exclusively private actors/partnerships that fulfil public goals by (partially) functioning as transition agencies. There are signs that a 'new generation' of Dutch temporary work agencies is taking on roles of intermediaries and coordinators in developing TLMs. Thus, within the right institutional context, self-regulation can serve public goals by relying on private-for-profit actors as the primary (or even exclusive) local transition agency. Of course, the long history of apprenticeship, where individual firms are in fact the most important local transition agency, implies that this, in itself, is not a completely new development. However, the aforementioned recent developments in the Netherlands indicate that this type of self-regulation may have more promise to offer than we tend to realise. This creates new questions to be answered in future TLM research. To name just one: is it foreseeable that private actors do internalise public goals to such a degree, and synchronise these with their own private operations and goals, that a new version of the 'invisible hand' will arise that is more congenial to public social goals?

Note

[1] Another example, the growing role of temporary employment agencies in training at the school-to-work and other transitions, will be discussed in Chapter Thirteen of this volume.

References

Coleman, J. (1990) *Foundations of social theory*, Cambridge, MA: Harvard University Press.

Gelderblom, A., de Koning, J. and Stronach, J. (1997) *The role of apprenticeship in enhancing employability and job creation*, Rotterdam: NEI.

Gelderblom, A. and de Koning, J. (2001) *Werken en leren in een transitionele arbeidsmarkt* (www.e21e.nl).

Muffels, R., Wilthagen, T. and van den Heuvel, N. (2002) *Labour market transitions and employment regimes: Evidence on the flexibility-security nexus in transitional labour markets*, Berlin: WZB.

Nagelkerke, A.G. and Wilthagen, T. (2003: forthcoming) 'Wie durft er nog ESF geld uit te geven?', *NRC Handelsblad*, 24 June.

Schmid, G. (1992) 'Flexibele coördinatie: de toekomst van het duale systeem uit oogpunt van arbeidsmarktbeleid', *Cedefop beroepsopleiding*, vol 1, pp 53-8.

Schmid, G. (1998) *Transitional labour markets: A new European employment strategy*, Berlin: Wissenschaftszentrum Berlin.

Schmid, G. (2000) 'Transitional labour markets: a new European Employment Strategy', in B. Marin, D. Meulders and D. Snower (eds) *Innovative employment initiatives*, Aldershot, Brokfield, Singapore and Sydney: Ashgate, pp 223-54.

Schmid, G. (2002) 'Foreword', in K. Schömann and P.J. O'Connell (eds) *Education, training and employment dynamics: Transitional labour markets in the European Union*, Cheltenham: Edward Elgar, pp xiii-xv.

Schömann, K. (2002) 'The theory of labour market transition applied to the transitional labour market of education and training', in K. Schömann and P.J. O'Connell (eds) *Education, training and employment dynamics: Transitional labour markets in the European Union*, Cheltenham: Edward Elgar, pp 8-38.

Schömann, K. and O'Connell, P.J. (eds) (2002) *Education, training and employment dynamics: Transitional labour markets in the European Union*, Cheltenham: Edward Elgar.

Streeck, W. (1992) *Social institution and economic performance*, London: Sage Publications.

van Lieshout, H. and van Liempt, A.A.G. (2001) *Flexicurity: Recent developments in Dutch vocational education and training*, Amsterdam: Max Goote Kenniscentrum.

Wilthagen, T. (1998) *Flexicurity: A new paradigm for labor market policy reform?*, Berlin: Wissenschaftszentrum Berlin.

Wilthagen, T. (2002) 'Managing social risks with transitional labour markets', in H. Mosley, J. O'Reilly and K. Schönmann (eds) *Labour markets, gender and institutional change: Essays in honour of Günther Schmid*, Cheltenham: Edward Elgar, pp 264-89.

EIGHT

The third sector: ghetto for the disadvantaged or springboard toward integration?

Paul Burgess

Introduction

With regard to transitional arrangements for young people, it has been speculated that the so-called 'third sector' of non-profit organisations, between state and market, can play an important role in developing labour markets: first, through the increase in employment opportunities within the third sector (these might be seen as a diversification of entrance options to the labour market in general); second, individuals, and especially young people in the third sector, can make valuable personal contributions – without being subjected to either market rules or formal qualification regimentation; third, tangentially the third sector is embedded in young people's biographies (life worlds) or at least provides bridges of familiarity compared to the bureaucratic logic of state institutions; and fourth, due to the lack of formalised structures, many third-sector organisations are open to individually shaped forms of engagement and participation.

The contextual background of this chapter can be located within a collaborative project funded by the EC under the Third System and Employment programme from 1998 to 2000 and involving a comparative analysis in four EU regions: Baden-Württemberg (Germany); Merseyside (UK); Cork (Ireland); Emilia-Romagna (Italy)[1]. The research examined the role of local third-sector networks and initiatives in the area of social and youth services (for example, youth work, youth policy, community work for young people) and their success or otherwise in supporting job creation for (disadvantaged) young people.

This chapter seeks to adapt some of the key findings of the project, particularly in the areas of comparative analysis of regional reports in the search for an understanding of those policies, experiences and processes that best embraced solutions and 'good practice'. Moreover, the potential of the third sector for young people's transitions to work – especially in an Integrated Transition

Policies (ITPs) perspective – is assessed as well as the constraints that limit the full exploitation of these potentials.

Employment: what is the role of the 'third sector'?

The third sector

> Our systems of employment, education and training, economic development, taxation, social security, were built upon assumptions about work and society which are now out of touch. We must introduce structural reforms into our employment, social protection and taxation systems .... This presents the third system with a new responsibility in one important element of the strategy: the need to make a decisive shift from passive to active policies. (Flynn, 1998)

As a feature of this new thinking, policy makers have sought to investigate and adapt the 'third system' as a means by which new avenues of job creation and training might usefully be explored. The term 'third system' – or third sector – refers to the economic and social fields represented by cooperatives, mutual bodies, associations and foundations, as well as the whole range of local job creation initiatives whose aim is to respond – through the provision of goods and services – to needs for which neither the market nor the public sector currently appears able to make adequate provision.

The EC has identified the third sector as a major source of employment. In a global perspective, such hopes are confirmed by the findings of the Johns Hopkins Comparative Nonprofit Sector Project, according to which the employment growth of the non-profit sector was three times faster compared with overall employment trends (Salamon et al, 1999).

The introduction of structural reforms into European employment practices, social protection and taxation systems, might variously enable a number of advances. For example, in the areas of employment:

* more diverse forms of contractual arrangement;
* wider definitions of economic activity that are valued and promoted;
* innovative training systems that continuously equip people with new skills and competencies (relevant to local labour markets and attuned to the wider range of economic activities now developing).

European trends in transitional structures of youth employment

Transitions between school and work have for a long time been the subject of both research and political attention. The (reductive) concentration on this part of the transition derives from the constitution of modern societies as functionalist labour societies in which social integration highly depends on gainful employment. In contrast to rather smooth transitions in the Fordist era, the contraction of labour markets since the 1970s and 1980s has exposed young people to risks of marginalisation. In this respect, four main patterns have been identified:

- pressure on European labour markets caused by processes of technological rationalisation, neoliberal shareholder value-structures and intensified global competition;
- increased labour market participation of women due to the need for independent sources of income and cultural emancipation;
- the construction of labour markets and welfare systems that protect male breadwinners rather than young people entering the labour market;
- a mismatch between competencies and qualifications provided by the education and training systems and the labour market due to modernisation of production and the shift from the manufacturing to the service economy (Reich, 1991; EC, 1998).

In Europe, the effects of these trends have been made visible by dramatically rising rates of youth unemployment. In most countries, young people represent the largest age group of unemployed people. From a comparative perspective, however, we find remarkable differences: in 1999, youth unemployment varied between 4% in Austria to as much as 40% in Spain. The picture diversifies even more when one looks at the social composition of unemployment. Whereas in some Southern European countries the rates for young women are much higher than for men (for example, Italy), we find the opposite trend in the UK. These differences are influenced by general labour market performance in the respective countries, cultural patterns (for example, regarding female employment), and by the actual constitution of particular transition systems. In Germany, for instance, youth unemployment has been always lower than the total unemployment rate because the dual apprenticeship system of employment training and education at school integrated a high percentage of young men and women in transition. In Southern Europe, and also in the UK until the late 1970s, school leavers entered the labour market directly and were trained on the job. Since the end of full employment, the youth labour market has been most affected by restructuring (Pugliese, 1993; Roberts, 1995).

Despite structural differences, the inherent difficulties in entering the labour market have led to an increase in educational participation across Europe. Not only have individuals stayed longer at school in order to expand their qualification profile, but governments have also actively introduced policies to make young people more 'employable' (EC, 1997c). A major policy priority has focused on the implementation and/or development of vocational training systems, either as a part of the public school system or in different models of company-based apprenticeship systems. Alongside these 'mainstream' training opportunities, various schemes for 'disadvantaged' young people have been designed. These policies start from the assumption that a certain percentage of

Table 8.1: Change of status of young people in Germany, Ireland, Italy, the UK and the EU between 1987 (1990) and 1995 (%)

	Germany		Ireland		Italy		UK		EU	
	M	F	M	F	M	F	M	F	M	F
Active										
1987	39.0	38.0	53.0	46.0	50.0	40.0	56.0	50.0	47.0	41.0
1995	33.0	32.0	43.0	36.0	41.0	30.0	50.0	43.0	38.0	33.0
Unemployed										
1990	4.3	4.7	20.4	18.2	23.3	32.4	11.9	9.6	13.9	17.6
1995	8.9	8.7	20.7	17.9	29.1	38.7	18.0	13.3	20.1	23.2
In education or training										
1987	59.0	55.0	45.0	46.0	46.0	44.0	42.0	36.0	50.0	48.0
1995	65.0	61.0	54.0	48.0	52.0	56.0	47.0	44.0	58.0	58.0

Note: M = males, F = females
Source: EC (1997a, 1998)

young people fail in entering regular training and employment due to individual deficiencies that have to be compensated for so that such young people are 'mature' or 'prepared' enough for participation in regular training programmes. However, the status of such schemes varies nationally as there are also examples (Italy or UK) in which participation in pre-vocational schemes leads to accredited partial qualifications that can be combined with further education or training (EC, 1997b; Chapter Fourteen of this volume).

European research has shown that integrative policies underlie institutional assumptions of normality (for example, the legitimacy of individual aspirations or individual ascriptions of failure), which, combined with their bureaucratic application, may actually lead to 'misleading trajectories' (see Chapter Two of this volume; EGRIS, 2001). As a result, the criteria of eligibility for participation may have too narrow (or too wide) a definition of the target group. This leads to the exclusion of individuals. Schemes aimed at compensating for individual deficiencies, therefore, may have a negative impact in so far as they may actually encourage stigmatisation. They may well restrict individuals' liberty of choice, while providing measures that apparently do little more than contain the superfluous labour force in order to 'clean-up' or 'massage' the unemployment statistics. Such policies often reproduce discourses of full employment, standard work arrangements and standard biographies that are simply unrealistic on a political, economic and a personal level. The transitional systems in which young people operate are dominated, therefore, by a series of in-built assumptions to which young people have to adapt – or perish.

Therefore, young people's biographies seem to be characterised, above all, by paradox. Young people have to cope with a situation in which they are both young and adult at the same time, but in different life contexts. They can indeed be said to live in a form of transitional purgatory. Many young people simply feel that they do not fit in, which represents a source of considerable confusion and uncertainty. As Bauman (1995) argues, this can be interpreted as a consequence of the fragmentation of individual biographies and social life. This remains an aspect of contemporary life that is especially pertinent to the everyday experiences of young people who have often been described as barometers of social change (Jones and Wallace, 1992).

Research has shown that young adults perceive their lifestyles as threatened by formal institutions, such as school, vocational counselling, training or social security – even if these institutions are intended to provide support with regard to social integration. Young adults prefer informal contexts and support relationships: family, friends, youth culture, and all contexts in which membership and participation can be negotiated and shaped individually. I do not want to equate identity work with individual involvement in informal contexts, but I do want to say that potentially (and especially in youth transitions) informal contexts are an important means related to identity work, providing an important source of belonging, meaning, orientation and experimentation. Informal contexts can be perceived as underpinning the social arenas in which transitions take place and being closely linked to 'sociality' (Bauman, 1995), a term that expresses the informal everyday practice that actually creates society. It is clearly the case that social innovation and social transformation have to be located at least partly at the level of everyday agency. This is especially true in the case of young people who may be perceived as disengaged or disadvantaged.

My hypothesis, then, is that the third sector carries a high potential for young people in developing a sense of 'biographicity' (Alheit et al, 1995). Individual strengths and ideas are negotiated and realised in the community; that is, a real context without measuring individual agency according to market exchange values or formal qualifications. This exchange between the individual and the community potentially leads to the very core of biographicity, in that it provides a context in which individual life histories can be legitimised. In this setting and in this social network, young people are able to relate individual experiences and orientations to the local opportunity structure as regards education, training and employment. In short, young people can reflect and develop their own biographies in a social context in which those biographies are accepted and nourished.

One of the perspectives of this research then, is to begin to come to terms with some of the needs young people have in an ever-changing world: the need to belong and to feel secure and in control of their own lives. It is for these reasons that young people's orientations and practices have to be taken into account when researching youth transitions. They are not simply relevant in terms of the construction of individual identity, but also as social arenas that interface with transition systems.

Unfortunately, these areas remain under-supported in so far as they lack institutional recognition. The training mindset is such that the *acquisition of competencies or potential employment* is a key concern. The less explicit benefits to be had from the training process are therefore neglected. Training agencies understandably prioritise measurable outputs, but by doing so undermine the effectiveness and potential richness of the training they provide.

A comparative analysis of young people's transitions and the third sector

Case studies into national contexts of third sector and transitions to work

It is against this contextual backdrop then, that the project 'Advising local networks of third-sector initiatives: job creation for (disadvantaged) young people in the area of social and youth services' sought to locate the effectiveness of third-sector interventions/opportunities in relation to young people's transitions to adulthood and to the labour market. The project followed an action/research approach, examining both the role and effectiveness of local third-sector networks and initiatives in the area of social and youth services in supporting job creation for (disadvantaged) young people and reinforcing existing potentials. The methods applied consisted of a questionnaire with local third-sector initiatives, qualitative interviews with both project workers and young people, and the introduction of a self-evaluation method for the initiatives. By the latter we were able to assess the biographic effects of the involvement of young people in the initiatives as a step in their transition to work.

All organisations in each of the countries examined are typical third-sector organisations, or, in other words, non-profit organisations, with one exception: the social cooperatives of Italy. Following the research of the Johns Hopkins Comparative Nonprofit Project on the structure and trends of the third sector (Salamon et al, 1999), the criteria that characterise non-profit organisations are:

- formal structure (they are all institutions with a legal status);
- private structure (formal and institutional separation of the state);
- self-regulation;
- voluntary participation;
- no distribution of profits.

The last criterion differs for the social cooperatives in so far as such organisations do make profits, although these are reinvested into the organisation.

Nevertheless, there are major differences in relation to the political and socioeconomic contexts in which the organisations have to act. Considering the general context, the third sectors in Germany and Italy are described as largely conservative combinations of welfare organisations that are very strongly influenced by the state. The dominant legal forms of organisation are associations and cooperatives in Italy and associations or semi-public bodies in Germany. In Germany, a corporatist structure has emerged creating huge welfare companies. The stable structure of the 'big five' (the major welfare organisations maintaining linkages with the churches, the labour movement, and the Red Cross, with the German case study referring to the fifth one as representing a lobby and roof organisation for 'free' initiatives) is due to the extensive application of the principle of subsidiarity in the structure of social services which allows for profits from subsidies and an involvement in policy making. Since German reunification, this structure (which is typical for our target region of Baden-Württemberg) has been expanded from the West to include the eastern regions, where the third sector plays a major role in the restructuring of the labour market, often without being socio-culturally embedded in local communities.

In Italy, the origins of many third-sector organisations are related to the Catholic Church. However, there has been a considerable process of 'secularisation' by which, in a first step, organisations linked to the trade unions, and in a second step, independent initiatives have evolved, especially at the local level. State policies have supported the development of the third sector by introducing new laws in favour of the third sector, including fiscal aid, the possibility of various sources of finance for voluntary associations (for example, 'partly' commercial activities) and greater fields of activity for the cooperatives. However, there are considerable regional differences with a very strong and dynamic third sector in the north east (for example, the Emilia-Romagna region, to which the Italian case study related) and in the southern regions inasmuch as third sector initiatives succeed in making a difference with regard to both job creation and providing young people with meaningful opportunities.

In Ireland, the third sector has been fashioned by the religious-political historical developments of a post-colonialist state. This had its origins in a symbiotic relationship between the Catholic Church, conservative social institutions and the state. The rural and religious links of third-sector organisations evolved from the cooperative tradition and were based on parish organisation and a self-help ethos. Alongside the organised church-based charities, the third sector was historically an integral provider of essential social services such as education, healthcare and childcare.

Essential to understanding the development of the third sector in Ireland is the recognition of the influence of the Catholic Church and its social teaching. The institution continues to have a significant role to play in many voluntary organisations today as well as in the provision of social services. The Irish third sector has also experienced, however, a concomitant process of modernisation in terms of urbanisation and secularisation. A diverse range of locally based democratic voluntary projects has augmented organisations. The significant difference between these organisations and the more traditional agencies is evident in the core issues of youth and community work: animation, negotiation and enabling. Indeed, these core issues have changed the emphasis of the third sector towards "working alongside and *with* people rather than *for* them" (Burgess, 1996, p 1, emphasis in original) – something that can be viewed as an increased politicisation within the third sector.

Since 1997, an attempt has been made by the Irish government to redefine the relationship between the third sector and the state towards a partnership model, which requires the government, the third sector and the private sector to play an active part in civil society. The state, however, due to the financing role of the government and such agencies as FÁS (the state employment agency) and the Community Employment Scheme, often supersedes its role as an active partner when voluntary, community and youth organisations compete for a limited amount of resources.

The UK's third sector is legally based on the welfare concept of the common law. It is characterised as an ideal typical Protestant liberal construction of the third sector in which the state tries to restrict involvement in welfare activities. The third sector usually acts in a very market-oriented fashion. The voluntary sector will probably increase within the next few years, if only because the state shows no desire to expand. Our UK case study was located in the city of Liverpool. The history of Liverpool's under-performance has led the city to become something of a laboratory for anti-poverty regional policies pioneered by successive national governments. Liverpool is extremely dependent on the public sector, while at the same time the politicised nature of the city means that partnership between different organisations remains a difficult thing to achieve. The size of the public sector and the partnership context provides the backdrop against which many individuals in the city have been working in the field of regeneration, of both their own careers and their organisations.

Comparing all those different sectors examined, the third sector in Italy, and especially in the region Emilia-Romagna, seems to be the most effective in a number of significant respects. The sector is well recognised and supported by public authorities, the population and through a new legal framework. With the cooperative as a specific form of third-sector organisation, it has developed as an intermediary between market and non-profit orientation, and seems to be very powerful, economically and socially. It is important to highlight that this development has strong cultural and historical roots and the political contexts, therefore, are highly supportive.

Nevertheless, all investigated organisations – even the Italian agencies – are under specific forms of pressure. In essence, this pressure takes the form of competition to – and marketisation of – the third sector, but takes different forms according to context. In Italy, the pressure for the third sector organisations comes through the need to be viewed as *competitive*. In the UK, the public and political pressure brought to bear on the third sector (in acting as successful private enterprises) affects third-sector organisations. Although voluntary organisations are working in disadvantaged areas with disadvantaged target groups – and are a key part of new institutional relationships that are attempting to regenerate these areas – there is no blueprint to work from. Although the third sector in Ireland has achieved more recognition by the state, the sector is still a separated and marginalised one. The state publicly asserts the intention of becoming a partner of the third sector in major social initiatives, but in reality this partnership is limited to a funding role. This leads to a greater dependency on the state and to competition between third-sector organisations for support. Moreover, the increasing influence of the burgeoning private sector competes with the third sector for the recruitment of (cheap) young workers (for sometimes better paid, black market jobs). A trend is being established whereby young people prefer to work in the buoyant private sector instead of being a volunteer or worker within the third sector.

Impact on young people's skills, competencies, qualifications and employment opportunities

In general, the young people of all the researched third-sector organisations accrued many benefits, but, above all, skills and competencies. They all gained socio-cultural competencies such as communication skills, self-confidence, sense of responsibility, ability to deal with conflicts, and teamwork. Moreover, they often acquired work-related competencies like punctuality, reliability and organisational skills, and professional competencies, such as those related to pedagogical work with children, young people, disabled people, or drug users. Furthermore, some of them learned how to produce drama and musical performances, while others acquired agricultural or handicraft competencies, and learned how to market their own work. The way in which the organisations achieved this revealed a trend strongly influenced by the respective regional and national structures of both the third sector and the transition system.

In Germany, the third-sector agencies offered pre-vocational training and counselling with regard to potential apprenticeships or professional education (accommodating a return to full-time education if necessary). This could be because employers usually prefer employees with a professional education.

In Italy, the young people got to know the organisations – especially the cooperatives – as real, potential and possible working places for the future. This socially and economically well-integrated sector offers acceptable working conditions and working places for the future. Moreover, the culture of the sector inspires young people while they are pursuing self-employment.

In the UK, we found a similar situation, but against the backdrop of different preconditions. The third-sector agency here was also focusing on self-employment for young people. However, this was necessitated by the lack of viable alternative employment. Therefore, the young people concerned have been trained to develop a realistic assessment of the labour market, and a particular way of looking at their personal and professional abilities.

In Ireland, the young people profited by the application of a 'journal of learning', a portfolio documenting a process of self-evaluation which increases employability by raising young people's self-confidence and self-reflexivity competencies. The portfolios used during this process were designed to be accessible but also challenging to the participant. The portfolios required the participants to fill in information on their own personal background, their agency and their hopes for the future. Additionally, they required them to reflect weekly on their experiences in work and the skills they used to fulfil their work goals. Through this portfolio mechanism, the project sought to enhance the existence of a learning/skills development base within agencies by 'sub-contracting' young people to work indirectly for this research project on information/data gathering, recording, observation and analysis.

The portfolio provided a method where individuals could build up, on a week-by-week basis, a catalogue of their positive and negative experiences of working in the third sector. It was adapted from an existing model of my own for work with adult learners on a Youth and Community Work Skills Training Programme at University College Cork (Burgess, 1996).

Besides this, all participating organisations focused their efforts on the empowerment of the young people with regard to their most difficult professional and personal situations. This highlights the fact that young people need more than simply a 'professional orientation'; they need general support regarding their experiences of exclusion and their rarely recognised biographical needs. They need encouragement and motivation to proceed with their biographical and professional careers, and in most cases that is exactly what they got from the third-sector organisations. These support mechanisms include the development of stable relationships, mutual trust and a general culture of solidarity. Emerging throughout this area was a consideration of the value of these benefits, namely in regard to the designations of 'employability' against the more 'concrete' concept of actual 'job creation' (the latter being a more desirable outcome for market-led/state-funded initiatives).

Moreover, the young people became aware of their skills-based knowledge. This created biographical direction and perspective, which often led to participation in further education (since most of the participants were early school leavers). In general (and in keeping with the current emphasis on the private sector), their view of the third sector was that the skills they learned would act as a springboard to transfer or channel their new-found employability into the private sector, and therefore a better-paid job.

It is not possible to document all the young people's further biographic decisions, because in many cases – at the time of interviews – they were not yet known. This highlights a transnational-shared assessment that the effects of the project on the employability of the participants will only really be illustrated over the coming years.

It may be prudent here to reflect on the specific appeal of youth work organisations with regard to the sample of third-sector agencies examined. The professionals of the organisations were very important to the young people. They represented women and men with the experiences and authority of adults but without the controlling power of parents. The young people often talked about the professionals as positive role models:

> "Well I can imagine having a lifestyle like hers later on. I don't know how to express myself, but she seems to be full of joy of life, so self-confident, she's doing her work as if it were the most natural thing in the world, that impresses me...." (Female, 18, Germany)

For the young people, the professionals are a mixture of friend, colleague, counsellor, sister or brother, sometimes mother or father relating to the needs and/or problems the young men and women concerned. In general, the most important part of all relationships was the trust that the young people usually developed toward the professionals. This served as the basis for many learning situations within informal settings.

The third sector as a springboard towards integration

The impacts on employment within the third sector – and in our case within child and youth work – cannot be assessed very optimistically, except in Italy, where we can point to a clear increase of employment due to an outsourcing of public employment to third-sector agencies and a new legal framework. All other countries show a lack of legal and financial instruments, which are necessary preconditions for employment development. German, Irish and UK third sectors are highly dependent on state sources of funding, a situation that does not allow the development of real scope for job creation. All researched third-sector organisations have to compete hard in order to get some resources for employment and/or job creation. Another barrier that should be recognised is the lack of political and societal recognition for the status of employment within third-sector organisations. Ireland shows the effects of this barrier most, whereas in Italy the Emilia-Romagna region does not exhibit this barrier at all.

Job creation versus 'employability'

Within the project's overall duration, the potentials of the different third-sector organisations – stimulated by the EC – were discussed against the backdrop of the question 'job creation versus employability?', which, in our opinion, came to be viewed as a *false dichotomy* and a misleadingly posed question in regard to the limited legal and financial scopes and contexts of most of the third-sector organisations (ECOTEC Research, 2001).

Employment policies oriented towards the third sector as a new source of sustainable employment are often critically assessed in terms of addressing job creation; that is, additional work places or individual employability. Against the backdrop of the biographical experiences documented and analysed in our research, this question can be characterised as a mistaken alternative. At the same time, employability in general is a rather misleading and abstract term, as it refers to the individuals' self-responsibility; that is, a term for individual capabilities to be employed *objectively* by someone else. It became apparent in examining young people's transitions to work that only *subjectively* relevant perspectives, which can be achieved by self-actualisation, generate intrinsic motivation. In the contexts of flexible, individualised and fragmented structures of social integration, intrinsic motivation is one of the most important resources (du Bois-Reymond and Walther, 1999). This means that 'employability' cannot be achieved without being involved in 'real' work and community experience. On the other hand, the third sector seemed to a large extent to be overcharged or burdened with job creation in the strictest sense. With the exception of Emilia-Romagna (where tax legislation and financial incentives enable at least some cooperatives to develop more sustainable jobs), all projects depended on public funds, which had to be reapplied for on a one- to three-year basis (and thus were highly vulnerable). Additionally, outsourcing of local welfare responsibilities has generated a great deal of third-sector activity. Often there is an emphasis on allocating local budgets. Therefore, the resources of third-sector organisations can provide only temporary or indefinite jobs with inadequate salaries, limited social protection and a lack of meaningful training. Our findings suggest that the third sector's potential with regard to young people's transitions is misunderstood and undervalued if measured within the scale of job creation versus employability.

In each of the projects, *career opportunities* could be provided, rather than jobs or work places in a conventional Fordist sense. Many of the young people involved have used this as a 'springboard' for developing subjectively relevant and viable pathways for their personal and working lives. This means that their employability has been raised, but only because of being involved in community or market activities and having the opportunity and support to explore activities and directions in the 'real field' of the local community and market. In order to achieve this and put this on a more solid grounding, third-sector organisations require more reliable funding and at the same time recognition in terms of status with regard to the competencies that young people develop *informally*. Put simply, jobs for young people within the third sector are rarely an end in themselves.

Perhaps there could be improved recognition of third-sector organisations and actors as 'social entrepreneurs', connecting different individual and social or community interests to a network with springboard effects for the individuals involved, while simultaneously possessing a communal value, rather than that of employers in a conventional sense.

Following the assessment of the Johns Hopkins Project (Salamon et al, 1999), it can be seen that there is a considerable lack of information about the potentials of the third sector worldwide and within the European countries themselves. Additionally, many politicians and economic leaders are unaware of the meaning and the potential resources offered by the third sector. There is a growing bureaucracy caused by the long tradition of public funding, and a concomitant increasing commercialisation caused through the growing need for competition within the sector and between the third sector and the private sector. The John Hopkins Project recommends a return to the original (philanthropic) values of the sector in order to ensure that the real needs of the citizens involved are met.

However, this description is largely superficial and there are some important implications characterising the sector's situation, which are often ambivalent.

These ambivalences can be better understood when considered under the designations of potentials versus constraints of third-sector development.

Potentials of the third sector

Third-sector organisations provide social services and reproduce the social capital of communities. This can take the form of providing services for target groups, creating and stabilising local networks, the integration of professional and voluntary work, providing (paid and unpaid) employment possibilities for unemployed young people, providing the support of employability as a self-evident part of work, the building of 'trust and confidential relationships' within the community, the developing and realising of democratic working and participation structures. In other words, third-sector organisations (having access to different [target] groups, administrative or political working agencies and enterprises of communities/regions) are able to mobilise those resources of cooperation and engagement that were formerly latent. Moreover, with the help of this specific access, these organisations are able to identify unmet needs and to encourage individuals, groups, agencies, and enterprises to express themselves.

A very specific potential strength of the third sector has to be recognised in the ability of the sector to combine social and economic objectives, tasks and issues as well as a democratic approach to paid employment (as we can well see in the example of the Italian cooperatives). Therefore, the third sector is potentially able to combine:

- labour market policy-oriented tasks (such as qualifications and employment agencies) and tasks of employment policies (such as job creation);
- tasks concerning the development of new structures related to changing needs;
- tasks related to the specific needs of different target groups;
- (as a horizontal task) social integration of participants in all processes around the different third-sector organisations.

In conclusion, third-sector organisations could take the role of a 'neutral' moderator that arbitrates between the claims and demands of the variety of community-related needs and issues that arise from many different interests and actors. They represent an intermediate perspective on transitions to work between those of individual life worlds and of systems such as the labour market or the welfare state (Habermas, 1987). Thus, they may qualify as indispensable elements of Integrated Transition Policies (ITPs) aiming to address young people's transitions in a more holistic way corresponding to the complexity of their biographic perspectives.

Constraints of the third sector

The strengths of the third sector are simultaneously counterbalanced by numerous shortcomings. Due to its peripheral situation in relation to the mainstream transition system, the third sector is often not known and recognised by public authorities within the private economy and the public in general. The sector is treated (as evinced by its own name) as a residual category of policy and provision – and depending on public funding – unable to act proactively or innovatively and is considered subsequently of little *real* importance.

The importance of the social capital potentials of the sector is virtually ignored. By 'social capital potentials' is meant the specific competencies of the sector to combine social and economic objectives, the closeness of the sector to its target groups and the ability to get access to the resources of communities and individuals.

There are some circumstances that push the third sector towards increasing competition and into the private market: in some cases, levels and sources of public funding are in decline and there are increasing numbers of commercial providers of social services. Additionally, in Germany, there has been a change in the meaning of the principle of *subsidiarity* (a move away from automatic validation of public funding to the necessity of legitimating work in order to qualify for funding).

Conclusions

In conclusion, it is important to point out that key findings of the research were posited on the premise that some third-sector employment initiatives seem intended to fill the vacuum created by the identified but unmet needs of many target groups. However, investigating the third sector's potentialities for

Figure 8.1: The third sector as intermediate field in the system of transitions to work

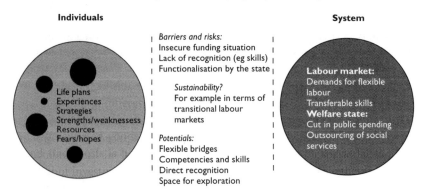

Class/education, gender and ethnicity as principal structuring factors

Individuals   **System**

Barriers and risks:
Insecure funding situation
Lack of recognition (eg skills)
Functionalisation by the state

Life plans   *Sustainability?*   **Labour market:**
Experiences   For example in terms of   Demands for flexible labour
Strategies   transitional labour   Transferable skills
Strengths/weaknessess   markets   **Welfare state:**
Resources   Cut in public spending
Fears/hopes   *Potentials:*   Outsourcing of social services
                                    Flexible bridges
                                    Competencies and skills
                                    Direct recognition
                                    Space for exploration

young people's transitions via the bi-polar terms of 'job creation' versus 'employability' offers a false dichotomy and misleadingly poses an unrealistic context in regard to the limited legal and financial characteristics of most of the third-sector organisations. The sector does not secure the resources necessary to prosecute this in a number of ways: most notably, political and public recognition which would help to organise social capital within the communities and regions; a legal framework which would support the creation of new intermediate organisational structures combining economic and social issues, designating them as equally important and significant; and finally, the need for the development of newly formulated support criteria for third sector organisations.

Perhaps one avenue through which this 'springboard potential' of the third sector could be developed and exploited is in the concept of transitional labour markets (TLMs) in which not only the status of employment but also transitions between different socially recognised activities are recognised and secured (see Chapter Seven of this volume). Given the increasing diversity and flexibility of labour markets, the concept of TLMs perhaps could be said to pose the following objective: namely, that the risk of long-term unemployment and social exclusion has to be tackled by organising 'bridges' between different socially relevant activities, occupational commitments and sources of income – thus creating what can be called a 'breathing labour market' (Schmid, 1996).

> As a *normative concept*, TLMs envisage new kinds of institutional arrangements to prevent those transitions from becoming gates to social exclusion and to transform them into gates for a wider range of opportunities (*integrative and maintenance transitions*). '*Making transitions pay*' requires institutions that realise in one way or the other the following principles: *work organisations* which enable people to combine wages or salaries with other income sources such as transfers, equity shares or savings; *entitlements* or *social rights* which allow choices to be made between different employment statuses according to shifting preferences and circumstances during the life cycle; *policy provisions* which support multiple use of insurance funds, especially the use of income (unemployment) insurance for financing measures that enhance employability. (Schmid, 1996, pp 4-5)

The key elements of transitional labour markets that are coordinated with gainful regular employment are part-time arrangements, wage subsidies, family (private) work, education and training, voluntary work and self-employment. In such a context, the specific strengths of the third sector can be exploited. These provide socially embedded support structures and biographic perspectives, while linking local labour markets with social communities. In these ways, the potential of the third sector can perhaps be fully utilised in this context and contribute to ITPs that respect the needs and aspirations of the young people concerned.

Note

[1] Contributing partners involved were IRIS e.V. (Institut für Regionale Innovation und Sozialforschung), Tübingen (Germany); GENESIS srl, Bologna (Italy); Hope Street Ltd, International Arts, Training and Development, Liverpool (UK); Department for Applied Social Sciences, University College Cork (Ireland).

References

Alheit, P., Bronn, A., Brugger, E. and Domenice, D. (1995) *The biographical approach in adult education*, Wien: Volkshochschule.

Bauman, Z. (1995) *Intimations of postmodernity*, London: Routledge.

Burgess, P. (ed) (1996) *Youth and community work: Course reader*, Cork: Centre for Adult and Continuing Education.

du Bois-Reymond, M. and Walther, A. (1999) 'Learning between want and must: contradictions of the learning society', in A. Walther and B. Stauber (eds) *Lifelong learning in Europe, Volume 2*, Tübingen: Neuling, pp 21-45.

ECOTEC Research (2001) *Evaluation of the third system and employment pilot action, Final Report to European Commission* (www.europa.eu.int/comm/employment_social/empl&esf/3syst/final01_en.pdf).

EC (European Commission) (1997a) *Youth in the European Union: From education to working life*, Luxembourg: Office for Official Publications of the European Communities.

EC (1997b) *European Employment Observatory: Tableau de Bord 1997*, Luxembourg: Office for Official Publications of the European Communities.

EC (1997c) *Employment Summit of the European Council 1997*, Luxembourg: Office for Official Publications of the European Communities.

EC (1998) *Employment in Europe 1998*, Luxembourg: Office for Official Publications of the European Communities.

EGRIS (European Group for Integrated Social Research) (2001) 'Misleading trajectories: transition dilemmas of young adults in Europe', *Journal of Youth Studies*, vol 4, no 1, pp 101-19.

Flynn, P. (1998) *Third system and employment. Seminar proceedings*, European Commission (www.europa.eu.int/comm/employment_social/empl&esf/3syst/index_en.htm).

Habermas, J. (1987) *The theory of communicative action, Vol 2*, London: Beacon Press.

Jones, G. and Wallace, C. (1992) *Youth, family and citizenship*, Buckingham: Open University Press.

Pugliese, E. (1993) *Sociologia della disoccupazione*, Bologna: Il Mulino.

Reich, R. (1991) *The work of nations*, New York, NY: Knopf.

Roberts, K. (1995) *Youth and employment in modern Britain*, Oxford: Oxford University Press.

Salamon, L.M., Anheier, H.K., List, R., Toepler, S. and Sokolowski, W. (1999) *Global civil society: Dimensions of the nonprofit sector*, Baltimore: Center for Civil Society Studies.

Schmid, J. (1996) *Welfare organisations in modern welfare states in historical comparative perspective*, Opladen: Leske+Budrich.

Stauber, B. and Walther, A. (eds) (1999) *Life-long learning in Europe, Vol 2*, Tübingen: Neuling.

NINE

The art of learning: empowerment through performing arts

Steven Miles

During a period in history in which young people's lives are apparently increasingly tenuous, the balance to be drawn between the training needs of the economy and those of young people themselves is particularly delicate. By evaluating three performing arts training programmes based in Mannheim (Germany), Liverpool (UK) and Lisbon (Portugal), this chapter aims to outline the benefits to be had from what will be referred to as 'secondary learning effects'. In what follows, it will be argued that mainstream youth training can benefit immensely by learning from alternative programmes that put young people's freedom and self-belief at their core. Above and beyond the ability to perform, the suggestion here is that these training programmes give young people the confidence to be themselves and hence to be the authors of their own training.

The European context

This research, which was funded by the Youth for Europe programme in the period 1997-2000, was concerned with the extent to which formal education and training prepare young people appropriately for the demands associated with entering the labour market[1]. In particular, the research group was interested in the extent to which training provides young people with the necessary raw materials with which they can develop their own personal biographies in an assured and self-confident fashion. Many commentators have pointed out that young people's transitions into adulthood are less secure and less easily defined than they may have been in the past, and in this context various commentators have described the 'yo-yoing' nature of contemporary youth transitions (see Chapter Two of this volume; EGRIS, 2001). The suggestion here is that young people's transitions have become destandardised and fragmented. In this sense, there is not a single transition, but a whole raft of transitions through which a young person has to navigate, notably in the context of family and intergenerational relationships, sexual and gender relations, education and training and the labour market, in local and regional, as well as in cultural, contexts. Perhaps the most important characteristic of youth transitions is that young people are obliged to develop appropriate and complementary coping strategies that are sophisticated enough to cope with the contradictory nature of their own experiences:

> in other words, young people's lives seem to bounce back and forth like a yo-yo. These oscillatory and reversible movements suggest that what has happened is the yo-yo-isation of the transition to adulthood. As if young people had gone to live in the skies and migrated like birds. (Pais, 2000, p 220)

Transitions between school and work have for a long time been the subject of both research and politics. The problem here is that modern societies have largely been constituted, arguably, as labour societies in which social integration not only depends on, but often is also reduced to, gainful employment. In contrast to rather smooth transitions in the Fordist era, the contraction of labour markets since the 1970s and 1980s has exposed young people to risks of marginalisation that have been made visible in the form of dramatically rising rates of youth unemployment. In most countries, young people represent the largest age group of unemployed people. The inherent difficulties in entering the labour market have led to an increase in educational participation across Europe. Young people in this context are currently under increasing pressure in coping with the risk of personal failure. They find themselves in a situation where they have to make important decisions about their futures, without necessarily having the appropriate support mechanisms to make that experience as straightforward as possible. In addition, in making such decisions, young people are often forced to seriously consider how to best balance family obligations with personal ones. Meeting these demands requires social, financial and educational resources that are simply not available to many young people. There are major variations – that is inequalities – in terms of the resources young people can call upon in order to cope with the demands of risky transitions that cannot be dealt with as straightforwardly as may have been the case in the past.

A particular concern is that, in these circumstances, young people are liable to be demotivated. Being realistic about his or her employment potential may result in a young person lowering their aspirations in advance. Many young people with limited qualifications take anything they can get. A coping strategy might therefore involve shifting one's personal aspirations and expectations to other areas of life, and by doing so replacing a subjective professional orientation with a mere 'job orientation'. For instance, a young person may aspire to work as a barperson in a trendy bar or club. The ambiguity of such processes of adaptation is clear: it either may work out as the (only) appropriate way to preserve one's self-motivation, dignity and self-confidence. Alternatively, it may encourage a process of disintegration and/or marginalisation due to a lack of opportunities for further progression.

A key phrase here is that of 'individualisation'. Economic and social change is such that failure in the transition to work has become a general risk that has to be dealt with on an individual basis. This problem is sustained by institutions that perceive young people as 'carriers' of deficiencies that 'cause' such problems. Getting used to a system in which young people are rarely respected and in which they are more often than not perceived to be troublesome will encourage a set of circumstances in which the individual conceives of counselling agencies or training opportunities in a negative light. In contrast, young people actually often feel pressured to accept specific options in order not to lose social benefits. More generally, the opportunities available to young people simply do not 'speak' to their everyday lives.

Young people currently have to balance the inequalities associated with traditional trajectories, which undoubtedly still exist alongside new risks, uncertainties and opportunities. In this chapter, I am concerned, therefore, with the broader life skills that young people may learn in a training environment that may allow them to cope more easily with the ups and downs of social change. Concern in this respect is with the degree to which informal learning – especially in the context of performing arts – provides an environment in which young people are best able to cope with the uncertainties of their everyday lives. The focus, therefore, is on three projects of varying informality. The British case study, for instance, is more bound to the mainstream educational system than that of Mannheim in Germany, but less so to the Portuguese example. However, all three projects are built on informal learning in terms of the open character of learning processes and the nature of skills young people acquire in such contexts. In other words, it is the contention here, conventional training programmes are over-occupied with measurable outcomes. But as far the young people we interviewed were concerned, what was most important was not whether or not they completed the course and received a certificate, but rather the meanings they invested in their experience of that course. The projects, therefore, provided non-formal settings in which educational objectives were paramount. However, such objectives were dependent upon the flexible nature of informal learning. The process underpinning and the content and form of learning outcomes are not, in this context, predefined.

The three projects

As a means of contextualising the issues discussed so far, it would be useful to outline briefly the three projects concerned and to consider the broader transition systems within which they operate. The unemployment rate for young people in Germany has for a long time been the lowest in Europe and, indeed, lower than the national unemployment rate. However, in contrast to other European countries, unemployment rates in Germany do not appear to fall after the age of 25. As such, youth unemployment carries a high risk of continuous exclusion. The problem with the German transition system as a whole appears to be that training opportunities that may actually serve young people's own needs are actually highly *normalising* in nature. The German system appears to be structured by powerful assumptions about the normality of work and of gendered life courses (Stauber and Walther, 1999; Biggart et al, 2002). The assumption that lifelong occupational careers are 'normal' is a highly male-oriented one, and exacerbates a situation in which new training opportunities (apart from the limited supply of apprenticeship places, which are still dominated by manufacturing professions) towards employment in the service economy are precluded (Baethge, 1999). Those who fail to live up to the expectations of the dual system are channelled into pre-vocational schemes. The tendency within the German system may therefore be said to blame the individual for the disadvantage he or she may experience.

Mannheim is an industrial city of approximately 300,000 inhabitants and is located in the region of Baden-Württemberg in southern Germany. JUST, which is the most informal of the three evaluated projects, is a community youth work project located in an inner-city neighbourhood. It was set up in the mid-1990s, at a time when youth unemployment and the consumption of hard drugs was rising notably among the young immigration population that attends the course. JUST is run by a community centre that offers a variety of social services to a variety of neighbourhood groups, most importantly the local Turkish and Italian populations. The main focus of our empirical work in Mannheim was a drama group located in this centre. The majority of those young men who belonged to the group had previously participated in training schemes for disadvantaged young people that lead either to a training or a school certificate, but that provide little in the way of genuine labour market prospects. When interviewed, they laughed off any suggestion that a career would be a possibility for them. When asked what was their dream job, a particularly telling reply was "if we get one at all, that one will be our dream job".

The Portuguese transition system is very much based on an ideology of enterprise in so far as its primary aim appears to be to provide young people with the skills necessary to support a thriving economy. However, unemployment is still a considerable concern and for many young people it could even be considered to be the norm. Young people from ethnic minorities are especially vulnerable in these circumstances. The persistently high number of early school leavers is a particular problem. Even those young people who do secure jobs are likely to be subject to the insecurities of jobs with short-term contracts or, indeed, no contracts at all (Almeida et al, 1996; Plug et al, 2002). In terms of training, the Portuguese government's strategy in fighting youth unemployment is to promote professional training among the most vulnerable of young people through the Professional Training and Employment Institute and to finance temporary programmes in which companies and organisations provide young people with temporary contracts of employment. Some commentators argue, in fact, that professional training is simply too specialised and as such has limited 'broad' value beyond the benefits received by the companies – as opposed to the young people – it serves (Moniz and Kovács, 1997, p 86).

Chapitô, based in Lisbon, the Portuguese capital, first began to offer a course in circus expression for street children in 1990. Since then it has developed into a student-centred environment that aims to prepare its students for the working world and, more specifically, the world of entertainment. Chapitô, therefore, trains young people in various forms of artistic expression including music, dance, circus arts and theatre. It is also formally recognised as a professional school that provides vocational training in circus performance and stagecraft. The project is targeted at young people who have problems fitting in with mainstream education. A typical student would have nine years of compulsory education behind him or her. Students come from all over Portugal, and indeed internationally, to attend the school, but are more likely to emanate from Lisbon and its peripheries. As the training the school provides has become more formalised, there has been an associated shift in the target group. Most young people at Chapitô are actually likely to be middle class and would have probably experienced difficulty in applying their artistic bent in a conventional educational setting.

There is a strong argument for suggesting that young people in Britain have been affected more than any other social category by the ramifications of recent economic change. In this context, Ashton and Maguire (1989) found that many young people's early careers were very likely to involve a series of shifts between government training schemes, semi- and unskilled work and, most worryingly, unemployment. In short, employment in general – and employment for young people in particular – is especially insecure. Indeed, during the mid- to late 1990s, unemployment among 16- to 19-year-olds remained at a steady 17.5%, but rising from just over 10% in 1989 (see Furlong and Cartmel, 1997). Perhaps the most interesting aspect of recent transitions in Britain is that more and more young people are pursuing their education, either through a traditional academic route or through alternative training programmes and less and less are going straight into the job market at the age of 16 (Biggart et al, 2002). Meanwhile, there is a tradition in which much youth training appears to have failed to capture the imagination of young people. There is also a grave concern among those involved in youth work that such schemes are intended to offset youth unemployment rather than provide young people with the skills they actually need (France, 1998; Hall et al, 2000).

Liverpool, located in the county of Merseyside, is an industrial city of just over 450,000 inhabitants. Similar to Mannheim, Liverpool has struggled to deal with the problems associated with deindustrialisation and has one of the worst unemployment rates in the UK. The British case study is based in Hope Street, and offers a performing arts training programme for unemployed young people in Liverpool. Originally set up in 1989, Hope Street sought to provide distinctively practical courses such as Acting Up, which is particularly informal in nature with the main emphasis being on engendering those skills necessary for the preparation of a public performance, but more generally, for life in a more and more flexible labour market. The provision of certified training in workshop skills, therefore, has become increasingly central to Hope Street's training provision. Participants are not only trained in drama and music, but also in transmitting these skills to other groups of young people. Rather than being purely artistic in nature, young people at Hope Street are encouraged to pursue culturally oriented careers in youth and community work, for instance, as well as other third-sector initiatives.

Evaluating the projects

Empowerment through informal learning in performing arts contexts

In comparing the three projects, the research grouping was concerned with the benefits of training in the performing arts. Why the performing arts? First, we start from the assumption that young people have a highly subjective interest in performing that, certainly at an informal level, plays a key role in the construction of youth cultural lifestyles and identities. Second, we contend that young people develop knowledge and skills in these aspects of their lives. Third, we argue that such competencies are in actual fact highly appropriate given the changing demands of the labour market and the changing shape of individual biographies. They are, in turn, in line with what have been identified as modern key competencies: creativity, networking and group skills, learning to learn, improvisation and flexibility. And they potentially deliver a very important resource for transition processes: motivation. In addition, the performing arts in particular potentially provide equally invaluable and yet undervalued qualities such as self-confidence, personal standing, more open attitudes to fellow human beings and more flexible attitudes towards gender relations.

It is worth noting that, in each of the three projects, the young people concerned had no guarantee of securing jobs in performance at the end of their training, this being especially true of Mannheim, which was the most informal of the three. Rather, the projects seemed to provide young people with a unique set of skills that allowed them to approach the prospect of adult life with far more confidence and assurance than they had done in the past. In order to address the success or otherwise of the three projects, we deployed a qualitative, multi-method, case-study approach that incorporated the following:

* interviews with identified experts/trainers;
* observations of training and performance;
* documentary analysis of course literature;
* group interviews with young people (which we saw as absolutely pivotal to being able to come to terms with the meanings these young people invested in their training);
* an evaluation of an actual theatrical performance via videotape, as a means of developing further discussions among the research team and with the project worker concerned.

This research is self-consciously qualitative and as such reflects our concern that a quantitative approach to intercultural comparison was likely to be far more superficial than an in-depth qualitative approach, which in turn, is likely to glean a richer set of results. In this context, our aim was to establish a well-rounded understanding of young people's experience of this form of training and in doing so to provide young people with a 'voice' in a world in which they felt that, in actual fact, they were very rarely heard. The specific questions we wanted our case studies to answer were as follows:

- How far do the three projects work for the young people concerned?
- How effective is their work with regard to providing prerequisites for young people?
- Which elements of the three projects might be usefully transferred and applied to mainstream training and youth policies?

In analysing our results, it soon became clear that the ability to 'find oneself' lies at the core of each of the three projects. Phrases like, 'coming out of my shell', 'brings me out of myself' and 'the freedom to learn' regularly cropped up during the interviews and, as such, hinted at the ability of these courses to allow young people to take responsibility for their own learning and, crucially, of their own long-term futures. Many of the young people we interviewed talked again and again about how disillusioned they were with their previous experience of education and training and how they felt like units who had to complete a particular course rather than human beings with particular needs.

> "I think with the course I was on before I wasn't really noticed. I felt like they barely knew my name. At Hope Street they did. And they could recognise my talents as well. If you had talent they'd push yer. They'd go, 'You're good at this, you should do this', or, 'that's your responsibility'."
> (Male, 21, Hope Street)

In a sense, the active and personal nature of performance appeared to provide young people with a sense of authorship of their own training:

> "When you are acting you have to dive into it completely, you have to forget everything around you. That leads you to yourself, it brings you out of yourself." (Male, 19, Mannheim)

The young people we interviewed did not appear to need a lot of persuading to join the training programmes concerned. It is true to say that, in the case of Hope Street, young people attending Acting Up would receive benefits depending upon their attendance. However, the camaraderie involved and the opportunity to be creative and to be themselves appeared to be more significant factors in ensuring these young people's active participation. Indeed, the programmes we evaluated appeared to work in so far as they gave young people the space within which they could develop a broad spectrum of skills.

> "Concentration is the main thing you learn here. Before the course started I could never concentrate on one thing, I always thought of a thousand things at a time. But now, I have learned to concentrate. You will see when you see us perform." (Male, 19, Mannheim)

In particular, the trust that those running the training programmes put in young people to negotiate the process involved in putting together a performance was something that these young people found very liberating. They found they had abilities and skills that had previously laid dormant, but which had been brought out of them through performance:

> "In difficult situations like in the interviews I had with employers, I know how to cope with this kind of situation. I think of what I want to say before I go into such situations. I no longer find it difficult to talk in front of people. I am much more relaxed than I was before I started here." (Male, 19, Mannheim)

The benefit of performance, therefore, appeared to lie in the process as opposed to the end product of that process. Although young people did learn the traditional performance skills, such as acting or singing, what appeared to be more important was the ability of the course concerned to bring these young people 'out of themselves'. These 'secondary learning effects' included: how to negotiate with others; how to work in a team; meeting deadlines; working independently as well as part of a group; being honest about making mistakes; discipline and time keeping; report-writing skills; communication skills and, perhaps above all, a sense of self-confidence and self-belief. This element of self-belief was clearly manifested in the interviews that we undertook with our respondents at the beginning and at the end of their experience of the training programmes described earlier in this chapter. The increased confidence that young people had garnered over such a period was clearly evident in this context through young people's self-confident attitude towards the interview situation. Meanwhile, the progression records maintained by Hope Street, for example, illustrated that young people were able to put that confidence into practice. Most importantly, as one young person at Hope Street put it,

> "I don't think 'Acting Up' is just a course on acting. It's a social course. It teaches you how to communicate, to talk to people and the idea is that when you go to work you can sell yourself. It is all about holding yourself and believing in yourself." (Female, 22, Hope Street)

Most important, then, is that these courses provided young people with the sense of self-belief that they could, in fact, be creative:

"I find this school is so open.... I can develop my own ideas. And in other schools I have things stipulated.... It is a school open to new opinions and ideas." (Female, 19, Chapitô)

In considering our data, we interpret each of the three projects as a source of 'meaning'. In short,

Learning – whatever form it takes – changes who we are by changing our ability to participate, to belong, to negotiate meaning. And this ability is configured socially with respect to practices, communities, and economies of meanings where it shapes our identities. (Wenger, 1998, p 226)

Participating in these training courses appeared to provide young people with a space in which they could begin to negotiate their place in the wider world. The three courses, therefore, can be said to constitute what Wenger has described as 'communities of practice': they provide a common enterprise through which individuals can begin to establish their own identities. For instance, the projects provided young people with a context in which they could challenge preconceived ideas about gender. These courses provided an open environment within which, among other things, the respective and respected abilities of men and women had equal standing. The point here was that these courses provided a lifestyle or a way of relating to the world that put young people in good stead for dealing with whatever might come their way, in the context of gender or otherwise.

"What does this course teach me? It teaches me everything. It teaches me how to relate to the outside world.... I like to be with people who can teach me, so that one day I can also teach. And I find this school teaches me so many good things.... It helps me to get to know my own body, it teaches me how to be, and it helps me to know myself a bit better and to know the others too." (Female, 19, Chapitô)

In this context, the three projects can be described as what Skelton and Valentine (1998) call 'cool places': they provide environments with which young people readily identify.

"We are all equal and this is a family [laughs]. Because this is a smaller school, all teachers know each other and know each of us. It's my second home [laughs]. I spend more time here with teachers and friends than I do with parents and my family." (Female, 15, Chapitô)

Chapitô offers young people a lifestyle with which they want to be actively identified. All three projects, in fact, provided the young people we interviewed with a common source of identity. It was this quality that made these projects stand out from the mainstream.

Differences in empowerment through informal learning: the impact of context

The projects under discussion deal with the symptoms of risky transitions. They help young people learn to find their own way in life and they motivate them to actively search for this in their own way. However, the risks inherent in the transition to adulthood will remain nonetheless. By adopting a comparative perspective, this research was able to provide a multifaceted perspective on the effects of participating in such projects on young people's biographies. The three projects differ in the form and the extent in which they are recognised by and linked to the formal transition system. While all young people have described the learning effects with regard to their personal and social competencies, these learning processes are made visible, accredited and recognised to a different extent. These differences are reflected in the destinations of the young people after leaving the projects. At this stage, it is important to consider the broader contexts in which the three projects operate, and their relationship with the local community on the one hand, and the biographical effects they have on young people's lives on the other.

Chapitô has a close relationship with the city of Lisbon and its surrounding area while simultaneously operating a variety of national and transnational networks. Its development coincided with a fundamental reform of the Portuguese education system. In order to increase the participation rate in education and training, it was transformed into a regular professional school providing a more practice-related alternative to conventional academic pathways, yet keeping the young people within the confines of the mainstream education system. The process of formalisation, therefore, was rapid in nature in terms of external funding, curricula and qualifications. Having said that, at the same time the organisation managed to keep the internal structures relatively informal. However, it has to be noted that, compared with the initial phase when addressing mainly street children, the target group has shifted to a milieu of alternative middle-class young people who feel marginalised by mainstream schooling.

When leaving the course, young people obtain a qualification that is comparable to qualifications from conventional training. Those who complete their courses of training at least have some hope of being able to secure a job in their chosen area of performance. On average, about two thirds of the students from the arts course who graduate pursue jobs in professional artistic productions (such as circus, theatre, or TV) or in social or community-based arts organisations. The others, due to the extended length and quality of training, have at least the possibility of applying their skills to setting up their own circus or theatre company.

Acting Up/Hope Street serves the city of Liverpool, while also organising international exchange projects. The substitution of the Acting Up project by the Workshop Leaders programme (which involves students organising and running drama workshops in the local neighbourhood) clearly states the investment Hope Street has in its local community. It is very important to maintain local links, because it is in this locality that young people are most likely to secure jobs and careers. It is very unlikely that many of these young people will become stars of the screen and the stage. They are more likely to secure jobs in local community projects. The development of Hope Street, however, has also to be evaluated with regard to wider trends in the UK in the 1990s. The education system has been more flexible in terms of broader access and qualifications have become modularised in a way that single elements of education and training can be accredited and combined in an individual education portfolio; and, significantly, most options are combined with education or training allowances. This made it easier for organisations like Hope Street to become formally accredited without having to undermine their underlying educational ethos. On the other hand, especially in the deindustrialised cities of the north of England, cultural industries and the community initiatives of the third sector have experienced a considerable growth and as such provide many new employment opportunities. Thus, it was possible for Hope Street to keep the focus on performing arts while maintaining strong links with the local community. However, in contrast to the largely pre-vocational incarnation of Acting Up, its successor, the Workshop Leaders programme, provided a higher level of training.

These young people do not acquire a proper qualification comparable to that provided by Chapitô, but at least they gain qualification credits that open their access to further education and training. So, rather than qualifications for jobs, Hope Street provides career opportunities. Sixty per cent of those students who finished the first Workshop Leaders course at Hope Street managed to secure a career in the arts or community sector. It appears that the New Deal for Young People (see the Chapter Six of this volume) has had a positive impact in this regard, despite the bad press it has received in Britain for its inherently bureaucratic nature. Due to additional European funding, it has even been possible for the organisation itself to support some young people in making their careers more sustainable after the course.

JUST represents the smallest and most localised of the three projects. As part of a youth and community centre, it largely depends on local youth policies and those integration measures that are implemented on behalf of local migrants. Being strictly separated from the education system in institutional terms, youth work in Germany is not recognised as a formal part of the transition system and there are no signs that this will change in near future. Indeed, it is fair to say that employers continue to trust more in formal qualifications than in more informal recruitment strategies. As part of a national programme for drug prevention, in the mid-1990s this open and informal approach was recognised for its efficiency in reaching the target group. By the end of the 1990s, the project was included as part of a local network for employment funded by the National Ministry of Labour. In order to secure this funding, stronger formalisation and standardisation were required and as such there was no award or accreditation for informal learning. On the positive side, however, the project was able to address the needs of the most marginalised young people in the neighbourhood without having to adapt to the demands of a formal curriculum.

The achievements of the project were illustrated by the group's success in a local theatre festival for students and in its selection as a pilot project for 'a neighbourhood-based prevention of labour market exclusion' by the German Ministry for Labour. However, this project was the least vocational of the three and none of the participants in the drama group secured a job on the basis of their involvement. Involvement in the theatre group did not pay off for the participants in terms of qualifications or even in terms of a subsequent transition into the regular education and training system. In the best-case scenario, the young people succeed in translating their experiences, increased self-confidence and motivation into improving their school qualifications or into 'performing' well in interview situations. In the worst, the young people concerned may in fact be forced to deny the salience of their experiences and to make an unavoidable sacrifice, in a sense denying themselves the freedom to 'be themselves' in order to secure jobs (or, if they are very lucky, careers) that are unlikely to fulfil them in the ways they might wish.

These comparisons show that the potential and limitations of informal learning strongly depend on the structural context: the local labour market as well as the national education system. In this context, we can identify systems that are less institutionalised as being more flexible than the norm. Under these conditions, informal learning projects are more likely to achieve funding and recognition. However, this also makes them more vulnerable to being subsumed by the mainstream that tends to be far more prescriptive in nature. A side effect of such formalisation is the rise of the entrance threshold, which privileges those who are more likely to cope with a vocational education curriculum. In addition, there is considerable evidence to suggest that current transition systems are rigidly structured by standardised vocational training. Here, informal learning is highly unlikely to become recognised by both the education system and the local labour market. If funded at all, such learning is likely to be perceived as part of pragmatic short-term policies as opposed to constituting an integral part of mainstream educational reform.

The extent to which informal learning is entirely compatible with the mainstream depends upon the local circumstances in which it operates. From one perspective, this tension certainly seems to be manageable, notably in the Portuguese and the UK contexts where the education systems are open enough to include arts-based courses. However, the price to be paid in these contexts is that the very young people who perhaps need such informal approaches most urgently, because of their extremely negative experiences at school and other state institutions courses, are more and more excluded from the projects. As far as the German example is concerned, the rigidity of the transition system and the policies that underpin that system inhibit the recognition of informal learning as a valid educational strategy.

Conclusions

In conclusion, the success of these three projects might be said to reflect upon the inflexibility of more traditional forms of training that tend to be less than entirely responsive to young people's needs. This research has illustrated that drama and performance provide an especially effective means of providing young people with an arena for self-development that is not usually provided for them by the mainstream.

> "I don't like the other normal schools, the way of functioning, the relations with the school, the fact of people making things they don't like. In the other school, I was doing something I didn't like. It is very good coming to a school and to be doing a thing that we like. Different ways, different people to be with who like the same things…." (Female, 15, Chapitô)

> "Here we are practically equal, the teachers just know more than we do, that's the reason they are above us. The lessons aren't impersonal and you are encouraged to discuss any problems you have both in and out of the class." (Male, 20, Chapitô)

The training that the Youth for Europe research group evaluated can be said, therefore, to constitute a deeper and more ambitious form of learning based on the construction of identity rather than the learning of measurable skills. These projects hint at a future in which educational models have the needs, motivations and creativity of young people at their core. To sum up, the courses provide a framework in which young people can begin to pursue their needs. The ability to do so is the by-product of secondary or indirect learning.

The projects:

- provide space for *negotiated experience*, precisely because they follow participatory curricula, where young people's interests and concerns are prioritised;
- promote *community membership*, in so far as they establish a group experience that becomes increasingly influential in the way in which it fulfils young people's need to belong;
- provide a *particular learning trajectory* that encourages young people to believe that they have some control over the direction in which their lives will go;
- represent one *important context* in young people's *everyday experience*, which they use positively to inform other aspects of their lives;
- encourage a *relationship between the local and the global*, in so far as they link personal concerns to broader social, political, cultural and economical ones such as immigration and social exclusion. The young people concerned may not describe themselves as political, but the projects encourage them to deal with these sorts of issues through performance and in relation to their own experience of them.

Drama and other performing arts actively facilitate the acquisition of these indirect skills in a variety of ways. Drama, in particular, puts young people in a situation in which they develop their own sense of creativity and the confidence that emanates from that creativity. Performing arts also provide young people with a means of self-expression, a 'safe space' in which they can perform with confidence and in which they are accepted as individuals. Public performance also encourages such students to believe that they have something worthwhile to offer the world around them. The fact that their work is deemed to be worthwhile boosts young people's self-belief. The process involved in performance and the way in which that performance grows is a great source of confidence. As one German participant put it, "We are getting better in our performing. It is great to observe this". This combination of explicit and implicit curricula gives young people a more rounded education and a broader spectrum of skills and competencies. Thus, such training can be described as an 'integrated' learning model that promotes individual autonomy, and therefore fits with the prerequisites of a model of Integrated Transition Policies as suggested earlier in this volume (Chapter Two).

It is worth reiterating the fact that the effectiveness of informal learning is dependent on young people investing such learning with the necessary commitment and motivation. However, informal learning does not work entirely independently. Its success is conditional upon it working alongside more formal aspects. The student benefits from the fact that the projects do not formalise certain aspects of their training; therefore, they are able to claim ownership of these aspects themselves. These projects provide young people, as one young person at Hope Street described it, as "a way out"; a way out from exclusion on the basis of social background, ethnicity and gender. These learning 'cocoons' provide an ontological security alongside a sense of belonging, often in environments whose only real sense of belonging was formerly based in a shared tradition of unemployment.

The rhetorical notion most applicable to this discussion might well be said, then, to be that of *empowerment*. The over-use of this term has tended to make it somewhat hollow, to the extent that the notion of empowerment is apparently used to legitimise any form of public socialisation or education. However, the origins of empowerment as a philosophy (Rappaport and Hess, 1984) are far more critical in nature. It is in this critical context that this term is appropriate here, in so far as there is recognition that many young people do not have the resources to take up many of the opportunities that are only available to them on a hypothetical basis. The three projects under discussion succeed in channelling individuals towards the resources they need in order to take advantage of such opportunities. They do so by respecting the individual regardless of how 'normal' or 'deviant' he or she may be. They also seek to raise young people's awareness of the opportunities available to them, encouraging them that they do have a future. They also focus on young people's strengths (which are often under-utilised or even ignored) rather than their weaknesses.

A key concern of ours is how far the mainstream can adopt some of the principles associated with informal modes of training without diluting their underlying principles. We are not advocating a single model of youth training here. Rather the intention is to call for a more holistic (as opposed to economistic) approach to youth training. Above all, there is a need to move away from a funding system that only rewards transparent economic pay-offs. There is too much pressure for such training programmes to produce immediate results when young people are developing in such a way that immediate results are not actually always in their best interests. A good training course is premised on the long-term benefits of that experience. Consequently, youth training policies should ideally be oriented towards a longitudinal perspective. Necessarily, this means a renewed openness to the possibility of investing in new drama groups and clubs (which may not normally receive such support simply because they are deemed 'unconventional' and therefore as not constituting 'serious' education) and arguably even a reassessment of the role of performance-related subjects in mainstream education (see also Chapter Twelve of this volume). In other words, risks – and, in particular, financial risks – need to be taken in order to give more innovative forms of training the recognition they undoubtedly deserve. The outcomes of informal learning are also less immediately tangible than more standardised curriculum-based learning. As such, there needs to be an explicit recognition that learning is very much distinguishable from teaching. This is one of the most striking conclusions to emerge from this study. These young people are able to learn, because they find themselves in an environment that motivates them to learn despite the fact they were deeply demotivated before joining the course concerned. These courses offer them a stimulating atmosphere that proposes alternative ways of relating to fellow trainees and adults and encourages them to develop their own interests. These courses are successful because they adapt to young people's sense of self. From this point of view, training cannot be designed to be an inevitable success, but it can be designed in such a way that young people find themselves in a position in which they want to make it a success. In this respect, as Wenger (1998, p 229) points out, "Learning cannot be designed: it can only be designed for – that is, facilitated, or frustrated". Our concern, therefore, is that the more standardised and rationalised the training programme the more likely young people are to be demotivated. Any notional economic pay-offs may also be undermined as a result.

In addition to all of this, it is also very important that the links between training providers, local authorities and communities are supported in order to ensure that the training provided matches up with the needs of the community itself. To varying degrees the projects we evaluated exist at the fringes. However, the principles they engender need to be brought into a much broader training landscape in order to provide the local community with what it may actually require. In this respect, the local community and the young people brought up in that community can benefit equally.

The rather static model of youth training that currently exists needs to be superseded by a more flexible, reflexive and pragmatic approach that actively embraces young people's personal biographies and hence the sorts of innovations evident in the three training programmes we evaluated in this chapter. Bona fide student-centred training programmes will produce their own economic pay-offs. Young people should not be seen as passive recipients of youth training. Rather, there needs to be something of a leap of faith in order that young people are entrusted to interact with their training in a far more proactive fashion than currently appears to be the case. Being a young person is by its very nature a complex experience. 'Youth' is in no sense a predictable stage of the life-cycle. Training programmes throughout Europe need to reflect this realisation and they need to reflect the potential richness of young people's lives. It is not always the case that young people are the passive subjects of disadvantage. They engage with such disadvantage in potentially creative and positive ways. Being a young person appears to be very much about maximising the moment and about feeling that you are fulfilling or finding yourself in that moment. Perhaps, indeed, an effective training programme is one that does not actually feel like a training programme at all: a programme that simply gives young people the room to be themselves. It seems to be the case that the only way transition systems are currently integrated, at least at a European level, is in so far as they prioritise the economic, apparently at the expense of the personal. In this sense, European transitions systems are more inflexible than young people are themselves. Many of the young people we interviewed during the course of this project were brave enough to put themselves on the line when they decided to take on the training programmes of which they were a part. Perhaps the time has come for youth policy makers and funding bodies to do the same.

Note

[1] The author wishes to thank the other researchers involved in the study – Axel Pohl, Barbara Stauber and Andreas Walther from IRIS Tübingen (Germany) and Rui Banha, Ana M. Gaspar, and Maria do Carmo Gomes from CIES Lisbon (Portugal) – for their comments on an earlier version of this chapter.

References

Almeida, J.F., Pais, J.M., Torres, A.C., Machado, F.L., Ferreira, P.A. and Nunes, J.S. (1996) *Jovens de hoje e de aqui, resultados do inquérito à juventude do concelho de Loures*, Loures: CMLoures Ed.

Ashton, D. and Maguire, M. (1989) *Restructuring the labour market: The implications for youth*, London: Macmillan.

Baethge, M. (1999) 'Glanz und Elend des deutschen Korporatismus in der Berufsbildung', *WSI-Mitteilungen*, no 8/1999, pp 489-98.

Biggart, A., Cuconato, M., Furlong, A., Lenzi, G., Stauber, B., Tagliaventi, M. and Walther, A. (2002) 'Misleading trajectories between standardisation and flexibility – Great Britain, Italy and West Germany', in A. Walther, B. Stauber, A. Biggart, M. du Bois-Reymond, A. Furlong, A. López Blasco, S. Mørch and J.M. Pais (eds) *Misleading trajectories: Integration policies for young adults in Europe?*, Opladen: Leske+Budrich, pp 44-66.

EGRIS (European Group for Integrated Social Research) (2001) 'Misleading trajectories: transition dilemmas of young adults in Europe', *Journal of Youth Studies*, vol 4, no 1, pp 101-19.

France, A. (1998) '"Why should we care?" Young people, citizenship and questions of social responsibility', *Journal of Youth Studies*, vol 1, no 1, pp 97-111.

Furlong, A. and Cartmel, F. (1997) *Young people and social change*, Buckingham: Open University Press.

Hall, T., Williamson, H. and Coffey, A. (2000) 'Young people, citizenship and the third way: a role for the youth service?', *Journal of Youth Studies*, vol 3, no 4, pp 461-72.

Moniz, A.B. and Kóvacs, I. (1997) *Evolução das qualificações e das estruturas de formação em Portugal*, Lisboa: IEFP.

Pais, J.M. (2000) 'Transitions and youth cultures: forms and performances', *International Social Science Journal*, LII, no 2, pp 219-32.

Plug, W., Kiely, E., Hein, K., Ferreira, V.S., Bendit, R., du Bois-Reymond, M. and Pais, J.M. (2002) 'Modernised transitions and disadvantage policies: Netherlands, Portugal, Ireland and migrant youth in Germany', in A. Walther, B. Stauber, A. Biggart, M. du Bois-Reymond, A. Furlong, A. López Blasco, S. Mørch and J.M. Pais (eds) *Misleading trajectories: Integration policies for young adults in Europe?*, Opladen: Leske+Budrich, pp 94-117.

Rappaport, J. and Hess, R. (ed) (1984) *Studies in empowerment: Steps toward understanding and action*, New York, NY: Haworth Press, Inc.

Skelton, T. and Valentine, G. (eds) (1998) *Cool places: Geographies of youth cultures*, London: Routledge.

Stauber, B. and Walther, A. (eds) (1999) *Life-long learning in Europe, Vol 2*, Tübingen: Neuling.

Wenger, E. (1998) *Communities of practice: Learning, meaning and identity*, Cambridge: Cambridge University Press.

Part Three:
Dilemmas and perspectives of
Integrated Transition Policies

Empowerment or 'cooling out'? Dilemmas and contradictions of Integrated Transition Policies[1]

Andreas Walther

What makes transition policies effective? What makes them fail? And what are the criteria for success and failure? Who defines them and from which perspective? These are the main questions addressed by this volume. After the presentation of findings of European research on the changes of transitions, the mechanisms of social integration and exclusion, and especially on recent trends in the effects of transition policies, the third and final part of the book reflects on some general contradictions and dilemmas that have appeared across the various chapters. First, the general contours of Parts One and Two of the book on the increasing discrepancies between state policies addressing the risks of social exclusion in transitions to work and the life perspectives of young men and women themselves are summarised. The second section confronts researchers' analysis with the views of national and European policy makers who have commented on some of the presented study reports[1]. Here a number of general policy dilemmas are introduced that can be identified as lying at the heart of the efficiency problems. Some of these will be dealt with in depth in the remaining chapters of the book. Section three advances the theoretical interpretation that the difficult relationship between changing transitions and current policies is a principal consequence of the structures of 'late modernity' or 'reflexive modernisation' (Giddens, 1990; Beck, 1992). The rising awareness of 'the informal' with regard to learning as well as to social support may be one (yet ambiguous) key to these challenges. The concluding section suggests that in order to find ways out of such dilemmas transition policies need to adopt a new communicative approach towards the assessment and the compensation of risk between individuals and society.

The gap between young people and transition policies

In the context of this book, transition policies have been conceptualised as the set of policies dealing with young people's transitions from education to work. This means, in particular, education and training, labour market policies, welfare and youth policies. Different policies refer to different aspects of youth transitions and at the same time youth transitions are only one part of their task. These different policies do not always act in a coordinated or integrated manner, therefore, but in a segmented and fragmented way which in the individual case may have unintended, even contradictory effects. This is what Manuela du Bois-Reymond and Andreu López Blasco have termed 'misleading trajectories' (Chapter Two of this volume).

Starting from this analysis, a main objective of this book is to explore the potential of the concept of Integrated Transition Policies (ITPs) to bridge the gap between the subjective and systemic dimensions of social integration. This concept explicitly refers to the changes in the objective structures of transitions to work and the subjective perspectives of the young men and women concerned. Young people's transitions from youth to adulthood that have for many decades been structured by more or less direct trajectories between school and work are being increasingly replaced by a more indirect relation between the end points of transition. This increasing "indirectness of youth" (EGRIS, 2002, p 124) and the emergence of 'young adults' as a distinct social condition – being neither youth nor adults, nor both at the same time – has undermined the potential of the normal biography to serve as an orientation for gendered life plans and social institutions concerned with the integration of the younger generation and of young people themselves. The presentations in Parts One and Two of this book share the assumption that institutional actors have either neglected or not yet recognised this change. This change consists of three major aspects:

1. The Fordist guarantee that any sort of education and training leads to a job and consequently to social integration in terms of both social and personal identity has been broken up. The decoupling of education and employment has revealed limitations of welfare or life-course regimes (to different extents as national comparisons show) as regards their integrative potential for all. Unemployment, but also the increasing necessity to change direction during a career, has undermined the idea that social integration self-evidently includes everybody.
2. The lack of reliability of provided trajectories and future perspectives has changed young people's orientation towards the future and the way they construct their lives. If the investment in formal education or training and the adaptation towards the normal biography does not guarantee future integration and full participation, if life decisions nevertheless have to be taken individually, if individuals are made responsible for their decisions regardless of the inequality of resources and opportunities and their compatibility with subjective needs, then biographic orientations and obligations become increasingly relevant. Authors such as Alheit (1995) and Böhnisch (1997) have referred to this as 'biographisation'.
3. State institutions (to different extents and in different forms depending upon context) feel the need to reinstall the structures of social integration that have been disordered by this destandardisation of transitions and life courses.

According to Kelly (1999), transitions have increasingly changed into 'wild zones'; that is, parts of society that are less controllable as regards integration and predictable outcomes. Due to the strategic function of transitions to work for the cohesion of present societies, European governments react to the challenge posed by these 'wild zones' by attempting to turn them into 'tame zones'. The directions and the extent of policy innovations are influenced by structures of 'path dependency'; that is, existing structures that have emerged from decisions taken in the past and from policy traditions that represent the raw material of reforms. Correspondingly, there are countries in which early labour market entry remains the prime objective of any transition policy as in the UK, while Scandinavian countries rely to a larger extent on general and higher education; in central European states (such as Germany), vocational training is conceived as the 'royal road'. Apart from that, policies can be located on a continuum between re-enforcing pre-existing institutional structures and fundamental reforms aimed at adapting to new labour market structures and life courses, the latter being characterised by an increased integration of – and flexibility between – education, training and employment-related approaches (see Chapters Four, Six and Seven of this volume).

With reforms, the problem remains that it is not totally clear in which direction they should point. Currently dominant discourses on 'employability', 'lifelong learning' and 'activation' can also be interpreted as expressing the embarrassment of education and training systems that have lost the ability to assess needs in terms of knowledge, skills and qualifications and therefore delegate the responsibility to the individuals concerned to constantly readjust their fit to labour market demands. The tendency towards individualising supply-side oriented measures for the so-called 'disadvantaged' – which in many cases focus on individual deficits, deficits that are constructed according to an ex-post evaluation from the race for scarce recognised social positions – can also be viewed as a result of the fact that national policies are simply too weak to restructure labour markets in a way that can provide integration for all citizens. While such strategies necessarily have a limited impact, the side effect is that individuals' active coping strategies are neglected and devalued in order to justify coercive measures. Formulated polemically, such policies concentrate on the task of managing scarcity by organising selection; by 'cooling' the aspirations of the less competitive individuals 'out', a perspective that will be taken up later in this chapter. However, comparative analysis shows that activation can – or has to – be conceived of in a holistic perspective as well: activation does not necessarily imply the reduction of 'activity' to paid employment. Compared with 'workfare' policies (for example in the UK, the Netherlands or, increasingly, Germany) that interpret 'activation' in terms of extortion – for example, "either you accept this job or we cut your benefits" – Scandinavian activation policies provide the unemployed with rights and with options for choice (see also Chapters Five and Six of this volume; Lødemel and Trickey, 2001; van Berkel and Hornemann Møller, 2002).

In a more general perspective, this discomfiting embarrassment of policy makers and institutions also stands for a decreasing certainty about the meaning of social integration. The labour market calls for a flexible and adaptive labour force, while state institutions are concerned with including all young people in something: education and training, jobs or (if nothing else is available) public schemes for pre-vocational education, lower-status training or subsidised employment. Although corresponding to different rationales and therefore focusing upon different aspects, these systemic approaches tend to reduce social integration to labour market integration. As regards the young people themselves, all research – be it quantitative surveys or qualitative studies – show that, for them, labour market integration is a central aspect of their identities (IARD, 2001; du Bois-Reymond et al, 2002). However, transitions are interlinked and fragmented at the same time as individuals are confronted with contradictory demands from other life spheres. Other decisions may be more important at a particular moment and may therefore influence transitions to work in a direction that in career-related terms seem to lack of rationality. At the same time, the development of biographies and identities through social integration does not only mean being part of the game in 'some' way, but requires being recognised as an individual with particular needs and wishes. In short, it requires identification.

Chapter Three of this volume confirms the multi-faceted structure of social integration/exclusion. Here, Kieselbach shows that economic and labour market exclusion are only one aspect of this, and that social isolation, institutional, cultural or spatial exclusion have to be considered as well. The finding that young unemployed in Germany (where the youth unemployment rate is low) experience exclusion in a more severe way and in more respects compared with young Italians (for whom unemployment or precariousness are much more the norm) may cause some controversy and debate: are family support, informal networks and informal work more efficient in preventing social exclusion than a diversity of training and support schemes? This is what the concept 'misleading trajectories' implies: not all education or training schemes actually lead to a job, and not all education, training or job experience can actualise social integration for each individual. In many situations, young people – without having alternatives – face subjective risks of demotivation and non-identification that may as effectively lead into social exclusion as the structural exclusion from any institutional or job offer (see Kieselbach's term of 'institutional exclusion'). Misleading trajectories emerge from the increasing gaps between these different aspects of social integration and the different power structures by which recognition can be gained.

Such findings are reflected in Chapters Eight and Nine of this volume, which are concerned with young people's experiences with third-sector organisations and performing arts projects. In their struggle to reconcile different aspects of their lives, to cope with denied perspectives and to protect their identities against being 'cooled out', many of those young men and women who have been labelled as 'disadvantaged' prefer more informal contexts in which they feel recognised as individuals.

Social theorists have referred to such discrepancies as the distinction between 'social integration' and 'system integration' (for example, see Habermas, 1981; Giddens, 1984). While social integration implies direct communication between individuals, system integration refers to the collective regulation of social relationships across time and space by more generalised procedures (money, law, qualifications and so on). However, as structures of system integration have emerged from the social differentiation towards more and more complex societies, they continue to depend on mechanisms of social integration in collectively shared and subjectively meaningful life worlds, such as the family, communities or public space. Labour markets depend on individuals' work ethics just as schools build on pupils' learning motivation, and the state on citizens' participation (Habermas, 1981). Yet, social and system integration do not necessarily contradict one another. Böhnisch (1994) argues that modern welfare societies experienced a high degree of coincidence between social and system integration in the Fordist period as long as the institutionalised (gender-specific) 'normal biography' was accessible to all. Obviously, this is no longer the case.

Dilemmas of transition policies

How do policies reflect the discrepancy between systemic and subjective dimensions of social integration and how do policy makers express the ambiguity of transition policies? Obviously, this depends on different factors.

1. There is a clear difference, of course, between national policy makers primarily concerned with problem solving, for example reaching the 'most disadvantaged', and EU policy makers engaged in developing more comprehensive visions. Due to the principle of subsidiarity, concrete competencies remain with the member states: "Integrating young people into work is a major national priority" (Smolar, 2002, p 1), while the EC perceives its programmes, in this case the Leonardo da Vinci programme for vocational training, as "a laboratory of innovation and experimentation" (Corman, 2002, p 1).
2. There are noticeable differences between policy makers from the different parts of Europe. Those from Northern or Western Europe are primarily concerned with policy efficiency, especially with regard to reaching the 'most disadvantaged'. On the other hand, the priority for those from Southern and Eastern Europe is the implementation of new institutions. For the latter, the debate about ITPs provides the opportunity to avoid the institutionalisation of misleading trajectories identified in the north and west of Europe.

3. Perspectives depend upon the respective policy sector they are centred upon. Labour market policies are clearly more concerned with the matching of supply and demand of labour, while youth policies focus more on young people's individual development and participation. The different policy perspectives may be visualised as operating along an ideal, typical continuum between 'soft' and 'hard' policies. At the soft end, we have youth policies characterised by a primarily subject-oriented and participatory approach that is organised locally and equipped with rather limited funding. At the hard end, labour market policies view individuals as one element of the more abstract relation of labour supply and demand, which is reflected by national institutions and rather large amounts of funding. Education and training as well as welfare policies can be seen as intermediating between the extremes as they try to relate individual development to systemic demands: qualifying the individual process of socialisation for participation in social and economic life; or compensating for social risks in individual living conditions. However, this varies according to the institutionalisation of selective mechanisms, of normalisation and the coverage of welfare provisions (Walther et al, 2002a).

The ambiguity of social and systemic integration, the different perspectives of policy sectors, and also the different views of research and policy, become visible in the discussion of some real or apparent dilemmas for transition policies and pedagogical practice (see also Chapters Eleven to Fourteen of this volume).

Employability and competence

It was mentioned earlier in this chapter that most transition policies can be characterised by supply-side orientation. Two concepts that have been recently put on the agenda in this regard are 'employability' and 'competence' (EC, 1997, 2001). However, do these concepts not stand in contradiction with each other? Policy makers legitimise the objective of employability because paid employment continues to be the key prerequisite for full participation in society (Schulte, 2002). Obviously, it is evaluated according to subsequent employment. This perspective contradicts broader concepts of 'contextual competence' or transversal skills developed in the context of the discourse on lifelong learning (see Chapter Eleven of this volume). It is debatable whether or not competence includes biographical skills ('biographicity'; Alheit, 1995); that is, the ability to relate wishes to opportunities, personal strengths and weaknesses to external demands, self-concepts to occupational roles and so on that normally would be recognised as prerequisites for a stable professional identity and career. However, individuals simply may refuse certain jobs if their content contradicts personal biographical assessment. Although the word 'employability' itself suggests a paradoxical individualised perspective ('being able to be employed'; see also Chapter Five of this volume), it may be compatible with competence if it is conceptualised as integrating structural and individual dimensions and combining different policy instruments as suggested by Gazier (1999; see also Chapter Seven of this volume), thus lowering the pressure on individuals to adapt to any demands of a constraint labour market. Comparative analysis has revealed huge variations in how national transition systems interpret employability and competence, thus displaying larger or smaller discrepancies between the two (see Chapter Six of this volume). This seems to be in line with the views of many policy makers both at European and national level. While, for a EU labour market policy maker, the quality of both training and jobs is the most crucial question (Wolf, 2002), a national policy maker responsible for programmes for disadvantaged youth argues:

> I think there is no reason for an either-or-postulate. Our schemes of support for disadvantaged young people have to be both: education and employment oriented at the same time. (Schulte, 2002, p 2)

The recognition of informal learning

Discourses about competence in the context of lifelong learning and vocational training (CEDEFOP, 1999; EC, 2001) increasingly refer to *informal learning* outside of formal education, as well as training that may even be unintentional – that is, taking the form of pragmatic, everyday-life learning. Informal learning is considered to imply intrinsic motivation due to its connection with life issues that the individual learners identify with. And it is seen as democratic because it occurs everywhere: in the family, the peer group or youth culture, in leisure activities, at the workplace or (more intentional in terms of non-formal education) in youth work contexts. However, the recognition of informal learning poses one central question:

> It is not always obvious how to 'measure' learning outcomes that have been acquired in a non-standardised and highly contextual form .... While solutions have to reflect the specific context and need addressed, there is a need to define and develop common principles supporting the credibility (and overall value for the user) of the various approaches. (Corman, 2002, p 4)

Apart from the difficulties in translating informal experiences for employers, labour officers or further training experts, any institutional approach of promotion and assessment risks undermining the informality of such learning, since such approaches require comparability and, therefore, supervision and control. While informal learning plays a central role in the concept of ITPs, the contributions of the third-sector youth initiatives and the performing arts projects (see Chapters Eight and Nine of this volume) have shown the consequences of this dilemma, lying between the lack of recognition on the one side and formalisation on the other (see also Chapter Twelve).

Balancing flexibility and security

Flexibility is another major catchword in current debates. It means increased access to options due to the fluidity and dynamics of labour markets, increased access to education and training and better adaptability to individual needs and labour market demands and tailored measures for disadvantaged youth to tackle multi-faceted constellations of vulnerability (Smolar, 2002, p 2; see also Chapters Two, Seven and Nine of this volume). Flexibility has to be viewed, therefore, as central to the destandardisation of transitions in a dialectical way; that is, as the source of destandardisation as well as a consequence of it. As in the case of informal learning, however, giving up standardised rules of organisation increases uncertainty and insecurity. One important question among many others is how to avoid delegating emerging risks as the sole responsibility of individuals. How can precariousness in work conditions as well as a consequence of education and training that are not recognised by employers due to a lack of standardised certification be prevented and/or compensated for? This opens up the debate to a consideration of the socio-political implications of flexibility, or vice versa: what are conditions under which individuals can and do accept flexibilisation and risk as reasonable? Under conditions of flexibilisation and fragmentation, individuals only maintain their autonomy, according to the sociologist, Zygmunt Bauman, if *security* is guaranteed. Bauman argues strongly, therefore, for a guaranteed basic income (Bauman, 2001; see Chapter Thirteen of this volume).

Addressing the needs of the most disadvantaged

The particular risks of so-called 'disadvantaged young people' have been referred to in Chapters Three and Six of this volume and are focused upon by policy makers and respective programmes. The preoccupation is that existing measures fail to reach all of their addressees. One reason is that, to secure their funding, many training providers 'cream off' those young people who have a higher probability to succeed in the measures provided. Another reason lies in the vicious cycles by which young people become alienated from public institutions during which multiple problems accumulate. Therefore, experts increasingly call for special measures for the most disadvantaged:

> taking into account the needs and deficiencies of the target group ... there must be a support system which is holistic, diversified and flexible. (Schulte, 2002, p 2)

The French programme Trajet d'accès à l'emploi (TRACE) has been identified as encapsulating an especially comprehensive approach, combining material and psychosocial support in various respects (Smolar, 2002). However, the need for special measures to regulate access in accordance with a specific target group does at the same time undermine the space for a flexible use of any particular measure, and as such, projects are easily identified as being for the 'losers'. One has to question if "in targeting training programmes on disadvantaged young people ... there lies a risk of (further) stigmatising them" (Corman, 2002, p 5)?

While stigmatisation may undermine both the motivation and identification of young people per se, workfare mechanisms are being increasingly introduced in order to make sure that the target group really is reached – something that makes it even more difficult for young people to identify with and motivated by such options. An alternative strategy would be to broaden transition policies and to equip them with mechanisms providing flexible support (Wolf, 2002, p 2). This would mean acceptance that transition-related risks concern young people in general; that is, those with more as well as those with fewer resources.

The dilemma of how to address the 'disadvantaged' relates to the more fundamental dilemma between competition and equal opportunities that is characteristic for societies based on capitalism and representative democracy. While capitalism needs competition in order to generate qualitative and quantitative growth, democracy is defined as providing equal opportunities for everybody. In this respect, Erving Goffman (1962) has described the education system as an efficient mechanism of 'cooling out'. It raises aspirations in terms of the belief that 'everyone can make it', which is true in theory but not in practice, since there are not enough well-recognised social positions that provide a reasonable life. In order to accept selection as fair and just, 'gate-keepers' apply criteria that are accepted as 'objective' diagnostics ascribing selection to individual performance and achievement – in order to reduce individuals' aspirations (Stone, 1992). It is obvious that schemes for unemployed young men and women have exactly this function, at least as a hidden curriculum that undermines and counteracts their empowering effects (see Chapter Fourteen of this volume).

Gender: with or against mainstream(ing)?

Gender is one of the main categories of social disadvantage affecting young women's and men's transitions to work, and it is an example of how structural disadvantage such as gendered labour market segmentation is individualised and reinterpreted, for example, in terms of gender-typical occupational choices of women. For decades, equal opportunities have been addressed by positive-action policies and measured with regard to female employment; and even in this reductive perspective the impact has been limited in most contexts (exceptions, such as the UK or Scandinavian countries, derive from much more fundamental alterations in structures of employment and welfare regimes that structure gender relationships). Currently, the new strategy is *gender mainstreaming*. This approach promises to reconcile values of gender difference and gender equality and to liberate gender issues from the ghetto of special measures for the disadvantaged in order to be included in a cross-sectoral way in all issues. However, it also entails the risk that, due to the lack of clear indicators (Behning and Serrano Pascual, 2001), gender issues may evaporate on their way from conceptualisation on a European level to national implementation. It also remains unclear how gender policies might address men. We still do not know very much about the personal and societal costs of young men being socialised towards the male breadwinner role – especially under conditions of competition that force many of them to compromise in this respect. And it is still quite unclear if there is a powerful political interest to break up the male (main) breadwinner model that, even in Scandinavian countries, is still a reality in the labour markets as well as in cultural identities of masculinity.

'Doing ethnicity' or promoting interculturalism?

Another important category of social disadvantage is *ethnicity*. In many countries the group classified as 'disadvantaged' overlaps to a large extent with youth from immigrant and ethnic minority backgrounds (see Chapter Fourteen of this volume). There is almost unanimous agreement among researchers and policy makers that the defining feature of 'disadvantage' for this group is derived from language problems. However, what about this group's bilingual, bicultural competencies? Interestingly, we can find both types of coping among these young people – ambitious adaptation behaviour and hostile disengagement with formal institutions – which probably depend on familial support, personal resources such as self-confidence and gendered peer mechanisms. One can also argue that, in the context of the elevator effect (increasing educational levels across all social contexts), western societies 'need' a new underclass and the education system is still an effective means in this respect. Therefore, part of the responsibility with regard to targeting 'disadvantaged youth' in general might be given back to schools due to their contribution in (re)constructing socioeconomic disadvantage in a meritocratic, apparently neutral way instead of simply motivating and empowering children for learning and active participation. However, as the recent PISA study has shown, there are considerable differences between national school systems (OECD, 2001).

Implementation: partnership or competition?

Policy dilemmas not only derive from a lack of knowledge but also from the difficulties of implementation in 'real' local contexts. 'Partnership' is one of the terms most often related to (Serrano Pascual, 2001):

> Integrated policy concepts have to ensure full partnership between all players; this is not only relevant in active labour market policies, but also especially in the fields of education and social cohesion. (Wolf, 2002, p 2)

Holistic and flexible support for the disadvantaged requires a "complex partnership involving the state, regional and local authorities, public services and social partners" (Smolar, 2002, p 1) enabling a "reliable system of different offers ... which combines all relevant local providers of support ... establishing what we call support synergies" (Schulte, 2002, p 3). Moreover, it also requires the recognition of informal learning in terms of acknowledged principles of "credibility" and "local level partnerships" (Corman, 2002, p 5). On the one hand, the unanimous calling for partnership can be seen as an indicator for the development of real partnerships. On the other hand, however, it also stands for the fact that – despite having been on the agenda for a quite long period – real partnership still has not been achieved except in unconventional single cases. In fact, there is lot of evidence that transition systems are increasingly characterised by economic criteria and by sharp competition among third-sector organisations and private training providers for scarce public funding. There is even competition between different public institutions, either about responsibilities and power or because bureaucratic requirements contradict one another (Low, 2001). In the end, both successful and inhibited partnerships consume a large part of the time, energy and also funding of actors that are intended to serve the young people concerned. Networking and partnership tend to become ends in themselves.

Assessing the effects of transition policies (or: the difficult liaison between policy and research)

A major concern of this whole volume is the *effects of transition policies* and the question of what kinds of effects are envisaged and how they are measured. In many contexts, the rate of former participants of policy measures in employment, or at least in regular training, is still the most important criterion of success and therefore the focus of evaluation and monitoring. This is an important aspect, of course. However, if it is the only one assessed, both the quality of jobs or training (according to subjective as well as to systemic criteria) and the conditions under which the individual operates, or the societal costs at which they are achieved, are neglected. Closely related to this question is the relationship between policy and research, which is characterised by mutual dependency as well as by constant misunderstanding: researchers feel either not heard or misinterpreted, while policy makers complain about inapplicability of research findings. This misunderstanding stands for a structural deficit in this relationship, consisting of diverging time perspectives with regard to both the production versus consumption of knowledge – long-term in case of research, short- or mid-term in policies – and the perspectives adopted for understanding social change. However, it can be assumed that restructuring the relationship between research and policy will necessarily fail if the particularities of knowledge, politics and social change in late modernity as well as their interplay are not taken fully into account. And such a changed relationship probably requires a form of dialogic and continuous integration rather than communication over research reports that either evaluate policies ex-post or model scenarios in abstract ways.

In the European context, the assessment of policy effects naturally stands in a context of comparison. Successful policies are likely to become models – 'good practice' – for other countries, especially if, as in the context of the European Employment Strategy (EES), common methods of benchmarking are applied. Consequently, European policy makers are interested in the transferability of success stories; or else they apply transferability as a criterion of success, mainly with regard to transfers from countries with strong labour market performance to countries with high structural unemployment (Wolf, 2002, p 2). There is often a complaint that existing databases are not properly used, while the European research discourse often appears as the search for the ultimate joint database that will overcome all problems of comparability and make transfer scenarios calculable. However, comparison and transfer may be more promising when limited to the understanding of structures serving as enabling prerequisites in specific cases that can then be transferred into functional equivalents in another context (Walther, 2000).

Having referred extensively to the single dilemmas and contradictions of modernising and implementing policies, it should be remembered that the scope of ITPs is related to the position of labour in the capitalist constellation that seems to be continuously weakened in the context of the ongoing advance of neoliberalism and globalisation.

Transition policies in late modernity: risks, reflexivity and informality?

Policy dilemmas stand for the fact that most policies have intended as well as unintended side effects that are often much less desirable than the intended goals. On the one hand, this arises from a lack of knowledge with regard to the assumed relation of causes and effects of political agency; on the other hand, it is related to conflicting values that, in the process of policy making, are often neglected through simple overruling or through a lack of time to develop comprehensive policy scenarios. Reviewing the research findings presented in Parts One and Two of this volume, it appears as if policies have to accept that, under conditions of late modernity and destandardisation, it is increasingly difficult to plan or structure career destinations. According to Ulrich Beck (1992), this is one aspect of the 'risk society' in which the predictability of the effects of institutional agency and planning decreases. In developmental terms, the complement of the risk society is 'reflexive modernisation', which means that risks increasingly emerge as side effects from human inventions, and that the rational model of linear causality and instrumentality is decreasingly reliable as a basis for policy making. For example, it becomes more and more difficult to distinguish between social 'disadvantage' emerging from deprived socialisation and the 'disadvantage' produced by the selective, stigmatising and demotivating effects of the policies that themselves address disadvantage. 'Status zer0' is a reaction of individuals against certain policies that itself generates new policy discourses in a cycle that will potentially continue ad infinitum. Institutionalised politics are 'delimited', while new forms of 'sub-politics' emerge from the institutional system, acting increasingly independently, while individuals themselves develop coping strategies. Evers and Novotny (1987) remind us that institutionalisation is a means of reducing insecurity in social life by transforming danger into calculable risk. Where, due to social change, institutions are revealed to be inadequate in compensating for risks, they argue:

> Under unstable, unexpected, and uncertain conditions behaviour is required which is innovative and able to generate adequate solutions. Every 'monocultural' behaviour therefore is pathological, a deformation. Organisations – and societies – must seek to maintain their 'response pool' and their ways of behaviour large and heterogeneous enough to be prepared for unexpected situations. Only enough variance in the reaction to unexpected changes may provide something as a fundament of security. (Evers and Novotny, 1987, p 323)

As a consequence, social spaces need to open for the active engagement of individuals to explore strategies of coping with insecurity and uncertainty, rather than being made subject to increasing control and standardisation. In the words of Peter Kelly (1999), experiments in surviving in the 'wild zones' of society should be encouraged, rather than trying to 'tame' such zones at any cost because the protective aspects of the latter are increasingly restricted to institutional structures themselves. These fail to protect the individuals concerned.

Generally, this fits the reflections of Anthony Giddens and Victor Turner. In his theory of structuration, Giddens (1984) refers to the 'interstices' between social structures; that is, the unstructured niches and spaces in society where, on the one hand, risks have not (yet) been controlled and included into cultural interpretation, societal provision and compensation, and where, on the other hand, there is scope of action, space to move and explore beyond institutional regulation. Giddens refers especially to processes of social change in which such interstices provide necessary buffers and manoeuvrability. In this he agrees with Turner, who relates the attributes of 'liminality' (the situation of being on the margins, at the threshold), inherent to both transitions in individuals' lives as well as in social transformations. And for young men and women who (have to) live their transitions under conditions of late modernity, liminality occurs exactly in this double sense: first, in relation to their transitional life phase as such; and second, as a consequence of the fading normal – achievable – biography: "The passage from lower to higher status is through a limbo of statuslessness" (Turner, 1969, p 97).

It is clear that formal structures – be they educational or support institutions – increasingly fail to address young people's needs, because they necessarily fail in considering living, learning and working situations that are structured by liminality.

The structural gap between policies and young people makes a perspective that is oriented towards 'the informal' in terms of social integration – or even better, the relevance of informal resources of social integration – more and more useful. According to Giddens (1990), the decreasing reliability of institutions and relationships in late modernity requires that individuals develop 'active trust' in order to cover their need for ontological security (Hartmann and Offe, 2001). This requires, however, contexts in which relationships can be actively shaped and lived. Therefore, the 'access points' of institutions – that is, concrete institutional representatives, and their trustworthiness, their credibility in the eyes of the individuals concerned – becomes crucial. It is in this light that Parts One and Two of this volume, which have highlighted the strength and the relevance of 'the informal' for young men and women, should be understood with the categories of *informal work, informal support* and *informal learning* being the most prescient.

Informal work has been referred to in particular by Thomas Kieselbach with regard to the coping strategies of long-term unemployed young people in Southern Europe (see Chapter Three of this volume). Despite the disadvantages with regard to income, status and work conditions, these young people use informal work because it makes them feel more active than relying on public institutions and/or formal work to which they have no access. They use their social networks to get such jobs, which implies that this work may be experienced as part of, or at least as overlapping with, their own life worlds. This does not say anything about the quality of such work with regard to their biographies. Kieselbach refers to the ambiguity between being trapped in precarious careers and the experience of empowerment. Referring to southern Italy, Enzo Mingione (1995) confirms the structural necessity of a socially embedded and flexible means as embodied in the partly formal and partly informal family economy to compensate for the lack of a developed productive infrastructure. And in the context of the situation in the north east of Italy, which is dominated by a dynamic structure of small enterprise districts, Vittorio Capecchi and Adele Pesce (1983, p 11) even refer to the emancipatory aspects of informal work:

> The informal economies however show ... markets on which the (independent) worker establishes a direct relationship with the consumer ... which includes a coincidence of life styles and of possible forms of solidarity (or compliance) which would not develop on the official market to the same extent.

However, understanding labour markets as fractal structures similar to a "spider's web" and not as "the aseptical and fenced around object" requires that labour markets first of all have to be addressed locally rather than nationally in order to assess and to match concrete demands and supplies (Accornero and Carmigiani, 1985, p 69).

Referring to the 'Brazilianisation of the West' in the context of neoliberal flexibilisation and globalisation, Beck (2000) calls for a valorisation of the pluralisation of (increasingly non-standard) forms of work. Far from neglecting the risks of precariousness, Beck claims to recognise the irreversibility of such trends and the need, therefore, to secure their liberating effects by the acknowledgement of their integrative potentials and the inclusion of all forms of 'socially useful work', such as care and family work or voluntary activities in a more universal and citizenship-based model of social security (Gorz, 2000). Opportunities for young people to engage in performing arts activities, which are not usually accepted as seriously labour market-related, may be reconsidered in this perspective.

Informal learning shares with informal work the lack of recognition, although it is less criminalised; except where informal learning in youth cultural scenes implies the learning of potentially risky and harmful deviant behaviour. There have been considerable attempts to assess and acknowledge informally acquired knowledge and skills. However, these approaches often have an instrumental bias inasmuch as they are related to a certification or accreditation of informal learning 'on the job' in terms of vocational qualifications (CEDEFOP, 1999). Learning in leisure time, in youth cultural contexts, in homework or in family work is much less taken into account. While many skills and competencies that women develop either as part of female socialisation in the parents' household or in their role as housewife and mother are included in formal curricula, for example in nursery teaching, such experiences are not usually assessed or certified in order to assist (re)entry into the labour market. Women are often channelled into pre-vocational or retraining courses in the area of home economics instead. The boundaries of formal education and training thus contribute to the dequalification and deskilling of individuals rather than to their empowerment (EGRIS, 2002).

With regard to young people, much more attention is paid to non-formal education in youth work settings than to their informal learning in everyday life contexts that are beyond public control. Still, such objectives appear to be less valued in the social hierarchy of skills and competencies compared to the formal repertoire on which the occupational system is built, as regards funding and recognition. Therefore, youth policies can be characterised as the 'soft' sector of policies addressing young people, since the young people lack the necessary power to impose their own standards on other policy sectors.

Informal support appears to be relevant on a material as well as a non-material level, and it is relied on either through choice or by pure necessity. Comparison between Northern and Southern Europe shows that young people in Southern European countries depend to a greater extent on their families because they do not have individual access to any kind of social security, despite the long duration of their transitions from education to work (see Chapter Three of this volume). However, many of them justify their staying at home even beyond the point of labour market integration – as an individual choice – because they feel comfortable at home and there is no need to move out, or because they feel responsible for their parents. At the same time, young people in Northern European countries increasingly use and rely on family and peer support. On the one hand, state support is more and more experienced as being connected to coercive conditions. On the other hand, the major effect of social exclusion in these countries is social isolation because family resources are less available and stable and because friendship and peer networks decline with the length of unemployment (Gallie and Paugam, 2000).

The message of such comparison is confusing and controversial and may be misunderstood one-dimensionally in terms of the damage done by the welfare state to the reproduction of social life worlds. Clearly, however, there is another lesson to be drawn that addresses the whole picture of social integration, one that requires the fundamental restructuring of the links between its different constituent parts. This involves connecting the different types of education and training to different types and forms of work based on a combination of income sources and reconciling work and education with family and lifestyles, systemic aspects of integration with subjective ones and the formal with the informal. This is the analytical framework of what has been called in the 'misleading trajectories' network ITPs (see Chapter Two of this volume). This becomes visible through the experience of approaches that leave space for a more informal negotiation between project makers and project participants, as in third-sector initiatives. Clearly, young people accept help as well as the responsibilities tied to this type of offer if there is a space for negotiation and for individual solutions that they experience as 'real', while they experience negotiation and contracting with formal institutions as token gestures from which they try to protect their identities.

Conclusions: perspectives of Integrated Transition Policies

For institutions, the demand to recognise the informal represents a paradoxical challenge. Institutions are a means to automatise and generalise social integration, to reduce uncertainty and to plan for outcomes that are identified or defined as desirable. In contrast, the recognition of 'the informal' means to accept uncertainty and to leave space in which the relevance of goals and the adequacy of means is negotiated. What is an appropriate policy approach with regard to 'the informal'? At present, three dominant policy reactions can be identified. The first one is to criminalise the informal by sanctions in the case of informal work. The second is to formalise the informal by incentives such as enlarging formal offers and certification, as in the case of informal learning. The third reaction is intentionally to include the informal into policy planning and rhetoric as the necessary social 'glue' without which institutions fail to achieve integration. This is particularly the case with informal support. At the same time, however, the conditions under which informal resources emerge are undermined: material provisions and psychosocial assistance for families as well as funding for youth work and cultural activities are cut down, while public spaces in which young people may congregate are functionalised. Under such conditions, a perspective towards 'the informal' means not only a reliance on its integrative potentials, but also a recognition and valorisation of individual strategies of (re)integration instead of neglecting or even punishing such strategies. Research has to contribute to this by identifying such strategies and by analysing the necessary resources and conditions that enable their advancement.

However, valorising the informal is only one aspect of the challenge for ITPs to close the gap between system and social integration – or to reduce both subjective and systemic risks of exclusion – as outlined in this volume. If it is true that (transition) policies depend on the active collaboration of their addressees – and the extensive advertising campaigns for programmes such as the New Deal in the UK or JUMP in Germany reflect this need – ITPs imply that young people's motivation, understood in its strict sense as *intrinsic* motivation, has to be recognised as a key success criterion of transition policies.

First, the increase of uncertainty in biographic perspectives results in the increase of individual responsibility for individual social integration. This means that social integration increasingly depends on the persistence and 'mobilising capacities' (Furlong et al, 2002) of individuals to constantly accumulate any kind of resources of social integration and consequently on their intrinsic motivation to do so. If motivation depends on the (subjective) relevance of a specific goal and the (subjectively) perceived probability to achieve it through personal action, as cognitive psychology suggests (for example, see Bandura, 1997), then individuals need the possibility to identify with desired social positions (something that implies choice); and they need free (that is, unconditional) access to competencies and resources to achieve these positions.

Second, most of the research on the relationship between achievement and motivation has been undertaken with regard to *learning* and education. The insight that learning requires learners' motivation seems to be banal inasmuch as learning happens as a cognitive process 'inside' the learner interrelated with social interaction. This means that motivation is a necessary prerequisite for efficient education and training. However, policies continue to design programmes to teach young people rather than to facilitate learning, and this is even more the case where learners are conceived as 'disadvantaged'. While this neglects the universally valid principle that "learning cannot be designed but only designed for – that is facilitated or frustrated" (Wenger, 1998, p 229), this approach becomes even more problematic under conditions of late modernity:

> Educational philosophy and theory face the unfamiliar and challenging task of theorising a formative process which is not guided from the start by the target form designed in advance; modelling without the model to be arrived at in the end being known or clearly visualised; a process which at best can be adumbrate, never enforced; in short, an open-ended process, concerned more with remaining open-ended than with any specific product, and fearing all premature closure more than it shuns the prospect of staying forever inconclusive. (Bauman, 2001, p 139)

In this perspective, the objective of 'learning to learn' shifts from a learning prerequisite to the most important learning objective, while education and training need to be (re)defined in terms of opportunities for experimental and explorative action and reflection rather than teaching specific skills and knowledge and providing qualifications.

This corresponds to the third and final aspect of young men's and women's motivation: the aspect of legitimate participation in late modern *democracy*. Public institutions are legitimised as the executive of democratic decisions, as the expression of a majority interpretation of the public good. Inasmuch as the growing complexity of social structures makes institutions contradictory and likely to fail, their credibility and legitimacy decreases, and " the growing practical impotence of public institutions strips interest in common issues and common stands of its attraction" (Bauman, 2001, p 205). This means that citizenship loses in concrete value and relevance that which can only be compensated for by redelegating power to individuals where they are concerned in their lives by public issues – power in terms of rights to negotiate with institutions about appropriate solutions, the appropriate definition of 'rights and responsibilities' in the individual case. Beck (1992) argues that to shape reflexive modernisation implies that institutions provide opportunities – spaces and resources – that enable individuals to learn, to act and to take decisions. It implies, as well, a renunciation of these processes to organisations according to normative plans that follow an outdated instrumental logic of linear causality. If policies are more likely to have unintended side effects than to achieve their intended goals, and if individuals are made accountable for their decisions – even when taken under conditions of restricted options – democratic legitimacy of institutions requires a maximum of *active participation* of those concerned: in terms of choice, in terms of influence, in terms of being recognised as the authors of their biographies (Walther et al, 2002a). It seems as if the process of institutionalising individual life courses has been developed too far. Taking a step back means reopening spaces for direct and symmetric communication in which young people and institutional actors communicate their views and interests rather than relying on benchmarks, indicators of disadvantage and bureaucratic rules of access and entitlements.

To conclude, making intrinsic motivation of individuals a decisive success criterion of transition policy, therefore, is both a normative consequence and a prerequisite of public efficacy in late modernity. Late modern transition systems entail risks for the young people involved, but it is not legitimate to tame the actors of such transitions when the structures are too wild to be tamed – especially if taming strategies imply the humiliation of those to be protected. Institutions have to take their share of risks by accepting open outcomes and by trusting (and not coercing) young people to be self-responsible.

Note

[1] Special thanks go to Marie Corman (EC, DG Education and Culture), Walter Wolf (EC, DG Employment), Erhard Schulte (German Ministry of Education and Research) and Roland Smolar (French Ministry of Employment and Social Affairs) for contributing and providing their written comments for this chapter.

References

Accornero, A. and Carmigiani, F. (1985) *Le paradossi della disoccupazione*, Bologna: Il Mulino.

Alheit, P. (1995) 'Biographical learning. Theoretical outline, challenges and contradictions of a new approach in adult education', in P. Alheit, A. Bronn, E. Brugger and D. Domenice (eds) *The biographical approach in European adult education*, Vienna: Volkschochschule.

Bandura, A. (1997) *Self-efficacy: The exercise of control*, New York, NY: Freeman.

Bauman, Z. (2001) *The individualised society*, Cambridge: Polity Press.

Beck, U. (1992) *Risk society: Towards a new modernity*, London: Sage Publications.

Beck, U. (2000) *The brave new world of work*, Cambridge: Polity Press.

Behning, U. and Serrano Pascual, A. (eds) (2001) *Gender mainstreaming in the European employment strategy*, Brussels: ETUI.

Böhnisch, L. (1994) *Gespaltene Normalität. Lebensbewältigung und Sozialpädagogik an den Grenzen der Wohlfahrtsgesellschaft*, Weinheim und München: Juventa.

Böhnisch, L. (1997) *Sozialpädagogik der Lebensalter*, Weinheim und München: Juventa.

Capecchi, V. and Pesce, A. (1983) 'Se la diversità è un valore', *Inchiesta*, no 59-60, pp 1-17.

CEDEFOP (European Centre for the Development of Vocational Training) (1999) *Making learning visible*, Luxembourg: Office for Official Publications of the European Communities.

Corman, M. (2002) *The art of learning: Empowerment through performing arts. The project 'Secondary Learning Effects'*, Discussion paper to the European conference 'Young People and Transition Policies', 6-8 June, Madrid.

du Bois-Reymond, M., Plug, W., Stauber, B., Pohl, A. and Walther, A. (2002) *How to avoid cooling out? Experiences of young people in their transitions to work across Europe*, YOYO Project Working Paper 2 (www.iris-egris.de/yoyo).

EC (European Commission) (1997) *Luxembourg Employment Summit of the European Council. Presidency Conclusions* (www.europa.eu.int).

EC (2001) *A memorandum on lifelong learning*, Commission staff working paper (www.europa.eu.int/comm/education/life).

EGRIS (European Group for Integrated Social Research) (2002) 'Leading or misleading trajectories? Concepts and perspectives', in A. Walther, B. Stauber, A. Biggart, M. du Bois-Reymond, A. Furlong, A. López Blasco, S. Mørch and J.M. Pais (eds) *Misleading trajectories: Integration policies for young adults in Europe?*, Opladen: Leske+Budrich, pp 117-53.

Evers, A. and Novotny, H. (1987) *Umgang mit Unsicherheit*, Frankfurt am Main: Suhrkamp.

Furlong, A. Cartmel, C., Biggart, A., Sweeting, H. and West, P. (2002) *Youth transitions: Patterns of vulnerability and processes of social exclusion*, Glasgow: Final Report to Scottish Executive.

Gallie, D. and Paugam, S. (eds) (2000) *Welfare regimes and the experience of unemployment in Europe*, Oxford: Oxford University Press.

Gazier, B. (1999) 'Employability: concepts and policies', *MISEP Policies 67/68*, European Employment Observatory: Berlin, pp 38-51.

Giddens, A. (1984) *The constitution of society: Outline of the theory of structuration*, Cambridge: Polity Press.

Giddens, A. (1990) *The consequences of modernity*, Cambridge: Polity Press.

Goffman, E. (1962) 'On 'cooling the mark out': some aspects of adaptation and failure', in A. Rose (ed) *Human behaviour and social processes*, Boston, MA: Houghton, pp 482-505.

Gorz, A. (2000) *Arbeit zwischen Misere und Utopie*, Frankfurt am Main: Suhrkamp.

Habermas, J. (1981) *Theorie des kommunikativen Handelns, 2 Volumes*, Frankfurt am Main: Suhrkamp.

Hartmann, M. and Offe, C. (eds) (2001) *Vertrauen. Die Grundlage des sozialen Zusammenhalts*, Frankfurt am Main/New York, NY: Campus.

IARD (2001) *Study on the state of young people and youth policy in Europe*, Milan: IARD.

Kelly, P. (1999) 'Wild and tame zones: regulating the transitions of youth at risk', *Journal of Youth Studies*, vol 2, no 2, pp 193-211.

Lødemel, I. and Trickey, H. (eds) (2001) *'An offer you can't refuse': Workfare in international perspective*, Bristol: The Policy Press.

Low, D. (2001) 'Sheffield Intermediate Labour Market Programme: a case study', in A. Serrano Pascual (ed) *Enhancing youth employability through social and civil partnership*, Brussels: ETUI, pp 191-205.

Mingione, E. (1995) 'Labour market segmentation and informal work in Southern Europe', *European Urban and Regional Studies*, vol 2, no 2, pp 121-43.

OECD (Organisation for Economic Co-operation and Development) (2001) *Knowledge and skills for life: First results from PISA 2000*, Paris: OECD.

Schulte, E. (2002) 'Comments on "Integration through training?"', Discussant paper to the European conference 'Young People and Transition Policies', 6-8 June, Madrid.

Serrano Pascual, A. (ed) (2001) *Enhancing youth employability through social and civil partnership*, Brussels: ETUI.

Smolar, R. (2002) 'Comments on "Long-term youth unemployment and risks of social exclusion"', Discussant paper to the European conference 'Young People and Transition Policies', 6-8 June, Madrid.

Stone, D. (1992) 'Gatekeeping experts and the control of status passages', in W.R. Heinz (ed) *Gate-keeping in the life course*, Weinheim: Deutscher Studienverlag, pp 203-20.

Turner, V. (1969) *The ritual process: Structure and anti-structure*, New York, NY: Aldine de Gruyter.

van Berkel, R. and Hornemann Møller, I. (eds) (2002) *Active social policies in the EU: Inclusion trough participation?*, Bristol: The Policy Press.

Walther, A. (2000) *Spielräume im Übergang in die Arbeit. Junge Erwachsene im Wandel der Arbeitsgesellschaft in Deutschland, Italien und Großbritannien*, Weinheim/München: Juventa.

Walther, A., Stauber, B., Biggart, A., du Bois-Reymond, M., Furlong, A., López Blasco, A., Mørch, S. and Pais, J.M. (eds) (2002) *Misleading trajectories: Integration policies for young adults in Europe?*, Opladen: Leske+Budrich.

Wenger, E. (1998) *Communities of practice: Learning, meaning and identity*, Cambridge: Cambridge University Press.

Wolf, W. (2002) 'Transitional labour markets and training', Discussion paper to the European conference 'Young People and Transition Policies', 6-8 June, Madrid.

ELEVEN

Competence and employability

Sven Mørch and Barbara E. Stalder

For some time now, 'employability' and 'competence' have been seen as issues of high importance for the discussion of policies for youth transitions. When this discussion is raised in relation to youth development, a number of current changes have to be considered. In a late modern world, changes are fast and all-inclusive. Labour market and qualification structures constantly evolve and the organisation of educational systems is subject to continuous political discussion and alteration. Moreover, individual development and individual learning perspectives are in constant flux.

Although they are often discussed, this does not mean that the issues surrounding competence and employability are clear and simple. The many perspectives expressed about modern development, labour market demands, youth life and individualisation make it difficult to clarify and agree about the meaning of the two concepts.

Competence may be defined thus:

> A competence is the ability to meet a complex demand successfully or carry out a complex activity or task. (Rychen and Salganik, 2002, p 5)

Hence, in this professional definition, competence refers to a context or situation, but is seen as a form of personal characteristic. Competence refers to the situation but may also be learned by the individual concerned.

Employability, on the other hand, is perhaps even more difficult to define. It may be defined as being useful or valuable in a labour market situation. In this way, it refers to a field of contexts without pointing to a specific context.

Competence and employability may be conceptualised as separate issues. In a labour market context, competence refers to the individual supply structure and employability to the labour market demand structure.

Looking closer, however, competence and employability appear to be the same issue seen from different perspectives. Both competence and employability point to the individual practice of knowledge and skills. From the demand perspective, employability asks what sorts of knowledge and skills are *required* for different persons in different positions in the labour market. From the supply perspective, competence points to *existing* personal skills and knowledge and the way in which they refer to labour market demands.

In everyday discussions, competence is often seen as some sort of private modern personality quality and employability as the demand of 'a total individual fit' to whatever is needed in the labour market. Individual development and social life, which are highly determined by labour market participation, are viewed as being opposed (see Chapter Five of this volume).

With such an understanding, it seems obvious that no simple solution exists to the theoretical challenge of combining the two concepts of competence and employability or to the practical question of how to integrate young people into modern social life.

In this chapter, we argue that competence and employability have to be understood as interdependent and intrinsically related to the general developmental aspects of processes of individualisation. Competence and employability should not be seen as contradictory concepts and practices that point to opposite interests; they should not be viewed as representing a personal and a labour market policy antagonism. Also, they should not be understood as being more or less the same, as some sort of a goal for a development of 'comployability'. Competence and employability are related concepts, not only in a theoretical analytical perspective, but also in practice and especially in youth life practice. They are different perspectives or questions to be asked of human practice, and as concepts referring to modern development they should be understood and clarified in relation to this development.

Employability asks how we are able to engage in the labour market, which is changing all the time. How should people develop engagement and motivation, knowledge and skills for a flexible job situation? And how should people themselves become flexible?

The concept of competence deals with a broader question. It asks what it means for an individual to act competently in modern life. What knowledge and skills should people have and be able to use in different situations and contexts? Here, the important question seems to be 'What should people be competent for?', or 'What does it mean to become flexible for a modern society and a flexible labour market?'.

When in our argumentation we address 'education' and 'school' in a general way, we refer to the wider settings of institutionalised and formalised learning through which young people go on to become both employable and competent for modern life. Apart from school in its stricter sense, this includes forms of training as well as schemes addressing assumed employability and competence deficits of unemployed or 'disadvantaged' youth (see Chapter Fourteen of this volume).

Modernity, competence and employability

To properly reflect upon these questions, it is important to have a more general perspective on how changes in modern life should be included in the discussion about competence and employability. It should be asked, 'What connections exist between labour market demands for employability and broad social competencies?'.

First, it seems important to understand that modern societies basically have changed their developmental 'logic' from production to consumption. Accordingly, the positions of and challenges for people have changed. Today, society should not only be reflected on or understood as a production-related class system, but increasingly as a consumer-orientated lifestyle world. This message seems to follow most late modern analytic frameworks. Already in the 1960s, Galbraith, in his book *The new industrial state*, wrote that production is planned today according to a new principle, which he called the 'revised sequence'; that is, consumer interests are developed before the commodity is produced. In this way, production is not dependent on demand and supply logic; rather, it creates its own demand (Galbraith, 1978). Other writers have underlined consumer society integration perspectives, pointing to the new importance of the need to construct oneself as a consumer by the use of lifestyle orientations.

Also, it has to be noted that the development of modern industries in late modernity follows the development of human capital. The point to human resource management is that production processes should be developed through the engagement of human resources. Thus, the individual capacities or broader competencies of employees are placed at the centre of modern development. In modern societies, employability should not only be defined according to immediate job demands, but has to include a broader understanding of personal competencies.

Hence, a new engagement in the 'human factor' of consumers and human capital influences the goals and agencies of personal development such as family and the school system. School curricula are particularly subject to change. Instead of only talking about disciplines and necessary knowledge and skills, schools now also emphasise multidisciplinarity and the development of individual competencies.

School life points to values such as democratisation, participation and the development of the 'qualified consumer of the modern world': a person who is able to reflect upon and choose among different alternatives in the development of his or her own lifestyle. Young people are made competent consumers, who are able to choose and select among different opportunities. Not only do they become consumers of commodities, but they also become consumers of modern life.

Today, especially in the Nordic countries, educational systems do not necessarily include curricula directly aimed at the development of skills and knowledge for the labour market. They try to engage young people in all sorts of human and social development by giving room for individual planning and interests. As a consequence, many educational trajectories do not guarantee that young people will be competent for specific jobs. They may focus on individual development and self-expression rather than on job perspectives. In the Nordic countries, it seems to be a general ideology both in school, among parents and in the public debate that young people should choose education according to what they 'like to do', and not according to labour market perspectives or unemployment statistics.

The interest in modern individual development is behind the current centrality of the concept of competence, but at the same time it also points to difficulties in unfolding its meaning and understandings. The question seems to be, 'Do modern educational trajectories make young people competent for jobs and their futures?' – that is, employable – or does education mostly engender misleading trajectories, where young people end up in jobs they do not like and/or in unsuccessful jobs (poorly paid, insecure, bad working conditions) (Walther et al, 2002)?

The late modern understanding of knowledge, skills and competencies points to a development where knowledge and skills are seen as reproductive qualities. Knowledge and skills belong to educational or school qualifications and not to individual development. They exist as large 'boxes' inside traditional educational institutions. At the same time, educational systems are viewed as ivory towers without any connection to real labour market demands. Therefore, young people should be cautious in spending so much time on educational curricula and the development of school-based reproductive knowledge and skills. Instead, they should develop their own 'knowledgeability' for the future – their competences. In this context, competence is seen as personal qualification, which can be unfolded in any particular context that somebody chooses to engage in.

The changes in educational form and content have in many situations made the question of planning education for the labour market only an indirect issue. Emphasis has been given to the perspective of individual competence, while the question of employability has become more like an issue of labour market discussions. This ambiguity of modern education is outlined in several late modern theoretical writings. Both Beck (1992) and especially Frønes and Brusdal (2000) underline the different relationships between education and job situation in former historical periods and today. Frønes and Brusdal describe how education was viewed before as having a high value: if people had an education, they could have a job. In modern society, this has changed. Today, education is not so highly valued (because everyone has some sort of education), but you cannot have a job without it. Thus, competence and employability seem to be concepts in the late modern world that direct attention to central issues and changes that lie at the heart of developmental processes in modern educational systems.

The political debate about employability and competence reflects the situation of changing 'traditional' educational systems and the labour market. The current engagement in understanding the relationship between employability and the development of competence is predicated on a fear that they will move away from one other. This means developing 'competent' young people who are not employable in the labour market.

Summing up the logic of understanding the relationship between competence and employability, it seems necessary to combine several perspectives (Figure 11.1).

On the one hand, in the development of the individual practice, employability refers to changing labour market demands while competence refers to the personal development perspective in a modern world. On the other hand, the relationship between competence and employability depends both on the general development of social integration or the question about how individual and society relate to each other, and on the specific development of youth life and educational systems.

Social integration and individualisation

Although late modernity (or post-modernity) is an important factor to be considered when analysing the challenges of social integration faced by modern individuals, it is imperative that we also think about the 'reality', meaning the concrete demands that an individual will face. For instance, people will be expected to live up to certain demands required by the labour market. Individualisation and the development of subjectivity are important issues in modern life, but certainly so are the issues of personal economy and career. Both competence and employability should be focused upon. The discussion of modernity must not stand alone as an abstract discussion of modern

Figure 11.1: Competence and employability from different perspectives

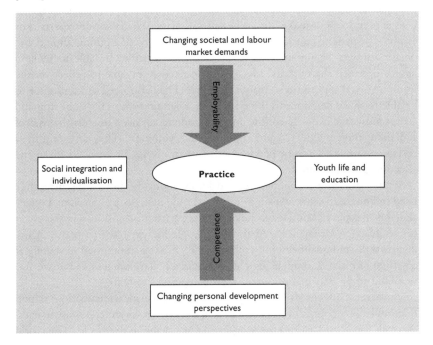

individualisation. In dealing with young people's lives, their development and future, it is essential *also* to contemplate the realities of the society we live in.

The question of modernity specifically focuses on the transition from 'the modern' to late or post-modernity. 'The modern' stretches from the creation of the bourgeois society to the postwar period. The post-modern or late modern era includes the past few decades. There are different stances on what post-modernity really looks like. Some social researchers prefer to see post-modernity as fundamentally different from the modern, while others prefer to view post-modernity as an extension of the modern; that is, as late modern.

Giddens, in his book *Modernity and self identity* (1991), presents a moderate position in the late modernity discussion. In his theory, he points to developments that constitute significant differences between the past and the present, as they can be looked at from a general perspective. In a very rough outline of Giddens' perspective, the important developments in late modernity can be summarised as follows.

People of today live like individual actors, and this calls for a self-understanding that facilitates the movement between a wide variety of different contexts. People need to think and act contextually, but they also need to understand themselves across the different contexts: they need self-understanding.

Late modernity requires people not only to *think as they go through life*, but also to *think about life*. People are expected to be able to rise above the situation, rise above the context, and think about the world from a distance. This distanced *reflection* makes it possible to talk about a condition, of *choosing* expertise or *choosing* social relations.

In modern society, we depend on experts. However, the fact that someone is an expert does not make him or her an authority. We *choose* our experts. For example, a patient consults a doctor, but gets a second opinion should the doctor's answer be unsatisfactory. However, in order to be able to make a choice between the doctors' advice, people need to be able to reflect on the issues involved, and to do so from a distance. They also need self-assurance to be able to make decisions in the end. After a certain time, reflections stop and action must take over. Therefore, modern individuals need to trust themselves and their choices (see Chapter Nine of this volume). They also require a certain minimum amount of knowledge of the issues in order to make the selection process fruitful.

At the same time as people need to know about life from a distance, they need to be able to work within a context. In the past, people developed once-and-for-all types of knowledge, linked to their particular positions in society as priests, teachers or farmers. At present, people are expected to master many diverse skills and qualifications, each of which may be summoned separately at any time or place. Competencies are contextually developed skills but are also supposed to be personal resources that span across contexts.

Moreover, Giddens makes the point that modern individualisation, which requires large amounts of broad social and knowledge-oriented competencies, also calls for a basic trust in the world and one's being in the world. The world must function as one expects it to. Giddens considers this basic trust to be an ontological prerequisite, a necessity for people to be in the world. Should these basic beliefs in the world not be upheld, people cannot develop their subjectivity and, hence, they cease to function socially.

Giddens sees his theory as a critical theory that includes various requirements that the world must fulfil. According to Giddens, the danger in late modernity is that people lose their self-identity and their faith in themselves. The answer is to develop social influence and influence on the conditions under which one's life unfolds. In late modern times, according to this theory, the individual is forced to take an active part in shaping the conditions under which he or she lives. *The individual must participate actively in the structuration process.*

Individualisation in modernity prepares the individual for the challenge of actively participating in social contexts. Giddens' analysis can be used to point to general competencies of individualisation in modern life:

- self-identity;
- reflexivity;
- self-assurance;
- knowledgeability;
- individual basic trust in the world and oneself;
- participation.

These modern requirements describe the general aspects of individual competencies in relation to an overall social integration perspective. They refer to our understanding of individual or personal competence. But at the same time, these competencies become aspects of a modern employability demand. However, they do not do so automatically. They are the basis of more precise expectations of employability. Human resource management expectations are very close to these requirements, but in other job situations other skills and knowledge are demanded. Also, different competencies should be balanced according to the labour market situation. Young people, for example, who have a very high self-assurance with only a low degree of knowledgeability, will have only limited success in the labour market (see Chapter Two of this volume; Walther et al, 2002). Therefore, Giddens' list points to single items, but as part of a general structure.

To summarise the modern challenge of individualisation or social competence, we finally have to consider the changing individualisation process.

In modern societies, individualisation is not necessarily increasing: it is changing. We may discern at least two different modes of individualisation. In the past 200 years, socialisation agencies such as families and school systems have been engaged in a special project: the making of the individual, first, as a development in the bourgeoisie and later as a broadening of individualisation extended to all young people (modus 1). In the new or contemporary situation, individuals are seen as actors in modern society, and as such, they are taken as individuals *before* they engage in education and social life (modus 2). Therefore, the new challenge is not to create individuals (modus 1) or to blindly support the individual, but to encourage individuals in the making of their society and new forms of social integration (Andersen and Mørch, 2000).

The described change may be illustrated very simply, as shown in Figure 11.2. Today, both modes of individualisation exist, but modus 2 challenges modus 1. Young people are not only the result of socialisation in education; they have become partners in the structuration of modern life (negotiation). Youth life is not only transition to adult society, but also contains demands for living in more modern social contexts. Therefore, individual learning and individual competence have become crucial for making people agents or constructors of society. What is experienced, however, are difficulties in creating social responsibility in modernity. All people – and perhaps young people especially – see the world from their own perspective, as worlds of their own, and it often looks as though individualisation has a tendency to create a very private perspective, a 'what's in it for me?'-type thinking' (Ziehe, 2001; see Chapter Two of this volume). This personal competence orientation may challenge the perspective of (modern) employability.

Youth life and education

According to our understanding, it is important to consider that modernisation refers not only to changes in labour market conditions and the conditions of social integration. Youth life itself and educational processes should be reflected equally. The possibilities of 'youth transitions' – the movement between family, education and labour market – and the problems and challenges that arise when transitional patterns change are particularly important aspects to consider. Structural perspectives on youth transitions point to various types of problems. Today, transition has become blurred in different ways. The classical idea of

Figure 11.2: Modern social integration and individualisation

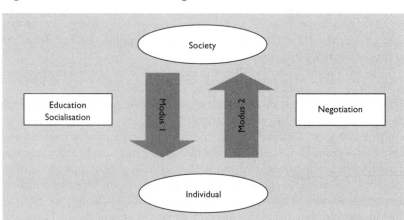

youth as a transition phase between childhood and adult life is questioned. This situation is caused by changes in educational patterns but also by changes in adult and work life.

Existing ideas and trajectories of social integration are part of the general understanding that transitions are successful when young people are placed in a secure job position. However, as the labour market has become more flexible, the idea of having a regular or steady job and position is also changing. The new labour market is not 'steady' and people have to change jobs and positions throughout their lives. Lifelong learning, therefore, has become a new reality. School and education is no longer reserved for young people.

Maybe the whole idea of youth as a transition is changing. In the modern western world, we are confronted by new circumstances of 'fragmented contextualisation' (see Figure 11.3): we live in a world in which more contexts are functioning as a network producing different aspects of development (Mørch, 2001, 2003). Developmental demands are overall demands of living in a post-modern world, where traditional structures have broken down and the individual has become the central focus of interest. All aspects of development are in some way informed by and combined with these challenges of 'post' or 'late' modernity.

Today, social integration does not only point to one major trajectory or normal trajectories between childhood and adult life. Many more routes or pathways may exist and become trajectories inside and between different or fragmented social contexts. The only objective for such transitions is that trajectories should combine social and individual life success and satisfaction (see Chapter Two of this volume; Walther et al, 2002). This means that the

Figure 11.3: Fragmented contextualisation

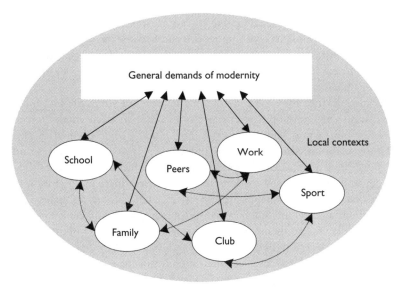

trajectory problem falls back upon the individual. The individual forms his or her own trajectory, and in this way contextualises aspects of development in her or his youth life inside societal conditions and perspectives. Thus, the trajectory challenge for young people is not only to participate, but *to find out what they should participate in and for what reason.*

To understand this trajectory challenge, it is important to have a broader view of youth life and youth trajectories. Modern youth life asks for a better understanding of individual activities and trajectories and how they create and contribute to individual development. Logic and sense do not objectively exist in formal transition trajectories – rather, the individual has to develop them. The individual has a new responsibility for creating his own trajectory, and this calls for a better understanding of how young people cope with given conditions. Specifically, it has to be investigated *how they should be empowered* to make choices inside youth and social life. Therefore, the second new challenge of youth seems to be 'the construction of sense and competence' for manoeuvring in a more open world. Young people should learn to 'cope', or else they should develop forms of 'expedient' life management (Mørch and Laursen, 1998).

However, even in a 'fragmented contextualisation' situation, some contexts may be 'reserved' for specific age groups. It is still possible for outsiders to observe youth and for young people to see themselves as youth. Youth still exist as an objective and subjective social category.

All in all, youth life has become more and more important to young people's developmental possibilities. Youth is the time for individualisation and learning is the most important means for individual success or failure. Young people who abstain from using opportunities available in this period will experience relative deindividualisation and will not become competent and employable. However, at the same time, youth has lost its direct transition qualities; it is no longer formed and developed directly in accordance with clear adult life demands. It has acquired its own importance and become its own (prolonged) time of life. Youth is no longer only a stage in a developmental perspective, but a set of contexts to which people belong for a period (longer or shorter depending on the individual) of their life.

Young people, therefore, use and combine contexts of youth life in a more personal way. They develop private trajectories inside modern youth life and in between the various youth contexts. For young people themselves, this generates a new situation, which includes both great opportunities and difficulties. Young people may feel formal education (which is defined according to the demands of school and working life) to be increasingly in opposition to their 'personal' lives and biographical perspectives. They may feel an antagonism between labour market employability demands and personal competence wishes. If young people engage themselves in and learn from modern youth life and reject formal education because of its irrelevance, they may gain new competence, but they may also lose their connection to jobs and the future, their employability. Individual trajectories may become too 'private'. However, should youth life become autonomous, how might the relationship between youth and society look to young people and policy planners? Which guidelines would guarantee adult life success?

In Nordic school systems, the challenge of modern fragmented and 'indirect' youth life seems to be to construct *individual* skills for the job market of 'transversal' competence, the kind of competence that may be used in working life as well. It increasingly becomes an *individual challenge to integrate competence and employability*. Modern social developmental challenges have to be solved in and through individual biographies.

However, the youth situation is so indirect, it is difficult to see connections and individual planning can be very difficult. Therefore, when young people are developing a useful trajectory, 'sense-making' becomes important and in many situations both guidance and counselling are required.

For many young people, it is difficult to find out which activities and competencies in youth life are important for their future employment careers. One of the individual answers to this 'un-plannable situation' might be 'to get the most' education possible. In the Danish educational system, for example, more and more young people choose to go on to grammar schools, even if the educational orientations are not academic.

Our broad and common youth culture, which involves all young people, has a hidden agenda, of which not all young people are aware, however. At the same time as youth life should be fun, competition for the future exists underneath the shared youth culture. This is a serious problem in educational curricula, where many youngsters are not aware of the consequences of bad academic performance until they experience the barriers to further education and qualified jobs. Youth and educational life in themselves differentiate young people according to adult life perspectives. They create leading and misleading trajectories, but it is difficult to see which are leading somewhere and which are not (Walther et al, 2002). Therefore, educational systems are under pressure to change their curricula and to find new ways of planning and delivering education or – more precisely – learning.

Education, competence and employability

Educational systems, however, exist as gateways to the labour market. Therefore, their role in the development of young people's competence and employability is a serious issue. However, the focus on employability often leads to very closed or one-sided reflections from the perspective of educators and employers. Instead, there should be a broader understanding of the development of young people with regard to their employment perspectives. The key question seems to be how education and the labour market should relate to each other in order to secure both the competence and employability of young people.

Recent developments and reflections about qualifications, competence and technology may prove helpful when elaborating on the notion of competence. The role of modern technology, especially information technology (IT), is obviously important in the discussion of modern educational systems. This is because it questions the logic of contexts; IT itself generates increasing volumes of knowledge and provides almost unlimited access to huge amounts of it. Hence, IT challenges former knowledge monopolies, including those of teachers. To find knowledge itself may no longer be the problem; it is the use of knowledge or knowledge contextualisation that becomes important – the translation of knowledge to knowledgeability or, of 'knowing that' to 'knowing how'.

In this context, the concept of competence has largely replaced the concepts of knowledge and skills in questions of education and working life. Competence is the meeting point between structural requirements and individual capacities. It is dependent on knowledge; but the challenge is not only to have more knowledge, but rather to be able to translate contextual problems and competence demands into information and knowledge queries. This is what educators and young people, the educational system and the labour market will have to focus on: the contemporary developmental challenges of young people and educational systems.

Basic developmental perspectives

To discuss this issue, it is again necessary to have a broad picture of development as it relates to both the individual and to individuals as agents in structures; that is, to the structuration process. A basic model of development is outlined in Figure 11.4 (Walther et al, 2002; Mørch, 2003).

Development of competence should be seen as having a number of dimensions. The model in Figure 11.4 pictures development according to three dimensions: being, knowing and doing. The perspective of the model draws attention to the fact that development always involves all corners or dimensions. In practical life, however, different corners of the triangle have often been viewed as most important for young people.

Figure 11.4: Developmental perspectives

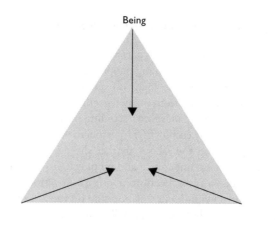

Being

Knowing   Doing

In the classic bourgeois school of the 19th century, the 'being' dimension was held to be the most important. Young people from the bourgeoisie should learn the Classics, Latin and Greek. These subjects and the correct educational manners formed the foundation of an educated person. To have a job, one needed to be 'educated'. Thus, social class was expressed in 'being' through qualifications and opened the way to adult life and employment. Being 'educated', in the sense of having the right bourgeois values and manners, gave opportunities for having a good job and a social position. Today, the 'being' dimension points to a more individualised 'being' perspective, meaning a certain kind of identity or self-understanding. Today it is important to know yourself and to 'be yourself', but only in special situations does it lead to a job.

Around the end of the 19th century, the 'knowing' angle became paramount. Industrialisation demanded qualifications; hence skills and knowledge became more important. Schools developed their own understanding of education and knowledge in school curricula. Knowledge about 'practical subjects' became central in this process; employment followed practically from educational trajectories. Education gave the knowledge, and knowledge gave the job. Today, knowledge is relatively 'unimportant', yet one will not have a job without it (Frønes and Brusdal, 2000). Education does not guarantee a job.

In contrast to the knowledge dimension, the 'doing' dimension was developed in everyday life through the apprenticeship model. It focused on the development of skills. 'Doing' was something that happened in real working life. In the apprenticeship model, skills were more or less contextual, and most skills were confined to a specific job situation. In this way, school knowledge and practical skills were opposed. They should work together as different forms of learning, but in practice this has not always been easy. Today it seems as if the 'doing' dimension has become the new challenge and a basic ingredient of development, although not in the sense that the value of being and knowing is declining. Today, educational systems have developed a high level of knowledge, and more and more young people stay in school longer and longer. Also, young people's self-understanding and self-reference, their 'being', has become very strong. 'Being' or 'knowing' do not seem to be the major challenges of modern development. The challenge now seems to be how the individual can use self-understanding and knowledge in a contextual way. Young people seem to be clever enough, but the question is: 'What are they clever for, or able to do?'.

This development underlines the general problem in educational systems of how to combine individual competence and employability.

The challenge of competence and employability

Discussion in education today centres round the issue of competence. In the developmental triangle this means that the perspective of doing has become a basic challenge, but not in the traditional sense of having 'skills'. Competence refers to what people should be able to do in a (post-)modern or modernistic world. Therefore, the being, knowing and doing perspectives are being challenged and changed. In a number of different critiques of school knowledge, this modernistic perspective has not been understood. Inspiration from Paulo Freire's liberation pedagogy (1973) or from Lave and Wenger's apprenticeship models (1991) lead, in this respect, to misunderstandings of the modern challenge. The challenge does not involve a contradiction between being, doing and knowing, but refers to the way they should be combined.

The dimensions have changed. The 'being' dimension has been individualised; today it points to personal and individual identity questions, not class affiliation. The knowledge dimension still indicates the different subjects in school, but knowledge on its own seems only to be a limited good. Education has grown, but its relevance and value has become rather uncertain (Frønes and Brusdal, 2000). The 'doing' perspective is also expanding. Many modern challenges and developments today seem to happen everywhere at once. Knowledge no longer seems to be the monopoly of education; doing is not the opposite of knowing. Theories of learning in practice have shown that learning happens in many everyday situations as non-formal or informal learning (Lave and Wenger, 1991).

Thus, the discussion on modern competence may circle around the sorts of competence young people should be able to ask for. Again, this gives rise to the question of how the three dimensions of development are emphasised.

If competence is seen mostly as a combination of being and knowing, then we are dealing with a very special or abstract competence. The doing perspective is weak or relates only to educational life itself.

When knowledge is reflected and combined with only the doing perspective or labour market demands, we may talk about labour market competence.

Figure 11.5: Abstract competence

Figure 11.6: Labour market competence

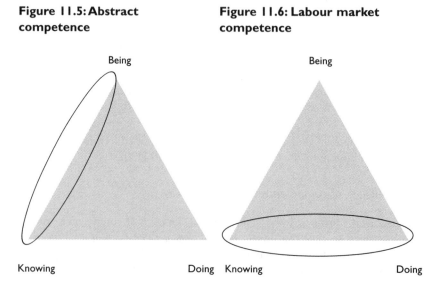

218

Figure 11.7: Social competence **Figure 11.8: Contextual competence**

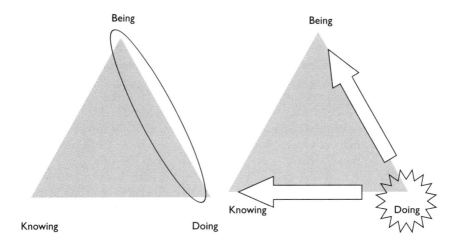

If, however, a relation is made between identity or social functioning and the doing perspective, we may talk about developing social competence.

These different 'competence' perspectives are discussed in various institutional settings. Abstract competence is discussed in the 'gymnasium' or school systems; labour market competence is discussed in political settings and in organisations and institutions of the labour market. Social competence is discussed in the labour market as well as in pedagogical settings such as youth work and everyday life (see Figures 11.5-11.7).

The discussions and reflections taking place, however, often do neglect an important aspect of the equation. Competence involves not only individual but also contextual qualities. Competence has to deal with challenges in social contexts and in the labour market. Again, the introduction of IT in modern companies is an illustrative example. It was mainly at that point that proper awareness of the competence perspective developed. The new work situation created different demands for employees, who needed to be able to use computers in the work situation. They needed to become competent in a very contextual way.

In this sense, competence refers to the context, and 'being' and 'knowing' may be seen as means for acting competently. In our understanding, knowledge and identity (or self-understanding) do not define competence, although competence is based upon them. The content of being and knowing should be developed according to contextual competence (see Figure 11.8).

Many aspects of modern life demand competence that in turn originates from knowing and being. This situation may not be new in any way; however, modern demands and new technologies have helped to focus our attention on the role of competence.

Competence and employability in Integrated Transition Policies

The modern challenge for youth and educational systems to combine competence and employability and to involve individual choices and labour market interests can now be reflected upon in a new way. It is now possible to point to a new perspective in the development of educational systems (see Figure 11.9) (Walther et al, 2002, p 148).

Figure 11.9 illustrates that it is necessary to develop a new meeting point. Educational systems and the labour market should develop a common understanding of the modern fields of competence. A discussion has to be launched to find out which competencies are expected from the flexible labour market and which personal competencies exist in modern social and youth life. The aim is to find fields of competence that relate both to general late modern developments and to local contexts. Negotiating fields of competence seems to be the new challenge everywhere. These fields might be seen as the melding of youth life and social life and should involve all who should be the partners of the fields of competence.

The task of education systems will be to focus on the relationship between those modern key competencies and the individual. Education will have to offer trajectories, which concomitantly allow for choice within both an individual perspective and within educational trajectories. School itself should not only 'modernise' its traditional curriculum, but also broaden it by focusing social questions. It should become more flexible. Teachers should not only support individual choices but the individual development of trajectories that lead to employability.

Figure 11.9: Planning for competence

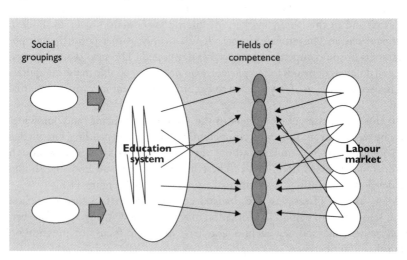

The labour market in turn should not only ask for more practical knowledge, but should also reflect upon the basic competencies needed in future productive and public life and define requirements and expectations to the educational system. Employers should be aware of the fragmented contextualisation people live in today and should support young people in the creation of their individual trajectories.

Generally, it is important to develop institutional reflexivity and more ideas for flexible coordination of policies in the labour market. Educational systems are asked to develop an institutional and social reflexivity according to how competencies may be linked to employability. For the moment, many things point to a culture of institutional self-centredness and a delegation of problems between different agencies and social sectors.

Research should be promoted to support the negotiation process of the education and employment sector. Specifically, it seems important to engage in research on modern transition practices and social integration, analysing and learning from good or bad practice. Also, it is necessary further to analyse different modern industries and labour market agents expectations and their pictures of what employability means in different situations. It is important to find out for accordance to exist between what is said and what is actually happening in recruitment policy. From here on, it seems important to study and analyse the more general perspectives that could draw together the different fields of competence, and to specify these according to different sectors of the labour market.

In the context of the European political debate, more questions arise. In Europe, modernisation is often seen simply as a process of Europeanisation, which challenges local development and creates a search for guidelines for all EU development.

This first picture of development refers to a political understanding of European development and as such it may reveal a political truth about modern Europeanisation. However, perhaps another truth – a second picture – also exists. Modernisation as such is not only a political process, but also an ongoing global and economical development that establishes political challenges everywhere. The Europeanisation process may be seen as some sort of political answer to this development.

The difference between these two pictures for the understanding of transition policy development is rather important. The first picture gives a portrait of European policy as a challenge to local development and policies. The second picture reveals that 'necessary' and global modernisation processes may be helped by European policies. In the first picture, a contradiction may develop between European development and local or national interests. In the second picture, all European countries may agree or disagree about the challenges of modernisation, because it is seen as a mostly economical developmental reality, and they might help to adjust political development to changing societies, such as by learning from 'best practices'.

To understand the development of youth competence and employability in

Europe, it seems important to reconsider the different understandings of policy and modernisation and their forms and consequences for youth transition. The 'modernisation' perspective refers to all countries. Before a European perspective may evolve, it is important to understand developmental or 'modernisation' processes as they challenge, in diverse ways, the different countries of Europe.

References

Andersen, H. and Mørch, S. (2000) 'Socialpsykologiens verdener', *Psyke og Logos*, vol 21, no 1.

Beck, U. (1992) *Risk society: Towards a new modernity*, London: Sage Publications.

Freire, P. (1973) *De undertryktes pædagogik*, Copenhagen: Christian Ejlers Forlag.

Frønes, I. and Brusdal, R. (2000) *På sporet av den nye tid*, Oslo: Fakbokforlaget.

Galbraith, J.K. (1978). *The new industrial state* (3rd edn), Boston, MA: Houghton Mifflin.

Giddens, A. (1991). *Modernity and self identity*, Cambridge: Polity Press.

Lave, J. and Wenger, E. (1991) *Situated learning*, Cambridge: Cambridge University Press.

Mørch, S. (2001) 'Some basic issues in youth research', in I. Guidikova and H. Williamson (eds) *Youth research in Europe: The next generation*, Strasbourg: Council of Europe Publishing.

Mørch, S. (2003) 'Youth and education', *Young*, vol 11, no 1.

Mørch, S. and Laursen, S. (1998) *At lære at være ung*, Copenhagen: Ungdomsringen.

Rychen, D. and Salganik, S.L. (2002) *DeSeCo Symposium*, Discussion Paper, 2nd International Symposium of DeSeCo (Definition and Selection of Competencies), Geneva: OECD and SFSO.

Walther, A., Stauber, B., Biggart, A., du Bois-Reymond, M., Furlong, A., López Blasco, A., Mørch, S. and Pais, J.M. (eds) (2002) *Misleading trajectories: Integration policies for young adults in Europe?*, Opladen: Leske+Budrich.

Ziehe, T. (2001) 'De personlige livsverdeners dominans', *Uddannelse*, no 10.

TWELVE

Of roofs and knives: the dilemmas of recognising informal learning

José Machado Pais and Axel Pohl

Redefining learning in a changing society

According to Deleuze (1990), contemporary social change can be seen as a historical passage from 'disciplinary societies' to 'control societies'. Institutions forming the disciplinary society – school, family, factory, hospital and prison – experience a decline in their ability to retain control. Although disciplinary logics continue to persist, they spread apart, fluidly, across the social tissue. It is within this process of change that the striated space that characterises disciplinary societies gives way to the plain space of the control society (Deleuze, 1980)[1]. While disciplinary society makes fixed shapes for institutions, control society is based on flexible and modulating networks.

The change from a disciplinary society to a control society was made possible by breaking down the obstacles that constrained the autonomy of institutions. The continuous removing of obstacles increasingly makes the distinction between institutions' inside and outside less clear. Concomitant to this process is a redefinition of power and its field of action. What will be discussed here in relation to these changes – because it has not yet received enough critical attention – is the socialisation that takes place *in between* institutions; that is, informal socialisation interrelated with informal learning (Pais, 2001).

As one consequence of this change, the world of labour increasingly demands of its participants the competence to organise and structure their own working lives and to develop the personal and social competencies needed for this. At the same time, education and training are less and less capable of producing these essential capacities on their own. They are highly dependent upon the world outside to generate resources like meaning, subjectivity and motivation (see Chapter Eleven of this volume). Informal and non-formal modes of learning, therefore, have gained popularity not only among educationalists but also among policy makers in Europe in the course of the past few decades (Bjørnåvold, 2001; Dohmen, 2001). These forms of learning are associated with great hopes of extending the boundaries of the formally organised and well-ordered guises of learning, and curing some of the negative effects that seem to be inherent in the latter. First, informal learning, it is hoped, should help in bridging the skills gap between the quickly changing demands of the economy for a qualified workforce and the relatively immobile output of education and training systems by providing flexibly acquired skills that are not available through formal training. Second, informal learning is viewed as containing the potential to ease the access to skills and competencies for young people who are alienated by the formal education and training system. Hence, it may be able to address the problem of unequal access to education and training resources. Third, informal learning seems to be a field where high potentials for the motivation of learners prevail, something which makes it more probable that biographic learning projects become subjectively more meaningful (du Bois-Reymond and Walther, 1999).

In this chapter, we critically assess, from a youth studies perspective, different strategies that try to make use of these potentials found in public policies in Europe at present. The first strategy is the most prominent among policy makers at European level and to a varying degree in several European countries. It aims to develop ways to officially acknowledge the skills and competencies acquired through informal and non-formal forms of learning. Sometimes the issues related to informal learning seem to be reduced to a rather technical approach and thus risk neglecting the deeper potentials of informal learning. Therefore, in this chapter, we suggest that transition policies should embrace two more options in recognising informal learning. The second strategy we examine starts from the observation that informal forms of learning happen not only in 'natural' everyday life contexts such as the family but also in the public sphere – for example, in community and youth work activities. Therefore, these types of strategy aim to strengthen such contexts in order to enhance the value of the learning processes to be found there. The third strategy we take into account is the renewal of learning in the formal education and training system that is informed by the knowledge gained on processes of informal learning.

Of course, this list of strategies is neither systematically elaborated in the sense that these are no more than roughly designed ideal types, which in reality might not occur in their 'pure' form. Nor is this list meant to be exhaustive – for example, policies in the enterprise world that are propagating informal learning are not discussed.

To conclude our chapter, we discuss the combination of these three strategies in the framework of an integrated approach to transition policies. In order to be able to analyse the strengths and weaknesses of these strategies, we have to recognise the multidimensionality of the contexts young people have to deal with in their transitions to adulthood today.

Current discourses on the recognition of informal learning

Policy makers and educationalists all over the world have become increasingly aware of the problems arising within the formal education and training systems

(Hager, 1998). In the context of the discussions surrounding lifelong learning, it has become apparent that informal learning has so far been a widely neglected potential. While scholars naturally have divergent ideas on which definition applies best to the nature of learning processes that happen outside educational and training institutions, the virtues of informal learning are nevertheless widely acknowledged:

- Informal learning is strongly determined by the learners themselves. It allows the learners to decide what is learned, when and at what pace.
- Informal learning is highly context-bound; as a problem-solving strategy, it fits very well with the needs of the situation in which it is happening.

In this section, we add more dimensions to this list by having a look at two different elements of policies that attempt to advance informal learning, before taking a more radical stance and analysing what these discussions could mean for the existing system of education and training.

Formal recognition of informally acquired competencies

The contextuality of informal learning is both an advantage and a disadvantage of informal learning. It is an advantage, because the knowledge and skills acquired are highly relevant to the situation and to the learner as well. Context-boundedness of knowledge and skills becomes a problem if there is not a social recognition of the learning outputs. For informally acquired competencies to be useful in socially shared situations like the labour market, they have to be converted into a socially legitimate exchange medium, for example, diplomas and certificates (see Chapter Eleven of this volume). At the European level, much effort is spent in developing means to assess and formally acknowledge skills and competencies acquired in informal and non-formal learning contexts. The primary objective of these efforts is to develop methodologies to assess competencies people have acquired in informal and non-formal contexts. The certification issue is central to many research and educational projects – for example, in the context of the EC's Leonardo da Vinci programme. We concentrate, therefore, on some issues related to the value of this strategy from our perspective without developing a comprehensive overview of the different aspects of the topic, which is covered in depth elsewhere (Björnavold, 2000; Dohmen, 2001).

One of the criteria we want to apply to our analysis of policy elements is whether they are likely to contribute to compensating for unequal access to educational resources such as formal training. And, indeed, there is some empirical evidence – at least for Canada – that informal learning is more equally distributed than participation in formal education. Unlike participation in further training for example, Livingstone (2001) found no difference in (self-reported) informal learning activity according to age, socio-demographic or formal education background. Therefore, well thought-out policies that try to make the outcomes of informal learning convertible in socially acknowledged goods can contribute to increasing the cultural capital of young people who are hitherto excluded from formal education and training for various reasons (see Chapter Two of this volume).

Although this strategy has its strengths on the side of balancing some inequalities in access to formal vocational and further training, some drawbacks and potential dilemmas should be highlighted relating to the other two dimensions we draw upon in this chapter to evaluate the potential impact of public policies.

For instance, we can shed some light on this strategy's impact on motivation. If we follow Kahane's definition of 'informality' (Kahane, 1997), two important features of informal learning are in danger of devaluation by a growing tendency to assess informally acquired competencies for the purpose of labour market insertion. First, what Kahane calls the 'expressive instrumentalism' of informal activities is one of the key motivational factors of learning. Expressive instrumentalism means that informal learning consists of a combination of activities that are, on the one hand, undertaken for their own sake and, on the other, include more purposeful activities that are more directly connected to problem solving. The balance between the two types is vulnerable, and if external purposes like those provided by the foresight to gain vocational certificates prevail, the 'symbolic surplus' gained through these activities may lose its positive impact on the individual's motivation.

Although an increasing demand for a better-educated workforce cannot be denied, an increase in certification may even have a paradoxical effect. A certain certificate inflation (Wallace and Kovatcheva, 1998, p 97) has already provoked in many European countries what is called the 'education paradox': increasing numbers of young people obtain higher education and training certificates, which in turn decrease in value for the purpose of stable insertion into the labour market. Therefore, it is questionable whether the extension of certificates granted will lead to less inequality in the balance of cultural/educational capital among young people. To avoid this alienation process, one could perhaps think of alternative 'dialogic' processes by which these competencies should be assessed. Partners in this kind of dialogue would be local stakeholders, such as enterprise representatives, public education and training bodies and the individuals themselves. Of course, a shift towards an education and training system that can adopt such processes depends heavily upon the nature of national transition systems (Chapter Nine of this volume). Within a framework such as the NVQ (National Vocational Qualification) system in the UK, such changes are more likely than in the German context, for example, with its highly formalised education and training system. On the one hand, the latter system features highly standardised certification for only a few standardised educational and training pathways, which makes more open processes of negotiating the 'true' competence gained from outside the system very difficult. On the other hand, more output-oriented systems like the British one seem to leave more space for the ways actual competencies are 'produced'. That the degree of regulation in the education and training system alone is not decisive can be shown, however, by the French case. Although France's education and training system is strongly regulated, the French 'bilan de compétence' shows that the political insight into the importance of opening up the concepts of what 'real' training is can be very efficient (Dohmen, 2001).

Thus, the processes of evaluation of informally acquired competencies has to be understood as a highly political process, and to a lesser degree as a methodological problem of inventing tools of assessment. One way of widening the perspective on informal learning is to shift from the macro level of certification of competencies to the meso level of societal arenas and have a look at institutions between the macro level of the education system and the sphere of everyday life where non-formal and informal learning are linked (Alheit, 1999, p 79).

Strengthening non-formal learning contexts

The emphasis on informal and non-formal learning implies a shift in the conception of learning itself: learning has to be conceptualised as being closely related to meaning and to identity. Learning cannot be thought of as something happening in young people's heads, but rather as something that arises out of social relationships (Wenger, 1998). Therefore, one key element of making better use of the potentials of informal learning and the social nature of learning itself is to support the contexts in which informal learning is happening. While a great deal of informal learning happens in the settings of everyday life, which are difficult areas for public policy interventions, some arenas of social activity are likely to provide individuals with opportunities for non-formal learning that are much more accessible to public policy management. So, institutions on this meso level between systems and individuals, which are neither state nor market, bear a high potential for some of the bargaining mentioned in the earlier section of this chapter. We can reduce our analysis here to dimensions directly related to informal learning because the third sector, as an important area for transition policies, is addressed in Chapter Eight of this volume.

On the 'pro' side, social institutions such as voluntary organisations, youth groups and the like share some advantages that make informal learning more likely to be embedded into more organised forms of learning. While informal learning cannot be planned, the non-formal types of learning happening on the meso level incorporate some important characteristics of informal learning processes.

They can pose lower access thresholds than formal education when they are set in young people's everyday life contexts such as local neighbourhood or youth (sub) cultures. Symbolic production, as an important aspect of some forms of informal learning, sometimes is the very purpose of such activities. The social aspect of learning is often met by the embedding of these activities in peer contexts. Hence, some of the major criteria of informality are fulfilled, which can provide a bridge between social integration (everyday life) and systems integration. Although participation patterns and conditions in these contexts are structured by inequality, they are more open to processes of interpretation and negotiation (Walther and Stauber, 1999). Indeed, in some cases, young people themselves hold power over the active environment.

There is some evidence that the incorporation of informal learning in formal institutions can produce a middle-class bias because more open learning settings (for example, in companies) "do not adopt a more open and inviting attitude vis-à-vis educationally excluded groups, but a more defensive stance instead" (Alheit, 1999, p 82).

All these factors make informal learning more probable than in other environments. However, there is a flip side: some of these organisations themselves suffer from low social recognition in terms of the power and money awarded to them. For example, all kinds of youth work provide young people with much of what we have mentioned to be prerequisites of informal learning. But, as they belong to a policy sector that can be labelled the 'soft sector' (Walther et al, 2002), the outcomes of learning processes happening there are rarely transmitted into a socially legitimate form of cultural capital. What is more, the organisations themselves are troubled with the consequences of being part of the 'soft sector'. They often work under conditions of financial instability, which makes their position even weaker. These organisations can become 'learning environments' in the sense of Alheit (1999), only if a change in societal attitudes towards their outcomes could be established that would mean a step away from short-term labour market success to mid- to long-term biographical outputs. To make these biographical outputs visible, strategies of certification of informally acquired competencies (as mentioned in the previous section of this chapter) would be very helpful, especially for those young people for whom these forms of outreach have become the only anchor that keeps them from losing touch.

The dilemma of reconciling formal education and informal learning

The challenge that recognising informal learning represents for (disciplinary) society becomes obvious with regard to the consequences it has for formal education. Hence, in this section, we take a more radical stance by considering a third strategy that consists of a deeper challenge to the existing education and training systems, including educational institutions from upper secondary schools to vocational education and training, and training schemes for young people who already have been rejected by mainstream educational institutions. Many commentators believe that failing consecutively in school is a problem. Yet, very few think about this problem beyond the narrow parameters of students flunking. Formal schooling repeats, year after year, many of its own, rarely addressed, inadequacies: the same unadjusted pedagogic models; the same boring classes; the same controversial evaluations; the same lack of preparation by poorly paid and demotivated teachers; the same punishments and the same concessions; the same unawareness and the same "it's always the same" (Benevides de Barros, 1997). Against this backdrop, some young people bet on the forbidden. Why do they 'play fight' in classes or throw paper planes? Why do they cheat teachers and schoolmates? Why do they talk about their tricks and jokes during break, the ones they did and the ones they are still going to do? The answer: because for many students the classroom is *dia*bolic, and for them what is more interesting is *sym*bolic creation. This is symbolic creation that can be found in doing things in a loose and spontaneous way, using imagination. Etymologically, the word 'symbol' is formed by *syn* (from the Greek, meaning 'with') and *balo* ('play') – as opposed to diabolic, in other words, *dia* (without) and *balo* (play). "The ability to create relations is the ability to create symbols" as Vaidergorn (2001, p 80) confirms. However, the architecture of formal education is diabolic: it does not have room for play, for relations, for the symbolic. While school bureaucracy values functional issues, young people experience a form of imprisonment.

Formal education: systems' permeability and liabilities

The education system is often disconnected from the reality around it. It encloses itself around an inside that is perceived as warranting its autonomy from an outside. But why do young people go to school? Thrown inside this system, young people shall 'prepare themselves for the future' (outside this system). Apparently, it is the future that legitimates the education system as it seeks to provide the education of 'tomorrow's adults': future citizens, parents, workers, professionals and leaders. In this perspective, young people are in a transfer process, with no present; or, their present is attached to the future: 'they go to school to become someone in the future'.

For formal education, the present seems to have only a transitional value, in other words, very little value. This way, young people's present is projected to the future in an unsure manner. And this happens even when young people choose the best courses available assuming that they will find the best integration route into the labour market. Once again the idea of 'exit' attaches the school to an interior (an inside), and to an exterior (an outside), the labour market. In today's society, educational careers do not end by obtaining a diploma. The objective of 'employability' presupposes 'lifelong learning', because of the permanent technological restructuring of the economy, which in turn determines that academic careers no longer have a definitive role for integration in the labour market – certainly not warranted for life (see Chapter Eleven of this volume). This happens because, beyond the tendencies we can project into the future, there remain large areas of uncertainty and insecurity – related to the maze-like complexity of our societies (Pais, 2001). In fact, European young people have polymorphic and ambivalent understandings of time, while at the same time admitting and recognising its linearity and its cycles (Pais, 1999).

Why, then, do young people go to school? To prepare for the future – as if the future already existed. In school, the future should not be something that has already happened. It is to be made, preferably in a participatory way, involving young people themselves. However, in formal school situations, a prescriptive culture prevails: study plans and subjects, disciplinary rules, global exams (standard), pedagogical practices inscribed in a philosophy of 'mass production' – all according to the function of education systems with regard to large-scale economies.

The education model, still operated by our societies, increasingly appears to be losing touch with the reality it tries to shape. This education model is based on a supporting philosophy in which education and training are understood as a waiting room with doors not yet opened to the upstream of professional integration. Young people are trained for active working life with the consequence that students are looked upon as 'inactive' (in a waiting situation). As odd as it may seem, official statistics reproduce this philosophy, by excluding the 'waiters' from the active population. By establishing a strict frontier between a time to educate (of supposed inactivity) and another time to work (of activity), the horizons of knowledge (knowledge limited to school certification) are in danger of becoming confined to obtaining a diploma and to the assumption that, with a better qualification, one can find a job more easily. Thus, school has been working as an artificial factor of employment contention, a parking lot for potentially unemployed young people. The misleading effect of contention is very clear: instead of reducing unemployment rates, this system increases the qualification levels of unemployed people (obviously, the reverse solution, nonetheless, is no better). However, some young people have the perception that school diplomas are like 'predated cheques', without any worth in the present and possibly of little or no worth in the future (see Chapter Two of this volume).

And since the future that school has to offer is so uncertain, and since young people reject the role of 'inactivity' applied to them by the system, many young people end up by valuing informal learning in contrast to a prescribed routine of school hours. This routine, an old vice of the education system, prevents a pedagogy of autonomy from happening, for which – in the words of Paulo Freire (1997) – to be able to teach does not mean to transmit knowledge but to create conditions for it to happen with, of course, the active participation of students.

New pedagogic goals: for a 'roof pedagogy'

The challenge of informal learning to formal schooling may be illustrated by an experience made during a research visit to a school in the surroundings of Lisbon, with a considerable share of gypsy students. The head teacher opened a drawer in her desk to show a number of knives she had taken from some of the children. Why do gypsy children bring knives to school? Why are they violent? Probably, gypsy knives are weapons of rejection, meant to fight against the submission to a school culture, by ritualising aggressive behaviours that are seen as a part of the gypsy culture. In this sense, gypsy knives are not only intimidation weapons; they are also an instrument of symbolic meaning that not only accuses the superficial structure of confrontation among students, but also the profound grammar of school education's contradictory culture.

Gypsy knives are not brought to school with the purpose of hurting or killing. The symbolism of the knife can be understood as mediation, enabling young gypsies to shape reality. Like every symbol, knife symbolism brings along a significant power element, justified by the fact that symbols themselves are multivalent, incongruent, polysemantic and splitting. The exhibition of a knife has the magical power to connote and denote visions of all the things it can represent. The act of taking the knife from the student does not empty its ability to confine the representation of all the tricks and blows it could cause, even if it is kept inside the head teacher's drawer. Symbols do have this structuring power; they structure imagination and proclaim or frame disorder, as well as order, invoking excesses of signification. The violence demonstrated by some gypsy children constitutes their particular way of showing their opposition to the frustrating learning models used in school. The meaning of life for these children can be found away from the official pedagogical discourses normally applied in the classroom.

The school head teacher who so carefully keeps the knives in her drawer recounted that during break, gypsy children, more than anything else, enjoy climbing on to the school's roof, as if searching for lost treasures. In fact, they are looking for birds' nests. The roof has a double meaning for gypsy children. From being a protection, a cover, it becomes a *dis*cover(y). Discoveries on the roof made us think that maybe the most significant things these children learn happen precisely outside the classroom where teachers' control can not reach them. The 'meaning of life' can be discovered (in a symbolic sense) on a school's roof, in a bird's nest.

The knowledge acquired on a roof is completely different from that acquired in a classroom, also epistemologically, because it is related to courage, risk, curiosity, adventure, transgression. What the children learn in the classroom usually seems foolish because it is embedded in an inflated rationalism, caused by a distance and abstraction from the real, experienced world. What can be done with children who find pleasure on the school roof, thus violating the normal rules of the education system? Do we begin disciplinary procedures?

What is important is the direction of organisation, arising from chaos and moving towards order. So, for children to understand the meaning of order, first they must understand chaos. If children are confronted with elaborated or stated information ('You can't go up to the roof!'), they will hardly understand its meaning. At most they will memorise it and reject it or assume 'that's the way it is'. When the head teacher, in a very clever manner, proposed to the gypsy children that, instead of killing the birds they should look after and feed them and gave them a cage, every day children brought in food to feed the birds. They were given a responsibility: to take care of little animals, a task they performed with enthusiasm and commitment. Then one day, they realised there was no sense in keeping those birds inside the cage, the same way they felt jailed inside a classroom.

In other words, the head teacher's idea renewed the learning process. She did this by accepting the children's innate curiosity, allowing them to face their world's strangeness, instead of considering the shapeless knowledge that places children in a passive role, as mere boxes where one places reified knowledge; as passive containers of uninteresting knowledge (from the children's point of view).

One of the major problems with the education system is the fact that we consider knowledge to be a predefined content, instead of considering it to be the result of questioning. When we make children repeat mechanically non-assimilated data, we are also inviting them to live in the absurd. Curiosity teaches us that the basic inquiry force is the window (Whitin and Whitin, 1997) or the roof, because by looking through the window or engaging in 'roof observations', students are faced with the world around them and in which they live.

We have seen before that formal schooling is like a prison for gypsy children. It is worth referring to the aphorism of cages and wings, stated by Rubem Alves: some schools are like cages; others are like wings. Cage schools are there so that birds forget how to fly. Wing schools dislike birds in a cage; they are there to stimulate and encourage children to fly. They do not teach how to fly, because it is innate knowledge: birds know how to fly from birth. Sometimes all it takes is a simple gesture like the one of the gypsy children: it is enough to open up the cage's door to encourage flight[2].

'Roof pedagogy' suggests that most of our schools are cage schools, keeping teachers and children imprisoned. Teachers are controlled by the contents of official programmes, tight to an obligation to keep up with official subjects and timetables, tight to pedagogical routines imprisoning freedom of knowledge. Students, too, are imprisoned, with disciplinary absences caused by flapping wings against cage walls, in an attempt to gain some free space, to gain freedom; a space that, eventually, can be conquered on the roof of the school. There, they feel free from the chaining of the body to the desk in the classroom. When their bodies move in the classroom, teachers rarely understand this body language; teachers only speak and listen with words. The schools we have do not teach children to be a body, to develop a body sensitivity, to be self-conscious (conscious of their own meanings). The violence in school can be interpreted in the sense that students react to being imprisoned and/or to being expelled.

Knowledge formally transmitted inside a classroom is knowledge that is focused on the individual and her evaluation. On the other hand, 'roof knowledge' is socially shared in the most beautiful asset of knowledge: discovery. The violent behaviours teachers usually ascribe to gypsy children can be, after all, the expression of a hidden fight for the opportunity to take up roof knowledge; in other words, learning by discovering, by collective creativity. It should be important for teachers to use to their advantage their students' life experiences; students, that is, that so many times rebel against an education system that silences them, that keeps them from discovering. Within this interpretative frame, their knives are also a symbol of power, or better still, counter-power against the way knowledge is usually transmitted in the classroom. Knives and fights during break-time help a frustrated energy to circulate that represents a sublimated potential for creativity.

We have seen that in traditional formal schooling, all training and education efforts, all learning contents, all behavioural rules, turn around a fixed goal: to prepare for future life demands (Pais, 2001). This model, however, only works when future demands can be established in an unmistakably clear way. If not, formal schooling is in danger of becoming an anachronistic reality or valued only for its cognitive capacity to transmit the functional contents of knowledge. Imprisoned in its own conventions, formal schooling is not ready to face new societal paths and challenges. A clear example of this lack of preparation is the difficulty that formal schooling has in dealing with the increasing heterogeneity of students, caused by a growing massification of education, but also by an intensification of (im)migration flows. Such heterogeneity – essentially socioeconomic in nature – is often transformed into a racial differentiation, not because students are different but because the difference is already predefined (as a consequence and not as a cause of differentiation) (cf Delgado Ruiz, 2002). This endemic inability to deal with difference contributes to school failures.

The formal school's inability to host 'the different' is reinforced by an ideology centred on school values, according to which the crisis experienced by the education system can only be solved by intensifying formal education. Relative failure of successive education reforms and the plain messianism of successive education reformers – who insist on ignoring the weight of school traditions and routines – prove that school is subordinated to a 'grammar' (Tyack and Cuban, 1995) of sedimented rules resistant to change. This resistance to successive reforms, over time, clearly shows that school is a 'persistent identity' (Nisbet, 1979). And as Nisbet argued (even though it may seem a paradox), there is not the least possibility of understanding the mechanisms of social change unless we understand or recognise seriously the fixation mechanisms of its persistence as happens in the education system. When governments change, they immediately change education programmes. However, these changes of programmes have no echo in the quality of the education system, or in the interests based on dominant corporation logic, or on the lack of preparation or demotivation of teachers – or on school failure. Programmes change, but routines subordinating pedagogy to the need to keep up with the programme remain: in terms of contents, means and time.

Should the ability to reproduce routines and resistance to change prevail, should schools only ensure devalued certification, to what extent do they have the ability to develop a democratic and egalitarian social order? Due to its persistent structure, schooling is organised through rituals that establish authoritarian structures. These structures only reward the most predictable students and those that show a strong compliance to the system routines. Socially disadvantaged young people experience difficulties integrating into this kind of school. In order to attenuate the tension caused by the presence of these intruders, the state develops "policies to control inequality" (Stoer, 2002, p 250). This is the case of the 'binary system' that unfolds itself in the academic path and the vocational path. Alternatively, sometimes that tension is subject to contention, accomplished by 'compensatory' measures developed to fight the school failure of 'misfit' students, usually labelled as 'dummies'. As happens in the game of cards called 'dummy' (a game of cards where players have to follow suit), the one who cannot follow suit has to get a card from the pack, risking being a 'dummy' for as many years as the cards he is holding, when the game is finished. Some non-formal education projects are like a pack of cards where 'misfit' young people try to obtain the good cards they are missing. Other times, 'compensation' occurs by a false play, which is protected by the system itself. Young people who cannot adapt to school carry on to the next school year (without knowing how they did it and without 'knowing' anything at all), based on an economic logic that pushes the head teacher towards the goal of 'continuous progression' (students failing a year may affect economic resources). However, this juggling is unable to fight school failure; rather, it simply ameliorates the symptoms. When statistics show a decrease in failure rates and school dropouts, it gives the impression that the problem of academic failure is being fought. Finally, compensation can be institutionalised by measures to support students with 'learning difficulties'. However, such compensatory measures rarely question the education system's learning contents or educational goals and establish themselves as a counter-hegemonic movement, since they are framed within the system reforms.

The relevance of 'knowledge for life' – one of the main educational goals – is seldom discussed, something that points to the need to discuss the central methodological presuppositions of a fundamental shift away from the traditional future-oriented school towards a new life-oriented school. Michael Brater (1999) discusses these presuppositions by suggesting not only a new formal pedagogy, but also explorative and life-oriented learning, and learning occurring in real-life conditions. Learning contents, as Brater claims, should no longer be educational goals, but instead must become learning pretexts. This new formal pedagogy should enable the selection of those subjects to teach according to the relevance criteria of such subjects; relevance regarding the formation of young people's competencies, as an impulse to individual development. Such a proposition implies the selection of qualification contents, revealing themselves as didactic motives to develop competencies that contribute to nurturing an autonomous human being: thus, operational skills in the cognitive domain are needed but also development of affection, feelings, willingness, and moral and social development. The second methodical principle to face the pedagogical task of enabling young people's active development can be found in what has been called 'explorative life-oriented learning' (Holzkamp, 1993). In this case, learning occurs within experimental situations in which subjects to be learned are put into practice ('learning by doing'). For this, the organisation of the education system needs to be rebuilt methodically by introducing learning processes centred on action. Interactive and non-centred learning processes allow contents to be experienced and explored, rather than absorbed and memorised cognitively. In such a model, students are invited to think, to know, to investigate, and to find out about new ways and new obtainable goals. The teacher no longer 'lectures', but commits herself to creating active learning situations, to help students themselves find solutions for problems, with a discovery logic (Pais, 2002). This exploratory learning – well illustrated in 'roof pedagogy' – stresses a process by which knowledge is produced, instead of defending a passive acquisition of transmitted and reified knowledge.

The third fundamental methodical principle centres on life-oriented learning, taking place in real situations. These conditions cannot be artificially simulated for didactic goals, or be divorced from real life, as often happens in conventional classrooms. In such contexts (divorced from real life), considerable losses are bound to happen, concerning meanings and motivation. These are important aspects that can only be found outside, in real life, on the 'school's roof'; because that is where real life takes place, and it is where one can see the expected training effects on skills, when they are released from school routines, life itself is shown to be the best place to learn.

As we have argued so far in this chapter, the education system can be looked at as a 'persistent unity over time', while persistence is well represented by the image of being imprisoned in a cage. Those living in a cage will hardly be free unless someone from the outside opens the door. In this sense, Nisbet (1979) argues that social change cannot be inferred from endogenous processes that, in nature, produce nothing but internal readjustments in the structure they refer to. Educational policies produce only small adjustments that cause little or no change in the education system because educational goals are seldom discussed. Robert Merton (1980) suggests distinctions between three models of achieving cultural goals (educational goals, in our case):

- The traditional model valuing 'institutional means' to achieve 'educational goals', which dominates current debates on educational reforms, creates, in fact, three kinds of student behaviour: *compliance* (educational success visible in the capacity to acquire all transmitted knowledge), *ritualism* (apparent compliance to educational system rules, but lack of motivation for learning) and *alienation* (withdrawal and clear demotivation regarding learning in school and compensatory quests in consumption and drug taking, among other things).
- The model –'alternative means' to achieve old 'educational goals'– is, beyond a doubt, innovative. However, it should be stressed that it is an innovation that does not question the old 'educational goals'.
- The third model states that educational reforms should not be confined to actions directed to 'means', no matter how innovative these might be. There is no educational change if its goals are not discussed. And a change of goals can only be accomplished under an impulse of exogenous factors to the so-

called formal school. This change can project a new reality caused by an action that transforms: *trans* (beyond that) *forms* (old form). The *trans-form-a(c)tion* is only possible through action and by the effect of a constellation of efforts directed to it: *questioning* (the education we have and the one we do not have); *inquiry* (of exogenous and endogenous factors, as a source of stagnation, renewal, or change in education systems); *information/circulation* (of pedagogical experiences that can be discussed and experienced); *interaction/cooperation* (among education agents, not only teachers, but also parents and students); *intervention/transformation* (concerning not only pedagogical means, but also new educational goals).

In this sense, good practices taken from so-called non-formal education and informal learning should be taken into account. By valuing non-formal education and informal learning, we are not suggesting that these should replace formal education – nor should they be developed against formal schooling (Apple, 2001). In return, however, schooling must open up to experiences it traditionally refuses to accept. In some non-formal and informal educational experiences, we find real challenges concerning educational goals and learning methods that can be demonstrated by roof discoveries and 'pedagogy of desire' (Garcia Castro and Abramovay, 1998).

Roof discoveries should begin with the teachers and students getting acquainted with and discovering one another. This implies that students are allowed to express their individuality, to make their existence real through concrete representations, for example by drawing. For that reason, gypsy children represent violence by exhibiting knives – the same way those who study very hard and memorise everything exhibit their knowledge by systematically putting up a hand every time a teacher asks a question. All subjects to be taught should either meet the drive for knowledge, the drive for discovery and learning about new things (as it happens in roof discoveries), or they should develop self-expression as it happens in body and music expression. Usually, self-expression in visual arts is encouraged by promoting public exhibitions of art creations – the classroom is seldom thought of as a room to free creative energy and participation.

However, when knowledge is a desirable asset – the 'pedagogy of desire' – the teacher stimulates the creation of a community of apprentices – and indeed, becomes an apprentice alongside the students. The teacher can set questions and problems, can create a climate of curiosity, encouraging discovery and, from then on, privileging student participation. The pedagogy of desire also takes place through playful pleasure. Some people think play also means mess, disorder and chaos. Nothing could be less accurate, because playful order has discipline and rules. However, perhaps as a result of a lack of artistic sensibility, education bureaucrats can only admit that a sense of discipline can be attained by the 'cage' logic. This is misleading because the presupposition itself is a key factor of indiscipline and violence. Also in this case, the 'wings' of freedom can provide flights of responsibility (see Chapter Nine of this volume).

Conclusion

Informal learning: the Swiss army knife of Integrated Transition Policies?

In this chapter, we have analysed the strengths and also the various forms of dilemma of three different approaches to push forward the recognition of informal learning from a youth transitions perspective. This exploration of terrain included perspectives of increasing human potential, of tackling inequality and of narrowing the gap between institutions and (young) individuals. It has become clear that these three approaches have to be seen as complementary elements in a more comprehensive framework of changing the ways society supports young people in their transition to the labour market.

The strategy of formally acknowledging competencies and knowledge acquired by informal learning runs the risk of simply doubling existing inequalities in labour market access if it is not understood as a political process of power distribution surrounding the issue of what kinds of learning should be awarded recognition and what kinds should not. Moreover it links to political questions surrounding contexts such as the third sector that bear a high chance of being able to empower young people in that process but are not given enough resources to do so. However, simply formalising the learning outputs of informal learning contexts would aggravate the danger that these contexts would lose some of the very virtues that make informal learning possible. We argue, rather, that Integrated Transition Policies (ITPs) as a more holistic approach should be aware of what we have analysed as the prerequisites of the integration of informal learning in transition systems:

- Learning cannot simply be conceived as passing on knowledge from one person to another, but its symbolic value and its social and collective nature have to be respected.
- Knowledge cannot be reduced, therefore, to a more or less fixed set of cognitive competencies. Integrated Transition Policies would rather conceive of it as 'landscapes of meaning', which is closely related to individual and collective identities as well as to 'learning biographies'.
- Today's youth transitions can no longer rely on fictitious rewards in the future as a collective resource to keep up individuals' most crucial resource in learning biographies: motivation, in the sense of the individual's own ability to relate his or her current situation and learning opportunities to an individual and collective past and future.

One practical consequence of this for ITPs is that learning cannot be organised and planned in rigorous curricula, but needs to be developed in a way that respects young people's biography and subjectivity. On the level of policies steering the transition sector, this would make it necessary to put more emphasis on formative success criteria than on quantitative output of policies. Due to the fact that each of the three presented strategies demand a high level of institutional reflexivity, a great deal of innovative energy will be needed if they are to become part of reality. As incorporating the 'informal' in each way will always mean the loosening of close-knit modes of planning and traditional ways of policy evaluation. One of the most important prerequisites for successfully developing integrated policies on this basis will be institutions' ability to accept uncertainty instead of emphasising short-term goals and rewards (see Chapter Ten of this volume). The complementary nature of the approaches we have described does not necessarily resolve the dilemmas that stem from the complexity of the given situation in today's education and training systems. However, each of them underlines what John Field (1998, p 1) has stated elsewhere:

> The idea of 'lifelong learning' draws attention not to education or training
> – traditional domains of policy-makers – but to learning, which is undertaken
> by individuals and organisations without much involvement by the state. A
> policy approach based on learning will be radically different from one based
> on education and training.

This means that concepts of transition policies that neglect the interrelatedness of these aspects, for example, by reducing the recognition of informal learning to an administrative tool, risk being stuck with the old model of education we have sketched in this chapter. An integrated approach would have to face the fact that discussing the means of transition policies without taking into account its objectives is a dead end. To put it in Peter Alheit's (1999, p 78) words: "A generally accepted informalisation of learning cannot be achieved without democratisation". In this sense, what has to be accomplished seems to reach far beyond a simple incorporation of some new methodologies of education and training, but requires an altogether fundamental rethinking of education and training as part of European societies.

Notes

[1] In the work of Deleuze, 'striated space' signifies "a partitioned field of movement which prohibits free motion. Smooth space refers to an environment, a landscape ... filled by events or haecceities, far more than by formed and perceived things. It is a space of "effects, more than one of properties" (www.rhizomes.net/issue5/poke/glossary.html).

[2] See www.rubemalves.com.br

References

Alheit, P. (1999) 'On a contradictory way to the Learning Society: a critical approach', *Studies in the Education of Adults*, vol 31, no 1, pp 66-82.

Apple, M. (2001) 'Away with all the teachers: the cultural politics of home schooling', *International Studies in Sociology of Education*, vol 10, no 1, pp 61-80.

Benevides de Barros, R. (1997) 'Subjectividade repetente', in E. Guimarães and E. Paiva (eds) *Violência e Vida Escolar. Contemporaneidade e Educação, Revista Semestral Temática de Ciências Sociais e Educação, Instituto de Estudos da Cultura e Educação Continuada*, vol 2, no 2, pp 116-35.

Bjørnåvold, J. (2000) *Making learning visible: Identification, assessment and recognition of non-formal learning in Europe*, Luxembourg: Office for Official Publications of the European Communities.

Bjørnåvold, J. (2001) 'The changing institutional and political role of non-formal learning: European trends', in P. Descy and M. Tessaring (eds) *Training in Europe. Second report on vocational training research in Europe. CEDEFOP Reference series (3 volumes)*, Luxembourg: EUR-OP.

Brater, M. (1999) 'Escuela y formación bajo el signo de la indivudualización', in U. Beck (ed) *Hijos de la Libertad*, México: Fondo de Cultura Económica (original German edn, 1997), pp 137-63.

Deleuze, G. (1980) *Mille plateaux*, Paris: Minuit.

Deleuze, G. (1990) *Pourparlers*, Paris: Minuit.

Delgado Ruiz, M. (2002) 'Estética e infamia. De la distinción al estigma en los marcajes culturales de los jóvenes urbanos', in C. Feixa, C. Costa and J. Pallarés (eds) *Movimientos Juveniles en la Península Ibérica. Graffitis, Grifotas, Okupas*, Barcelona: Ariel, pp 115-43.

Dohmen, G. (2001) *Das informelle Lernen. Die internationale Erschließung einer bisher vernachlässigten Grundform menschlichen Lernens für das lebenslange Lernen aller*, Bonn: Federal Ministry for Education and Research.

du Bois-Reymond, M. and Walther, A. (1999) 'Learning between want and must: contradictions of the learning society', in A. Walther, B. Stauber, E. Bolay, M. du Bois-Reymond, S. Mørch, J.M. Pais and A. Schröer (eds) 'New trajectories of young adults in Europe: a research outline', in Circle for Youth Research in Europe Circle (CYRCE) (eds) *Intercultural Reconstruction*, European Yearbook for Youth Policy and Research, vol 2, Berlin and New York, NY: Walter de Gruyter, pp 21-45.

Field, J. (1998) 'Globalisation, social capital and lifelong learning: connections for our time?', in A. Bron, J. Field and E. Kurantowicz (eds) *Adult education and democratic citizenship II*, Krakow: Impuls.

Freire, P. (1997) *Pedagogia da Autonomia. Saberes Necessários à Prática Educativa*, Rio de Janeiro: Editora Paz da Terra.

Garcia Castro, M. and Abramovay, M. (1998) 'Cultura, identidades e cidadania: experiências com adolescentes em situação de risco', in *Jovens Acontecendo na Trilha das Políticas Públicas*, Brasílis, CNPD, vol II, pp 572-9.

Hager, P. (1998) 'Recognition of informal learning: challenges and issues', *Journal of Vocational Education and Training*, vol 50, no 4, pp 521-35.

Holzkamp, K. (1993) *Lernen: Eine subjektwissenschaftliche Grundlegung*, Frankfurt-am-Main and New York, NY: Campus.

Kahane, R. (1997) *The origins of postmodern youth. Informal youth movements in a comparative perspective*, Berlin, New York, NY: De Gruyter.

Livingstone, D. (2001) *Adults' informal learning: Definitions, findings, gaps and future research*, NALL (National Research Network on New Approaches to Lifelong Learning) Working Paper 21, Toronto: NALL.

Merton, R.K. (1980) *Teoria y Estructura Sociales*, México: Fondo de Cultura Económica, pp 209-39 [original English edn, 1949].

Nisbet, R. (1979) *Social change*, Oxford: Basil Blackwell.

Pais, J. (1999) *Consciência Histórica e Identidade. Os Jovens Portugueses num Contexto Europeu*, Lisboa: SEJ/CELTA.

Pais, J. (2001) *Ganchos, Tachos e Biscates. Jovens, Trabalho e Futuro*, Porto: Ambar.

Pais, J. (2002) *Sociologia da Vida Quotidana. Teorias, Métodos e Estudos de Caso*, Lisbon: Imprensa de Ciências Sociais.

Stoer, St.R. (2002) 'Desocultando o vôo das andorinhas: educação inter/multicultural crítica como movimento social', in St.R. Stoer, L. Cortesão and J.A. Correia (eds) *Transnacionalização da Educação*, Coimbra: Afrontamento, pp 245-75.

Tyack, D. and Cuban, L. (1995) *Tinkering toward Utopia. A century of public school reform*, Cambridge, MA: Harvard University Press.

Vaidergorn, I. (2001) 'Sol e Ar, de solidariedade e de arriscar: a espacialidade e a sacralidade', in O. Rodrigues de Moraes Von Simson, M. Brandini Park and R. Sieiro Fernandes (eds) *Educação Não-Formal. Cenários da Criação*, Campinas: Editora da Unicamp, pp 79-93.

Wallace, C. and Kovatcheva, S. (1998) *Youth in society: The construction and deconstruction of youth in East and West Europe*, Basingstoke/New York, NY: Palgrave.

Walther, A. and Stauber, B. (eds) (1999) *Lifelong learning in Europe*, vol 2, Tübingen: Neuling.

Walther, A., Stauber, B., Biggart, A., du Bois-Reymond, M., Furlong, A., López Blasco, A., Mørch, S. and Pais, J.M. (eds) (2002) *Misleading trajectories: Integration policies for young adults in Europe?*, Opladen: Leske+Budrich.

Wenger, E. (1998) *Communities of practice: Learning, meaning and identity*, Cambridge: Cambridge University Press.

Whitin, P.H. and Whitin, D.J. (1997) *Inquiry at the window: Pursuing the wonders of learners*, Portsmouth/New Hampshire: Heinemann.

THIRTEEN

Flexibility and security: the supposed dilemma of transition policies

Barbara Stauber, Siyka Kovacheva and Harm van Lieshout

Introduction

How to balance flexibility and security? This question has been the implicit or explicit topic of the seven research projects presented in this volume, and it concerns one of the most central questions in current social debates, be it on the level of social policy in general (which kind of welfare state[s] do we need?); be it on a theoretical level (how can social constellations in general and young people's transitions in particular be conceived in the context of late modernity?); or be it on the level of practice (what kind of support do young people need?).

Flexibility in such debates is almost always equated with more freedom – a presupposition that is rarely explicated, and that connotes the idea of something to be achieved easily; that is, as soon as structures allow for more flexibility, freedom will automatically be enhanced. Apart from illustrating a rather limited understanding of freedom, this expresses perfectly the dominant one-sided view of flexibility, with the nexus of security constantly obscured.

The search for a balance between freedom and security is closely related to the history of modernity, as Zygmunt Bauman reminds us in his latest book, *The individualised society* (2001, p 55):

> The political history of modernity may be interpreted as a relentless search for the right balance between the two conditions for a postulated, and forever not-yet-found, 'point of reconciliation' between freedom and security, the two aspects of the human condition that are simultaneously contradictory and complementary. The search has been thus far inconclusive. Most certainly, it remains unfinished. It goes on. Its continuation is itself the *conditio sine qua non* of the modern society's struggle for autonomy.

Applied to the practical level of transition policies, the relation between flexibility and security at first glance seems to be a dilemma: apparently, there is a broad gap between those who complain about a lack of institutionalised transition structures (especially with regard to the system of education and training), and who therefore call for more standardisation in order to increase the security of trajectories; and those who criticise strongly formalised and normalising systems as overpowering and rigid and who therefore call for more flexibility. However, whenever one goes deeper into this discussion, the dichotomy of flexibility and security reveals an ideological division, with the call for more security being equated with 'old-fashioned welfare thinking' and the call for more flexibility with 'something modern and trendy' – at least in the dominant discourses (for a critical voice, see Bourdieu, 1998).

Looked at more closely, the concepts of flexibility and security may also imply very different and much more complex understandings. A more differentiated debate could clarify these different notions and could also find links where both concepts could be combined in order to overcome this dichotomy.

Discourses on flexibility and security

'Flexibility' is one of the major 'buzz' words in current debates about employment policies and the development of labour markets. It operates on both economic and subjective individual levels. On the one hand, the changed economical and technical conditions of work produce and enforce structural changes in labour markets and changed patterns of employment, thus leading to a significant decrease of 'normal work', the latter continuing to be the central reference point for social security rights in conservative welfare and employment regimes, such as Germany, Austria, or France (Esping-Andersen, 1990; Gallie and Paugam, 2000). On the other hand, and at the same time, changed living patterns, individualised life plans and pluralised ways of living require differentiated models of employment to complement new flexibilised lifestyles.

Translated into policy, flexibility becomes difficult because of these very different notions of what it should mean in practice. It refers alternately to structures and to individuals, and sometimes it seems as if the confusion of these levels of meaning is not unintentional. Hence to clarify, the following two main understandings can be distinguished.

First, flexibility exists as a term related to *structures*. As such, it is often combined with the diagnosis that employment structures or regulation of the employment and training sector are too rigid. In its more extreme conceptions, flexibilisation is dealt with as *the* (neo)liberal means against 'too much regulation' of labour markets in order to increase job facilities. Correspondingly, flexibilisation experienced as deregulation across Europe, and increasingly in the post-'socialist' countries, is the most prominent object of leftist and trade unionist critique. This is because it removes barriers for dismissal and allows employers to prey on low labour costs for young people (and other structurally weak social groupings) without submitting to training responsibilities – hence, flexibility in the form of deregulation makes young people particularly vulnerable and contributes to their prolonged dependency upon their parents (Kovacheva,

2001). However, there are also a few possible 'third ways' between the (neo)liberal and the structure-conservative streams that can be identified: for example, policies such as those in Denmark and the Netherlands that aim at improving access to employment, education or training in a way by which different types of (un)employment can be combined without losing the right to social benefits. In the Netherlands, also, part-time work is more secure and there are policies trying to balance the interests of firms and the interests of employees within the model of the 'breathing firm'. In the example of Volkswagen in Germany, external flexibility, often practised as dismissal, is replaced by internal flexibility where working times are adapted to the firm's needs, and where on the other hand the 'time' needs of employees are respected. Of course, such policies can more easily be implemented by large enterprises with appropriate structural facilities. Such examples show, however, that strategies of flexibilisation do not necessarily delegate risks to the individual, and that, if applied to specific aspects of the work relationship, they even may enhance (young) people's options.

Second, flexibility is also used as a term *to (de)qualify the individual*. This discourse supports flexibility as a systemic demand directed to those who want to enter, to stay, and to move within the employment system. It is inherent to the discourse about employability with its rather individualising logic (see Chapters Five, Six and Eleven of this volume), which is searching for an understanding of the misery of unemployment in the character prerequisites of the individual. The latter is consequently suspected to be inflexible, neglecting her or his personal potentials of flexibility in terms of time, place and content of work, and also of social insecurity (see overview of recent studies in Klammer and Tillmann, 2001). This discourse ignores a basic fact, however: that flexibility is a highly exclusive criterion which from the beginning sorts out those who are far away from being able to fulfil these demands.

Should both levels – the structural one and the individual one – be confused, one has to be careful not to end up in an highly individualising discourse, which makes individual young people responsible for their transition problems. This discourse accuses them of being too demanding, too lazy, too rigid, and so on. This logic of individual deficits prevents policy from necessary interventions, which are not necessarily contradictory to some forms of flexibilisation.

Aside from the two dominant discourses outlined earlier, there are also (seldom used) alternative discourses that understand flexibility strictly from the individuals' subjective perspective – asking what kind of employment structures they need to meet their changing needs and aspirations, or what individuals need to be enabled to act flexibly in facing new labour market demands. Such a subject-oriented perspective, in fact, represents a totally different understanding of what flexibilisation could mean. And it automatically brings the discourse closer to the one about security, because individual flexibility necessarily has to be backed with basic security structures (see Chapter Two of this volume).

While flexibility is *the* trendy topic, the question of *security* is far less fashionable and is mostly discussed as the annoying but inevitable addition when translating 'modern = more flexible employment strategies' into practice. Social policy as a safety net, therefore, is far less on the political agenda of almost all political currents – even more so now with the coming of New Labour in the UK and the new social democracy in Germany with conceptions of social policy explicitly aimed at increasing flexibility by meeting employers' demands for deregulation. In the context of post-'socialist' countries, security is still connected with the totalitarian version offered by state socialism, and is therefore extremely unpopular among political elites. Within the discourse of more flexibilisation, security plays an increasingly weaker role, even though it should be discussed at least as intensely as flexibility. Like flexibility, security may be understood on two levels.

First, it could be discussed on the level of securing structures and institutional procedures – which, of course, have some securing effects for the individual, but which may turn into a kind of structure-conservatism. One example of such structure-conservatism is German transition policy, with its rigid adherence to the 'dual system' as the only way of providing acknowledged training. It continues to do this despite its increasingly visible excluding effect that fails to offer sufficient opportunities for all young people without post-compulsory education for whom the dual system is the only access to skilled jobs. The increase in numbers of young people working without firm contracts in Southern and Eastern Europe, and also in the UK, clearly reveals the necessity for more security, at least in working contracts based on agreements between the social partners. In the liberal understanding of flexibilisation, social security is often suspected as being about over-regulation. Therefore, in such discussions, innovative social security concepts are underdeveloped or predominantly exist as 'poverty policy', for example, a very low basic security that should be introduced *instead* of all other income measures (Dean, 2002).

Discourses that focus on individual deficits rarely take into account that, in order to be more flexible, a person concomitantly needs more security. This is the insight of approaches that develop an alternative *subjective perspective*. Starting from (different) life situations (also within transitions from youth to adulthood or from education to work), such approaches take into account the different (security) needs of (young) people. Security is revealed to be a broad concept that includes income security but also includes security provided by reliable regulations and normative criteria such as *trust* encompassing the issue of personal security provided by social acknowledgement (see Chapter Ten of this volume; Hartmann and Offe, 2001).

Within these discourses, there are some other, more hidden ones, concerning questions, such as who is mostly affected by flexibilisation? Who pays the price for flexibilisation? And which price is to be paid in different working situations and at different stages of working biographies?

Women in all European countries are affected much more than men by flexible work, and research reveals that females tend to be the most flexible individuals in labour markets (see the UK as an example, where young females adapt much more easily to changed labour markets than young males, and where 'male underachievement' is increasingly understood as a social problem; Biggart et al, 2002). Young women can avoid unemployment, but what does flexible work mean with regard to their career prospects, to social security and to pension entitlements?

Immigrants in all countries are also much more affected by flexible work – like women this is a result of their generally weaker position in labour markets (see Chapter Fourteen of this volume). However, if they are refugees, they are also often forced to accept flexible (and sometimes illegal) work by restrictive residence allowances. Under which conditions can or do they benefit from this work?

And last but not least, *young people* are much more affected by flexible work than their older counterparts (for example, high rates of temporary work as in Spain, regardless of the level of qualification). Under which conditions do they benefit from flexibility and can they use their flexible jobs as a bridge towards the labour market (as, for example, in the case of those young people in Southern Europe whose family support mechanisms safeguard this bridge)? Why do young people need these jobs as a kind of Transitional Labour Market (TLM) (see Chapter Seven of this volume)? What does this mean with regards to perhaps even more flexible education and training facilities in the future?

Flexibility and security in youth transitions

Young people's transitions to the labour market and adulthood are often accompanied by insecure and flexible jobs (with a tendency to persist). This fact underlines the point that any flexibilisation (for example, of transitional pathways and access facilities) needs a concomitant enhancement of security in order to prevent the individualisation of transition risks. Equally, any enhancement of the safeguards within transitions needs at the same time to maintain space for individual freedom in order to allow the different needs of young women and men to be fulfilled and to enhance real forms of participation.

With regard to the situation of young people in flexibilised labour markets, findings from comparative European research that deals with the contradictory nature of the topic, show how – under the conditions of yo-yo-transitions between youth and adulthood (see Chapter Two of this volume) – flexibility is needed *and* has to be secured[1]:

- It is an all-European trend that young people are overrepresented in the spheres of flexible work both in the developed and newly formed labour markets. It is particularly the youngest age group (16-24) and often the oldest age group (56-65) among the workforce that have the highest shares of employees in non-standard jobs, including part-time work, fixed-term employment or work without a contract. Only self-employment, as a specific type of flexible work, is rarer among youth, but at the same time this is the group with the highest potential in terms of desire and values to risk starting their own business.

- In different national contexts (and different social policy regimes), different patterns of flexible work dominate among youth. Thus part-time work is more typical for Dutch and Scandinavian youth, and is also much better safeguarded. Work without contracts is almost absent in these national contexts, while it is widespread among South Western and South Eastern European youth, and increasingly so among British youth.

- The patterns of flexible work have different legal and financial conditions and offer different career prospects and different opportunities to combine paid work with other endeavours outside this sphere. Young people seem to be overrepresented in the more precarious types of flexible work, particularly on a fixed-term, 'on-call' basis in temporary work agencies, and 'only on a fee' basis and without any contracts. As these jobs are more insecure, with fewer career prospects and lower pay, young people are disadvantaged in these respects.

- Flexible jobs mean very different things for students and low-qualified youth in advanced societies. The first group accepts short-term, low-qualified jobs as they do not identify with them and views those jobs as a temporary source of income until they qualify for their desired secure professional occupations (van der Meer and Wielers, 2001). For the second group, however, flexibility is an imposed option, providing not only less security and less payment but also fewer training options and fewer career perspectives. The risks of flexibilisation thus disproportionately affect the lowest qualified (Gangl, 2002).

- In interviews, young people show a complex attitude toward this situation. On the one hand, they feel pushed into such jobs by unfriendly labour markets. They favour highly-paid, highly-qualified, challenging and secure jobs. On the other hand, they prefer more insecure, non-standard jobs to secure but low-paid, dead-end jobs. Often young people choose an insecure, informal job providing no social benefits but some money and skills, while waiting for a more qualified and desired job. Security is a valued goal, but its achievement is postponed to (hypothetical) future permanent and prestigious jobs, while currently accepting temporary and often precarious jobs (du Bois-Reymond et al, 2002a).

- This attitude of 'waiting' for the permanent secure job while doing precarious jobs is more typical for young people who can rely on strong family support, both financial and emotional, as is often the situation in South East and Southern Europe. In these regional contexts, insecure jobs are a route to social integration (see Chapter Three of this volume). In Northern and Western Europe, job insecurity more often results in feelings and experiences of isolation and marginalisation.

- Flexibility of work is viewed positively as a temporary solution by young people, preferred both to unemployment and to low-paid, low-qualified, uninteresting (albeit secure) jobs. Insecure flexible jobs are viewed as stepping-stones to more qualified, more challenging, more prestigious and secure jobs. Social policy and youth work can support young people in building their careers accumulating skills and experience, while recognising their subjective motivation in search of the desired work–life combination. Social research should contribute by studying youth careers over time and their personal needs and values in order to outline the factors for successful social integration and personal satisfaction.

According to the insecure labour market insertion of young people, flexible (and insecure) jobs are highly ambivalent. On the one hand, they are a chance to wait for qualified work – as long as they not only mean exploitation and as long as they provide some important learning experiences, they *could* be a door-opener to qualified jobs. On the other hand, they could turn into a trap, if they are the beginning of an insecure 'McJob' career (see Chapter Three of this volume; Lex, 1997; Braun, 2000). In the UK, this is discussed as the 'revolving doors' effect, with young people entering measures only to enter the next one and so on, but never getting access to regular work. As far as young people in transitions are concerned, some questions can be extracted from these research findings:

- How can risks derived from flexible work be compensated for?
- How can jobs be secured – at least on a basic level?
- What could be ways to acknowledge job experiences?
- How can professional prospects be developed out of flexible work for young people?
- What is necessary to make 'wait-and-see-strategies' pay off?
- What is necessary as an equivalent to a stabilising and secure background, that in some cultural contexts is provided by families or the welfare state?

The overall question remains, however: how can the interconnectedness of flexibility and security be transferred into policies appropriate to guarantee both sufficient flexibility and security for the individuals concerned? And how can it be transferred into the concrete context of transition policies? What are concrete needs of flexibility and security for young women and men? With a closer look, most of the studies presented in this volume in one way or the other are concerned with this question.

Manuela du Bois-Reymond and Andreu López Blasco (Chapter Two) point out that *misleading trajectories*, the contradictory effects of integration policies for young people, can result from a lack of flexibility as well as from a lack of security (or both). Therefore, they argue for a balance of flexibility and security within a holistic concept of Integrated Transition Policies (ITPs) that includes flexibilised education systems and basic security rights.

With regard to the *risks of social exclusion resulting from long-term youth unemployment*, Thomas Kieselbach refers to security in terms of psychosocial stabilisation (Chapter Three). At the same time, this requires flexibilised measures that give access to young people at different stages of their transitions. Flexibilisation thus implies a modular process of qualification to be achieved by networking with enterprises and better accessibility to training and work experience. These are the specific notions of flexibility within this project, to be carefully balanced with security.

In their comparison of *recent programmes against youth unemployment* in EU member states, Wallace McNeish and Patricia Loncle (Chapter Six) critically unpack their underlying ideological contents and contrast the ideology of flexibilisation, which underlies most of the analysed policies, with the often unmet needs of flexibilisation in terms of local labour market policies and tailor-made pathways for the most disadvantaged. The latter need to be backed both by security and a shift towards demand-side approaches: that is, job creation and basic income.

The concept of TLMs presented by Harm van Lieshout and Ton Wilthagen (Chapter Seven) directly refers to the question of employment strategies that are flexible and reliable. They show that the integrative potential of apprenticeship training under conditions of flexibilised and modernised labour markets, for example, depends on flexible links with other policies such as social benefits and temporary work agencies. Elements of the Dutch flexicurity policy will be also discussed in more depth later in this chapter.

Paul Burgess (Chapter Eight) underlines the need of young people for both more flexibility *and* more security. *Third-sector* organisations have the potential to adapt their activities to young people's interests and competencies and to allow for individual step-by-step learning processes. At the same time, there is an enormous lack of security for the third sector itself due to its weak structural position and the precarious wages and working conditions that characterise the tradition of voluntary work.

As a particular example of this ambiguity, Steven Miles (Chapter Nine) analyses the potentials of *performing arts* for the integration of young people with low training motivation. He argues that it is the training system itself that needs flexibilisation in order to be open for innovative approaches that are able to raise the creative and learning potential of discouraged young people.

These studies share the insight that, on the one hand, young people all over Europe need more basic security to be enabled to actively 'perform' their transitions, but that, on the other hand, they need at the same time much more space for such activities in order to unfold their competencies, to discover where to engage, to keep the fragile cycle of motivation turning. In all the projects, researchers were convinced that it is not adequate simply to cut the link between flexibility and security. As long as individuals are considered to be real actors and their different needs are concerned, one cannot opt for *either* freedom/more flexible structures, *or* security/more stable structures: individual actors need both. The projects already gave some hints of a possible combined approach of 'flexicurity' for young people in terms of places where young people find better conditions for their transitions. However, a lot of implementation work has to be done to transfer such experiences into political practice. With this regard, the new paradigm of flexicurity (see Chapter Seven of this volume) sounds promising.

Ways out of the dilemma: flexicurity as a new paradigm for European welfare policies?

Flexicurity is already on the political agenda of some European countries as a set of measures designed to cope with the effects of restructured labour markets (for an overview see Klammer and Tillmann, 2001). Flexicurity policies are mainly oriented towards the (re)integration of (young) people into work in order to develop a better balance between supply and demand in new labour markets. Under certain conditions, new labour market regulations and institutions could enhance the quality and security of job transfers. As young people are highly concerned by insecure jobs, these policies are extremely important to them.

Denmark is one of the countries that has undertaken considerable efforts in terms of an integrated restructuring of social and labour market policies. However, due to the level of benefits and the scope of choice that activation policies leave to the individuals concerned, the costs of deregulation are shared between the individuals and society. So, Denmark is usually referred to as a successful rebalancing of flexibility and security rather than an example of the neoliberal 'rights and responsibilities' discourses (Köhler, 1998; Greve, 2000; van Berkel and Hornemann Møller, 2002). Of course, these policies have produced other problems, especially for young people, where a trend towards activation for activation's sake can be observed, with the effect of activating measures turning into 'containers' for young people (Mørch, 1996). Nevertheless, some efforts had been made to support upward-mobility with social rights and to safeguard against downward-mobility with social protection.

In the UK, the New Deal represents a major policy drive to reintegrate different groups in the labour market. Here, however, there is an accentuated workfare approach where young people are forced to take part in activating programmes if they do not want to lose their benefits. In correspondence to the logic of liberal welfare regimes, the compensation and coverage level of social security is much lower than in Denmark, for example (Gallie and Paugam, 2000; van Berkel and Hornemann Møller, 2002).

Flexicurity policies in the Netherlands allow for a new understanding of flexibility as a new chance for unemployed young people. Apart from the extension and regulation of part-time work contributing to the redivision between paid and unpaid work (such as care), it is the specific policies for temporary work that represent an innovative answer to the flexibility–security dilemma. The latter are presented, therefore, in more detail in the next section (see also Chapter Seven of this volume).

The flexicurity paradigm in Dutch labour market policy

National and international commentators have judged Dutch socioeconomic performance quite favourably over the past few years. One particular aspect of the Dutch 'miracle' (Visser and Hemerijck, 1997) is the flexibilisation that has occurred in the Dutch labour market. Increased labour market flexibility is a policy guideline that many observers (such as the OECD) prescribe in order to combat persistent labour market problems – and in particular, high levels of unemployment. However, this flexibilisation has not caused a sharp increase in social inequality (which by international standards remains quite low in the Netherlands). This is due to the fact that the concept of flexicurity has not just cropped up in theoretical discussions but has structured labour market regulation and collective bargaining. The most obvious example is a new Flexibility and Security Act that re-regulates temporary agency work. On the one hand, it entails further flexibilisation as it has abolished the previous permit requirement for temporary employment agencies. On the other hand, however, it offers enhanced security for temporary workers – something that gradually increases with their tenure as a 'temp' worker (for other examples of flexicurity, see van Lieshout and van Liempt, 2001; van Lieshout and Wilthagen, 2002). This example is highly important from a TLM perspective, because Dutch temporary agency work is increasingly relevant for at least two (of the five) transitions highlighted in this theory: the transition between unemployment and employment, and the transition between education or training and employment, and – something that should increasingly be taken into consideration as well – the transition from one job to another (see Chapter Seven of this volume).

The recent employment growth (and unemployment decline) in the Netherlands has coincided with a substantial growth of temporary work, from 77,000 full-time equivalents (FTEs) or 112,000 actual jobs in 1988 to 147,000 FTEs or 248,000 jobs in 1997. In 1997, approximately 2.5% of the national workforce consisted of workers employed through temporary employment agencies. While the German population, for example, is roughly 5.5 times as large as the Dutch, the Dutch market for temporary work is four times its size (Wansink, 1997). In 1997, half of the temporary workers were younger than 25, and 29% had been unemployed previously to their current temp job. Thirty-four per cent of all temp workers had found a permanent job within a year; and 41% of this group (14% of all temp workers) had found one with the firm they had been working for through the temporary employment agency (van der Ende et al, 1999). In all, in 1997, an estimated 100,000 temp workers found a permanent job with the client firm they had been temporarily employed with (Arents et al, 1998). This corresponds to almost 20% of all persons that found a permanent job that year. Interestingly, temp workers who were older, previously long-term unemployed, or physically challenged had the same chances of finding a permanent job as other groups (van der Ende et al, 1999).

The Flexibility and Security Act for the first time classifies the relationship between a temporary work agency and a temp worker as a 'regular' employment contract. There is one important exception to the general rules of employment law for this specific relationship, namely that both parties may agree in writing that the contract of employment will end without notice when the client firm points out that there is no more work. Yet, this exception can no longer apply once the temp worker has worked for the temporary employment agency for

26 weeks. The act implies additional improvements in worker protection once the temp worker has performed temp work for an even longer period.

This act was not a state initiative; its way was paved by a previous central agreement on flexibility and security between the leading organisations of the social partners. Soon after this, the social partners negotiated a collective labour agreement (ABU) that entitled temp workers to pensions, assessment of their training needs, and a permanent contract once they had gained enough tenure.

The most important agreement, which covers about 90% of all temporary employment agencies (Verhulp, 1998; Grapperhaus and Jansen, 1999), distinguishes four phases related to job tenure as a temp worker. Phase 4 implies that temp workers are awarded a permanent employment contract with the temporary employment agency once they have worked for 18 months (including time spent in prior phases) for the same client firm, or for 36 months (including time spent in prior phases) for various client firms. Phase 3 already entitles them to fixed-term employment contracts for one or more three-month periods, and these contracts cannot be terminated in case the client firm runs out of work.

Article 34 of the agreement concerns training 'rights' for temp workers: as soon as a temp worker has been working for one temporary employment agency for 26 weeks (Phase 2), the agency must discuss the workers' training needs with him or her and workers gain pension entitlements. It also requires temporary employment agencies to spend a gradually rising percentage (0.92% in 2002) of the total (gross) wage sum they pay their temp workers in a particular year on their training. And it creates a training foundation for the sector that has to monitor compliance with the training rules stipulated in the collective labour agreement.

There are two key effects of the Flexibility and Security Act and the new ABU agreement that are highly relevant to our discussion here. First, they entail direct effects, as they entitle temp workers in Phase 2 and beyond – as a group – to discuss their training needs, and force temporary employment agencies to invest in temp worker training. Second, the act and the agreement jointly strengthen the employment relations between temp workers and temporary employment agencies after specified periods of time. This may cause an indirect, positive effect on temporary employment agencies' training investments, as in the final two phases they still have to pay a temp worker when they temporarily cannot place him or her with a client firm.

There are also two mechanisms through which temporary employment agencies protect their training investments. One is through the fees they receive for hiring out workers: as these are usually qualification-based, more qualified workers will entitle them to larger fees (MGK and NEI, 1998). The other mechanism is that temp workers themselves usually have to contribute towards their training costs, except when training is very firm and job-specific. In that case, the client firm will usually pick up the bill.

The national evaluation study of this policy found that positive experiences among both employers (including temporary work agencies) and flexible workers generally outweigh negative experiences (van den Toren et al, 2002). Workers who prefer flexible work are now able to do so in a more regulated and secure employment relation, while those for whom flexible work is a second-best option, the act has softened the rough edges of some of these flexible contract forms (temp agency work and on-call work) and offered an opportunity for mobility into permanent employment. Such mobility, however, is by no means guaranteed.

The importance of the Dutch example lies in showing how, under specific conditions, policies towards a better balance of flexibility and security are a realistic political option. It also shows that temporary work, which is always under suspicion of simply being an instrument of labour market deregulation, may provide a bridge into a more secure labour market sector (van Lieshout and Wilthagen, 2002). Moreover, it illustrates the potentials of temporary work agencies as 'new' actors, which could be labelled 'transition agencies' (Wilthagen and Rogowski, 2001), and which (although working as private firms) could be integrated in public policies for the labour market (for the German case, see Bericht der Hartzkommission, 2002).

One limitation of the Dutch example, however, is that the security aspect of flexicurity is still exclusively linked to the employment contract. The policy has indeed improved labour contract conditions for particular weak groups in the labour market – temp agencies workers as well as others. However, the policy did not improve security for those without a current employment relation. One reason for this may be that the Netherlands already starts from a rather high level of social security and belongs to the more universalistic type of welfare regime (although the level of benefits for young people is lower than that for adults; Esping-Andersen, 1990; du Bois-Reymond et al, 2002a).

Perspectives of transferability of good practice

As soon as examples like Dutch policies are regarded as 'good practice', transferability has to be discussed. It is an unavoidable issue when looking at the Dutch case, that the policies implemented have a contextualised meaning and a national context effect. They were developed within and hence make sense within a specific cultural and structural context. Flexicurity in the Dutch example is based on a rather long history of flexible work and of experimenting with ways to enhance qualification levels and provide qualified employment for young people. Dutch flexicurity policy could only emerge after a slow and sometimes painful learning process for all the policy actors involved. Hence, this policy is the result of a rather high level of institutional reflexivity, which is more likely to be attained within a small wealthy country that has what is a long, relatively cooperative and consensual industrial relations tradition (Visser and Hemerijck, 1997). Nationwide evaluations subsequently provide the information base that is necessary for further consensual political development. This specific context cannot be taken for granted in other countries. Therefore, strategies of transfer have to be flexible themselves in order to take different socioeconomic, political and socio-cultural contexts and uneven development between countries into account (Leibfried and Pierson, 1998; Walther, 2000). Thus, flexicurity may be adopted as a principle, which takes into account the premise that both flexibility and security are necessary. However, the concrete relationship of both components − flexibility and security − and their operationalisation in specific institutional arrangements have to be adapted and redefined according to the specific situation in other national contexts. In this regard, intercultural learning is extremely important: it means understanding the cultural context from which good examples emerge, and then 'de-contextualising' the respective experiences in order to 'recontextualise' them within a new context.

Despite such problems of transferability, certain aspects of the implementation of flexicurity policies do nevertheless allow for guarded generalisations:

- Most important for all these policies is the availability of (some) paid work or the realistic expectation that new job facilities can be created by such policies. While it is conceivable that this policy has, to some extent, helped Dutch employment growth of the past decade, it is far from the only explanation for this growth; furthermore, it is doubtful that such a consensual policy could have been developed among the state and the social partners in a period of rapidly declining economy and job losses for trade union members.
- While high unemployment may substantially hamper the development of such a flexicurity policy in other counties, there is one alternative that is more readily available. In all countries a lot of work is done without any pay; for example, informal care in families and through voluntary organisations. This highly gendered area has to be viewed as a significant pivotal point within the whole debate. Such work should be regarded as having the potential (if it could be generally acknowledged as important) to be redistributed and recompensed.
- Basic income and basic rights of social security remain decisive. The Dutch current example *is* more than the dominant European strategy that views security as embodied in a *permanent* employment contract − however, it nevertheless remains exclusively employment-related. A more radical strategy would be to secure life chances independently from reliance on paid employment. This would involve a generalisation of social security, which at the same time points towards the rebalancing of flexibility and security in terms of the flexibilisation of security (see later in this chapter).

Conclusions: young people, flexicurity and Integrated Transition Policies

This discussion brings us back to the concept of ITPs (see Chapter Two of the volume). Against the background of such a holistic model of transition policies that aims at combining flexibilisation with improved basic security for young people, some conclusions can be made.

Education, training and labour market policies strongly demand that young people react flexibly to social and economic change. However, if such policies do not guarantee a basic security, they do not act in favour of the individuals involved and put all the risks inherent to change on their shoulders. Integrated Transition Policies for young people must strike the *balance between flexibility and security* in all measures advertised and prevent illegitimate (and ineffective) demands upon the education system and the labour market.

It has been argued that a more holistic and biography-oriented approach requires the coordination of the different policies concerned with young adults' transitions in order to restrict segmentation and one-dimensional 'human capital' perspectives (Walther et al, 2002b). With regard to the relation between employment and welfare policies, this means that *employment policies* have to provide young people with access to more qualified work opportunities after an experimental phase of insecure jobs, for example by introducing a so-called 'qualification pass' giving evidence of their experiences (in a wide sense). Placing young people into existing or newly created jobs or schemes has not only to fit with labour market demands, but also with young people's everyday lives and lifestyles. This may imply support for young people in making informal activities formal and paid, to recognise not only formal qualifications but also informally acquired skills for entering employment and, in case of part-time or low-paid work, be matched by welfare payments to guarantee a decent living. As a principle, activating policies have to be balanced with *enabling* ones (Rabe and Schmid, 2000).

Welfare policies can be characterised as 'enabling' if they provide young people with individual choice and the possibility to experiment with different options. This means that the risks of insecure jobs can be minimised by adapting social security systems to the needs of young people, such as housing benefits for young people, a basic income for young people, grants for experimental working phases and so on. Such means of basic security would be most appropriate effectively to facilitate flexibility in the interests of young people. To enfold all potential actively to shape their transitions, young people need 'ontological security' (Giddens, 1991), which always has a material/economical component. André Gorz argues for an unconditional basic income, because it is especially appropriate to let both individuals and society benefit from the voluntary nature of competence building (Gorz, 2000). Although a lot of European research has been undertaken in this area (BIEN, 2000), until now there has been little reflection on the potential specific benefits for young people, let alone the political implementation.

Coming back to the initial question of flexibility *and* security, and asking for political prioritisation of this issue, we quote Zygmunt Bauman, whose position is unambiguous:

> As things stand at the moment, most attention needs to be focused on the security side of the sought union. Since an autonomous society is inconceivable without autonomous citizens, and since the autonomy of citizens is unthinkable anywhere but in an autonomous society – the efforts, to stand a chance of success, need to be applied simultaneously on the 'macro' and the 'micro' level. (Bauman, 2001, p 56)

Bauman expresses here the essential argument that substantive individualisation (flexibility) (see also Beck, 1992) is simply not possible without a certain level of support on which people can rely (security).

The fact that the need for this support is too often neglected (on a theoretical as well as on a political level) has its roots in the long tradition of the fiction of the autonomous subject, which has dominated Western thinking. This fiction depends on the traditional gendered division of labour – because social tasks in a broad sense (that is, all tasks concerning personal dependency) are separated from the sphere of public recognition and delegated to women and the private sphere where they are not valued in the same way as other necessary social tasks. Hence, bringing back this consideration of dependency together with security into political discourses represents a chance to rethink social responsibility in terms of an equal division of labour between the sexes, just as much as it represents a chance to develop new transitional pathways for young women and men.

Note

[1] The projects referred to are 'An evaluation of programmes to assist the young unemployed in East-Central Europe', ACE Programme, European Commission (1996-98); 'The young self-employed and their support schemes in post-communist countries'; Overseas Development Administration, UK (1997-99); and 'Households, work and flexibility'; Fifth Framework Programme, European Commission (still in progress).

References

Arents, M., Donker van Heel, P. and Polanen Petel, V. (1998) *Instroom uitzendkrachten 1997*, Rotterdam: Nederlands Economisch Instituut.

Bauman, Z. (2001) *The individualised society*, Cambridge: Polity Press.

Beck, U. (1992) *Risikogesellschaft*, Frankfurt-am-Main: Suhrkamp.

Bericht der Hartkommission (2002) *Moderne Dienstleistungen am Arbeitsmarkt*, Broschüre Nr A 306 des Bundesministeriums für Arbeit und Sozialordnung, Berlin.

BIEN (Basic Income European Network) (2000) 'VIIIth International Congress', 6-7 October, Berlin (www.bien.be/Archive/Congress/).

Biggart, A., Cuconato, M., Furlong, A., Lenzi, G., Stauber, B. and Walther, A. (2002) 'Misleading trajectories between standardisation and flexibility – Great Britain, Italy and West Germany', in A. Walther, B. Stauber, A. Biggart, M. du Bois-Reymond, A. Furlong, A. López Blasco, S. Mørch and J.M. Pais (eds) *Misleading trajectories: Integration policies for young adults in Europe?*, Opladen: Leske+Budrich, pp 44-66.

Bourdieu, P. (1998) *Acts of resistance*, Cambridge: Polity Press.

Braun, F. (2000) 'Übergangshilfen – Sackgassen, Umleitungen, Überholspuren?', in A. Pohl and S. Schneider (eds) *Sackgassen, Umleitungen, Überholspuren?*, Tübingen: Neuling, pp 35-48.

Dean, H. (2002) 'Business *versus* families: whose side is New Labour on?', *Social Policy and Society*, vol 1, no 1, pp 3-10.

du Bois-Reymond, M., Plug, W., Stauber, B., Pohl, A. and Walther, A. (2002a) *How to avoid cooling out? Experiences of young people in their transitions to work across Europe*, YOYO Working Paper 2 (www.iris-egris.de/yoyo).

du Bois-Reymond, M., Plug, W., Ferreira, V., Pais, J.M., Keily, E., Lorenz, W., Bendit, R. and Heim, K. (eds) (2002b) 'Transiciones modernizades y politicas de desvestaja: Paies Bajos, Portugal, Irelanda y jovenes immigrantes en Alemania. Revista de estudios de juvenshed', *Jovenes y Transiciones a Lavida Adultes en Europa*, no 56, pp 55-75.

Esping-Andersen, G. (1990) *The three worlds of welfare capitalism*, Cambridge: Polity Press.

Gallie, D. and Paugam, S. (eds) (2000) *Welfare regimes and the experience of unemployment in Europe*, Oxford: Oxford University Press.

Gangl, M. (2002) 'Changing labour markets and early career outcomes: labour market entry in Europe over the past decade', *Work, Employment and Society*, vol 16, no 1, pp 67-90.

Giddens, A. (1991) *Modernity and self-identity*, Cambridge: Polity Press.

Gorz, A. (2000) *Arbeit zwischen Misere und Utopie*, Frankfurt: Suhrkamp.

Grapperhaus, F. and Jansen, M. (1999). *De uitzendovereenkomst*, Deventer: Kluwer.

Greve, B. (ed) (2000) *What constitutes a good society?*, New York, NY: St Martins Press.

Hartmann, M. and Offe, C. (2001) *Vertrauen. Die Grundlage des sozialen Zusammenhalts*, Frankfurt and New York, NY: Campus.

Klammer, U. and Tillmann, K. (2001) *Flexicurity. Soziale Sicherung und Flexibilisierung der Arbeits- und Lebensverhältnisse*, Research project for the Ministry of Employment and Social Affairs of the Land Nordrhein-Westfalen, Düsseldorf.

Köhler, P.A. (1998) 'Soziale Sicherheit in Dänemark', *Soziale Sicherheit*, vol 47, no 6, pp 226-34.

Kovacheva, S. (2001) 'Flexibilisation of youth transitions in Central and Eastern Europe', *YOUNG*, vol 9, no 1, pp 41-60.

Leibfried, S. and Pierson, P. (eds) (1998) *European social policy: Between fragmentation and integration*, Washington, DC: Brookings, Institution Press.

Lex, T. (1997) *Berufswege Jugendlicher zwischen Integration und Ausgrenzung*, München: Juventa.

MGK and NEI (Max Goote Kenniscentrum and Nederlands Economisch Instituut) (1998) *Monitoring and financing lifelong learning. Country report: The Netherlands*, Amsterdam: MGK voor Beroepsonderwijs en Volwasseneneducatie.

Mørch, S. (1996) 'Individualisierung und "Container-Projekte". Probleme und Forschungsperspektiven der Konstruktion von Lebensphasen', in A. Walther (ed) *Junge Erwachsene in Europa*, Opladen: Leske+Budrich.

Rabe, B. and Schmid, G. (2000) 'Strategie der Befähigung: Zur Weiterentwicklung der Arbeitsmarkt- und Rentenpolitik', *WSI-Mitteilungen*, vol 55, no 5, pp 305-13.

van Berkel, R. and Hornemann Møller, I. (eds) (2002) *Active social policies in the EU: Inclusion through participation?*, Bristol: The Policy Press.

van den Toren, J.P., Evers, G. and Commissaris, E.J. (2002) *Flexibiliteit en Zekerheid. Effecten en doeltrefendheid van de Wet Flexibiliteit en Zekerheid*, Den Haag: Ministerie van Sociale Zaken en Werkgelegenheid.

van der Ende, M., Donker van Heel, P. and Arents, M. (1999) 'Het uitzendbureau als bemiddelaar', *Economisch Statistische Berichten*, vol 84 (4186), pp 56-8.

van der Meer, P. and Wielers, R. (2001) 'The increased labour market participation of Dutch students', *Work, Employment and Society*, vol 15, no 1, pp 55-71.

van Lieshout, H. and van Liempt, A. (2001) *Flexicurity: Recent developments in Dutch vocational education and training*, Amsterdam: MGK voor Beroepsonderwijs en Volwasseneducatie.

van Lieshout, H. and Wilthagen, T. (2002) 'Transitional labour markets in action: new developments in the Dutch vocational education and training market', in S. Rouault, H. Oschmiansky and I. Schömann (eds) *Reacting in time to qualification needs: Towards a cooperative implementation?*, Berlin: Wissenschaftszentrum Berlin, pp 133-49.

Verhulp, E. (1998) 'De uitzendkracht in het Flex(s)t(r)ijdperk', *Nederlands Tijdschrift voor Sociaal Recht*, vol 13, no 11, pp 322-34.

Visser, J. and Hemerijck, A. (1997) *'A Dutch miracle': Job growth, welfare reform and corporatism in the Netherlands*, Amsterdam: Amsterdam University Press.

Walther, A. (2000) *Spielräume im Übergang in die Arbeit, Junge Erwachsene im Wandel der Arbeitsgesellschaft in Deutschland, Italien und Großbritannien*, Weinheim/München: Juventa.

Walther, A., Stauber, B., Biggart, A., du Bois-Reymond, M., Furlong, A., López Blasco, A., Mørch, S. and Pais, J.M. (eds) (2002) *Misleading trajectories: Integration policies for young adults in Europe?*, Opladen: Leske+Budrich.

Wansink, W. (1997) 'Duitse uitzendmarkt wacht "Riesenentwicklung"', *Flexmarkt*, vol 1997, no 11, pp 35-7.

Wilthagen, T. and Rogowski, R. (2001) 'Legal regulation of transitional labour markets', in G. Schmid and B. Gazier (eds) *The dynamics of full employment: Social integration through transitional labour markets*, Cheltenham: Edward Elgar, pp 233-73.

FOURTEEN

'Disadvantage': transition policies between social construction and the needs of vulnerable youth

René Bendit and Dermot Stokes

Introduction

Our changing perspectives on young people's transitions across Europe are shaped by a complex weave of experience and circumstance. Of particular concern in this regard is the phenomenon of youth unemployment. This generates significant competition among those trying to enter the labour market, with two key outcomes. First, it makes the passage between school and training to work a very difficult and uncertain transition. Second, qualification requirements for jobs are currently inflating, which means that having a certain qualification does not assure a position in the labour market. This is seen to disrupt the transition to adulthood, a key factor in which is the adoption of an adult vocational identity (Hannan and O'Riain, 1993).

This concern has led to a wide range of measures in most European member states and the accretion of a vast range of experience regarding successful measures to assist young people to enter education and training and engage with the labour market (EC, 1996). However, among policy makers certain assumptions have remained intact. In particular, it is assumed that young people's achievement of independent adult identity follows a linear path – something that no longer holds true for many young people in all advanced economies. Indeed, the very idea of transition is itself in trouble. Social and economic conditions in economically advanced countries have created a paradox – young people take longer to make the transition to adult identity and independence and indeed 'yo-yo' back and forward between what we once knew as youth and adulthood (see Chapter Two of this volume). Although this appears to apply across all social classes, unqualified young people lacking the necessary personal, social, cultural and financial resources are most vulnerable to the enormous social and economic changes presently underway. Some of these individuals are extremely 'disadvantaged' and detached from social and economic integration. A key challenge for policy makers is to address their considerable difficulties regarding transitions. In this chapter, we try to analyse the phenomenon and the concept of disadvantage a bit more in depth; that is, how disadvantage is constructed and to which purpose, which individuals and groups are most likely to be classified as disadvantaged, and by which means risks of social exclusion linked with social disadvantage may be compensated.

The theoretical and social construction of 'disadvantage' and 'disadvantaged groups'

Since the mid-1980s, the concept of 'disadvantage' and related concepts like 'discrimination', 'vulnerability', 'social exclusion' and 'marginalisation' have become central to social policy planning of the EC as well as of national governments (EC, 1983). The concept of 'disadvantage' involves the recognition that:

> despite the drive to universal citizenship and welfare provision, several groups in the population experience systematic discrimination and unequal access to resources, that is work, benefits etc. which impact on objective life chances. On the other hand is the proposition that unequal status also has important subjective effects – lack of confidence, self-esteem, dignity and self worth. (O' Brien and Penna, 1998, p 123)

Although most theoretical approaches seem to agree on the existence of structural and personal or biographical factors contributing to the condition of disadvantage of a person or group, they differ in stressing one element or another.

Those examining the origin of 'disadvantage' from a socio-structural perspective put the accent of their theoretical discourses on the existence of a segmented social system where there are not enough opportunities for all its members. Given this structural lack of social integration opportunities, the system needs to elaborate a way of differentiating individuals and so regulate the access to the given possibilities within society. There is a relative unanimity that such differentiation should not depend on unequal social starting positions such as one's socioeconomic origin, but on individual performance. This reflects the idea of 'democratisation' of the social system, where success or failure should not depend on structural factors but on individual performance. However, as we shall see below, the individualistic perspective can lead to an individualisation of structural deficiencies; that is, considering the individual responsible for his or her situation because of supposed inadequate resources.

In this 'post-structuralist' perspective, where individuals are conceptualised as negotiators of their own lives, the general tendency is to place the origin of disadvantage and social exclusion in individual deficiencies rather than in the inherent limitations of the social structure and the insufficiencies of the institutions.

Furthermore, the concept of disadvantage has been used as an instrument to meet transitional problems. This, for example, is the case in Germany where, due to high levels of competition and lack of training and working vacancies for all applicants, there is a group of capable and employable individuals classified as 'disadvantaged' in order to accommodate them to social measures. Hence, it is possible to identify as another function of the concept of disadvantage the 'cooling out' or 'parking' mechanism; that is, the lowering of socially raised aspirations in a socially 'harmless' way.

It is also evident that the social and theoretical construction of 'disadvantage' cannot be interpreted without considering the different historical, economical, social, cultural and political contexts in which processes of social inequality, personal vulnerability and exclusion take place within Europe today. Notwithstanding the diversity of both educational and vocational training systems and labour markets in Europe, we can observe that 'disadvantage' and 'disadvantaged groups' are universally the outcomes of specific temporal and spatial combinations of structural and individual factors and of social challenges (expectancies) coming from society. The latter emanate from the labour market as well as from educational and vocational training systems. In addition, there are those factors emanating from the political system, for example, from the political-administrative definitions of the problem of 'disadvantage' as well as from their educational, labour market or welfare policies and programmes.

Structural factors and the construction of 'disadvantage'

From a sociological perspective, the concept of 'disadvantage' and the definition of specific 'disadvantaged groups' have been discussed as an unintended consequence of accelerated technological, economical and social changes, taking place all over Europe over more than three decades. In the context of such modernisation processes, structural theoretical analysis focuses on social inequality and on the social effects of segmented social systems. With reference to those experiencing social inequality in the form of problematic life conditions (for example, difficulties in accessing housing, health and welfare services, to paid work or educational, professional or vocational qualifications), this theoretical perspective prompts the hypothesis that such manifestations of 'social disadvantage' are the result of existing structural inequalities in society. They are the main cause of such problematic life conditions as well as of the lack of skills and competencies on the individuals' side, to cope with such situations. In this perspective, education tends to be viewed more or less explicitly as the key to social equality. It is also decisive, therefore, in the perception of disadvantage as a social problem.

This way of looking at disadvantage has been changing since the early 1980s. On the background of further emerging disadvantaged groups, new structural approaches were brought into theoretical discussion. Authors such as Geurts (1989) perceived a shift from the 'social inequality thinking' model towards an 'access thinking' model. From this point of view, and in accordance to the concept of 'starting qualification', disadvantage is seen to be a situation in which individuals or groups, because of different structural factors, appear not to have adequate levels of qualification baggage (for example, of knowledge, attitudes and skills) to get full access to the labour market or a position within the employment system. The same is also true for holding one's own position and developing personally and professionally once a regular employment is found (Hövels, 1999). Politically, this increased focus on the importance of adequately meeting future qualification demands in the labour market has led in almost all EU countries to their so-called 'qualifications offensives'.

A general review of sociological literature on this issue in European countries (mainly Germany, the UK, Ireland, the Netherlands, Spain and Portugal) identifies the main determining factors of disadvantage of young people and young adults. These are consistent with both structural approaches mentioned above:

- social class background (parents with low levels of educational; parents on low incomes or who are long-term unemployed; families with low economic and social capital resources, and so on);
- problematic housing conditions and other unsatisfied basic needs for certain groups (migrants and asylum seekers, homeless or ethnic minorities, such as travellers and gypsies);
- general disadvantage or discrimination by gender (for example, difficulties in obtaining access to part-time jobs and part-time training opportunities);
- gender stereotypes and parental attitudes towards and expectancies of education;
- unstable conditions in specific segments of the labour market, specifically those where early school leavers, young migrants without vocational or professional training and sometimes even qualified young unemployed adults can eventually find (precarious) jobs;
- unfavourable regional labour market conditions and training possibilities;
- poor institutional support at educational, professional and social level;
- unstable legal conditions of certain social groups (migrants and asylum seekers; residence and work permits; legal and illegal work); and finally
- cultural factors such as family cultural values and quality of family relationships; cultural background of migrants and of ethnic minorities; normative conflicts with majority value systems and discrimination according to ethnic-cultural origin.

Apart from this, political-ideological and sociological discourses on social inequality, equal opportunities and individualisation, as well as religious-ideological discourses (for example, in Catholic contexts with regard to gender equality), contribute to the theoretical and social construction of disadvantage and disadvantaged groups.

Individual factors in the construction of 'disadvantage'

Where structural deficiencies exist, and where in turn there are not enough opportunities for all, the individualistic perspective often leads to individualisation of structural deficiencies. In other words, the individual comes to be considered responsible for her or his situation because of supposed inadequate resources, while the real cause of exclusion is to be found in insufficiencies of the social structure (see also Chapter Six of this volume). The structural influence in conceiving the concept of disadvantage not only achieves relevance in the presence of structural deficiencies, it also is to be found in the definition of the personal factors that will be considered relevant in according the status of 'disadvantaged'. In this sense, it is the given social structure that determines the value of personal characteristics in order to achieve social integration and what is to be viewed as a personal inadequacy. This means that even such factors as sex, ethnic origin, physical or psychological handicaps or the possession or not of certain skills or abilities cannot be viewed as inherently disadvantaging, but as closely related to the system of values of society.

Considering this 'structural determination' of personal factors and the relative nature of their intrinsic value to explain disadvantage, it can be observed in the literature on this issue that the theoretical and social definition of disadvantage and disadvantaged groups has also been based on 'individual criteria', including risk-susceptibility factors. Our analysis shows that the principal individual factors cited in the literature on the theoretical construction of the concept of disadvantage are:

* physical or mental *disabilities*;
* problematic *family constellations*; lack of resiliency factors in family socialisation (for example, interest and influence of parents on educational careers of their children) and networks of social support;
* *critical life events* in the family (such as illness or death of parents, divorce, migration, legal problems, poverty);
* *psychological factors*, such as hierarchy of personal priorities, lack of intrinsic or extrinsic motivation, prevalence of 'non-adaptative' behaviour to cope with critical life events, low self-esteem;
* the lack of *social skills* and communicative competencies.

As interdisciplinary research shows (see Chapter Three of this volume), there seems to be a very complex and tight relationship between structural and individual factors, and neither set can be understood without reference to the other.

The political-administrative construction of 'disadvantage' as legitimisation of policies

The combination of individual and structural factors determining disadvantage was undoubtedly of major importance at the moment when state strategies to cope with this problem had to be defined. The confluence of the structural and individual factors mentioned earlier in this chapter has often been 'used' by administrations to define disadvantaged groups in accordance with their own political orientations and administrative priorities. From this perspective, persons and families belonging to such disadvantaged groups are frequently pathologised, or characterised as 'deficient', incapable of accomplishing educational tasks, in 'need of help'. Even if administrations sometimes legitimise existing special educational or training programmes for the 'disadvantaged' as part of a strategy to cope with societies' structural problems (for example, the EU's 'Qualifications-Offensive against Youth Unemployment'), in most cases they focus on young people's individual deficits. Such discourses take the perspective that compensatory programmes and measures should tackle personal deficits in order to integrate young people in risky life situations through training and qualification. This kind of psycho–pedagogical legitimisation of compensatory measures contributes to an individualising concept of disadvantage while structures of social inequality are neglected.

This political definition of disadvantage, which can be found more or less explicitly on all EU countries, is very problematic. On one hand, it helps administrations to legitimise and to promote the financial support of additional forms of 'second-chance programmes' (of whatever standard). On the other, it allows political administrations to avoid making decisions on concerted and long-term strategies and solutions for structural labour market problems.

Equally, the political construction of disadvantage does not operate without consequences for those concerned. The individualising approach and legitimisation of 'action programmes' make young people experience their status as disadvantaged in a very contradictory way. On the one hand, they feel that participation in 'second-chance programmes' may open up new possibilities of vocational training or financial support. On the other, they find that such participation can have a stigmatising effect when seeking a job or subsequent regular training. In the perceptions of political-administrative decision makers, as well as in private companies, the disadvantaged are mainly understood as 'problematic', for example those who are 'untrainable' and have to be maintained under social control by welfare and other 'disciplinary' institutions. For these reasons, the concept of disadvantage should be used very carefully.

New approaches: 'disadvantage', vulnerability and social exclusion as different moments of the same process

Current approaches to the problems of disadvantage and social integration (see Dubet and Lapeyronie, 1992; Bhalla and Lapeyre, 1994; Jordan, 1996; Schnapper, 1996) understand the concepts of 'disadvantage', 'vulnerability' and 'social inclusion/exclusion' as different moments of the same social process. This contemporary perspective allows not only a wider and more dynamic view but also helps to develop more integral and integrated concepts for social policies. Furthermore, this approach does not only focus on economic, social or personal factors influencing disadvantage and vulnerability, but also on questions related to civil rights and citizenship.

In the frame of this paradigm, personal, social, economical, cultural and political needs are defined as 'rights', which by extension means that, while *social inclusion* can be conceptualised as the access possibilities that persons and social groups have to social rights, *exclusion* must be defined as the *impossibility* or incapacity of certain persons and groups to implement these rights without external help. As we can see, this paradigm does not refer only to the question of access (to economic resources, social and civil rights) and to the adaptability of individuals and groups to new economic or social challenges, but also to the risk of becoming, over longer periods of time, dependent on social assistance or other forms of public support – the effect being a lowering of self-esteem and danger of exposure to exclusion and stigmatisation (EC, 1983).

This perspective of defining 'needs' as social and civil rights, and of considering also the risk of stigmatisation through 'help', offers a dynamic analytical framework within which those processes that could lead to exclusion can be better explained without falling into the dichotomy of absolute inclusion or absolute exclusion. This means that, for the interpretation of actual social phenomena linked to exclusion, very different forms of disadvantage and vulnerability, as well as the specific dynamic of social inequality and of 'accessibility' characterising our societies today, have to be included into the analysis. With reference to young people, it can be assumed that the gap between 'outputs' of the education and training system and the new demands of the labour market contribute to deepen the disadvantaged situation and the vulnerability of certain groups and persons, thus increasing their risk of developing 'misleading trajectories' and of social exclusion (see Chapter Two of this volume).

When speaking about social integration in general and about the integration of disadvantaged youth in particular, one usually refers to labour market integration, because work is seen as the key instrument to achieving social inclusion. Thus, disadvantage is considered to be closely related to the condition of being unemployed or having difficulties with access to education, which is considered the key instrument leading to integration into the labour market.

By comparing the situation of disadvantage in different European countries, it seems to be important to note that being employed does not necessarily mean integration into the system. In fact, in some countries like Spain, Portugal, Ireland or Italy, being employed can be considered as a disadvantage if the person enters the labour market too early, or accepts precarious working conditions or voluntary work. In this sense, social integration appears to be more related to the acquisition of a social status within the system than to the mere participation in the labour market. Therefore, work is perhaps viewed as necessary, but certainly not enough to attain a recognised position within society. This example shows that to link social integration exclusively to labour market integration or access to education can be too narrow an approach to understand the role 'disadvantage' plays in social processes that can lead to social exclusion.

'Disadvantaged groups' with regard to education, training and employment

The achievement of social integration by securing qualified employment can be represented as a process supported by several educational and vocational institutions. The main objective of this system is to provide the individual with skills and resources (qualifications) to compete in the labour market. In this sense, the system of education and training also represents a key instrument to overcome initial social inequality determined by structural and personal or biographical factors. In other words, each person encounters the demands of education, training and employment with a different 'baggage' (or lack) of resources.

Despite the level of complexity of the different national educational and vocational systems across Europe, one can observe certain 'critical transitions' within the institutional structures of education, training and employment. These passages refer to every situation in which the individual is confronted with a decision, evaluation or selection in order to pass to another level within the educational and vocational system or to move on into the labour market. At each of these passages, young people must use their resources to cope with the requirements of the situation.

As education and training systems become increasingly elaborated and subdivided into multiple different pathways, the transitions within those systems become more complex involving multiple options. The transition may become even more complicated if the consequences of the final decision lead to entirely separated pathways with little or no possibility of passing from one alternative to another, as for example in the highly stratified and subdivided schooling and training systems of Germany or the Netherlands. Of special importance is the transition from primary to secondary education where the age of the pupils at the moment of their first selection acquires significance regarding disadvantage. As a result of the relevance of such selection for future labour market integration, authors like Stauber and Walther (1999) identify early selection as a 'first trap' built into the education system. It seems very likely that any vulnerability will manifest itself at such transitional moments and that disadvantaged groups regarding education, training and employment will appear.

Another especially critical transition is that from compulsory education to upper secondary vocational education or training. As training opportunities are limited and tend to be colonised by those with higher qualifications, many of those coming from the lowest qualified segments of lower secondary education have fewer opportunities to progress to vocational training. They have to participate in pre-vocational education or compensating measures, some of which really only constitute 'waiting halls'. Moreover, access to some of those measures is only possible by being regarded as disadvantaged or 'vocationally immature' as is the case in Germany (Kiely, 1999; Stauber and Walther, 1999). From this perspective, the following main groups of 'disadvantaged' can be identified.

Early school leavers

Against a backdrop of general qualifications inflation, the phenomenon of early school leaving becomes even more significant. As mentioned earlier, a minimum qualification is necessary to obtain a job, but is not always sufficient. In the Netherlands this situation has generated a definition of the concept of minimum starting qualification as "an equipment of knowledge, attitudes and skills to get full access to the labour market or positions within the employment system and to hold one's own and develop oneself there (and elsewhere)" (Hövels, 1999). In this regard, Hövels distinguishes different types of dropouts:

- those without the bare minimum who do not manage more (or even less as in the case of child work in Portugal) than primary or special school;
- traditional dropouts who enter lower secondary education, but do not obtain the certificate for compulsory schooling;
- those who finish lower secondary education at the compulsory level (leading to vocational training and apprenticeships);
- those who finish upper education without continuing or those who drop out of vocational training.

For those in the 'under the bare minimum' category and the 'traditional dropouts', prospects of success in the labour market or vocational training are very poor. As a result, they are considered the 'hard core' of early school leavers, while those leaving school with a compulsory certificate are likely to cope more easily with their situation in the labour market (see for example, Hannan, 1998; McCoy et al, 1999).

The motives for dropping out of school are consistent across all the countries studied. From qualitative research on young peoples' views of education emerges a deep dissatisfaction with their school experience (for example, Willis, 1977; Banks et al, 1992; Bates and Riseborough, 1993; Doran and Quilty, 1998, Fleming and Kenny, 1998; O'Sullivan, 1999). We also find less value attached to learning itself (intrinsic motivation), which is likely to be determined or at least influenced by social class background and lower educational levels associated with the family of origin of early school leavers. In contrast, early school leavers attribute positive value to work as a means to earn money to become independent as soon as possible (extrinsic motivation). According to this, their level of aspirations is often low and they display a short-term perspective (Braun et al, 1999; Hövels, 1999; Pais and Santos, 1999).

It is true that these youngsters often manage to enter the labour market and apparently avoid unemployment more effectively than more qualified persons (especially in Southern European countries). However, they do so preferentially in the so-called secondary labour market, which is characterised by precarious jobs, low wages and impoverished career perspectives. As a result, they are still in a disadvantaged situation according to our definition of the concept. Child labour in Portugal is also related to early school leaving. Predominantly in rural areas, parents prematurely retire their children from education to support the family economy with the argument that work is the 'real school of life' and that nothing will be gained by staying longer in school (Pais and Santos, 1999). This is consistent with the 'rational choice' model first proposed by Erikson and Jonsson (1996), in which educational choices are seen to be made according to the perceived costs and benefits associated with continued participation. According to another categorisation proposed by Hövels (1999) using living conditions and prospects of the early school leavers as classification criteria, the characteristics mentioned earlier would be related to the group of 'money earner'. Another sub-group are the 'the problematic school leavers', characterised by multiple problems such as drugs, mental disorders, financial and residential troubles and lack of parental support in times of crises. They are highly disadvantaged because of their exclusion from key social systems (school, work and welfare regimes), something that makes prevention and support difficult since they are not known to official institutions.

Ethnic and cultural minorities

The category of ethnic and cultural minorities in the European countries includes young people from former colonies, migrant workers, refugees and asylum seekers. They originate from the Caribbean, East Asia, Africa (especially northern Africa), Turkey, the former Yugoslavia and increasingly Central and Eastern Europe, but also from southern EU countries. Apart from this, there are indigenous ethnic minorities like the travellers or the gypsies with similar economic difficulties and problems of social integration.

Ethnic and cultural minorities are often perceived as an undifferentiated group of 'foreigners' without proper acknowledgement of the diversity of different ethnic and cultural origins. They are sometimes considered not actually to be citizens (or 'full citizens') and/or not to share important cultural values or aspirations of the majority. Their situation within the majority society can be seen as half-integrated and half-excluded (Bendit et al, 2000).

The presence of migrants in different European countries is closely related to labour market conditions. The reasons prompting emigration often are related to job opportunities – be they on the primary or secondary (illegal) labour market (for example, former 'guest workers' in Germany). This also applies to their actual residence and legal situation in the receiving countries (work and residence permits), factors that are strongly linked to the labour market situation there (see Bendit et al, 2000). This often leads immigrants to opt for illegal residence, thus increasing the precariousness of their situation.

Concerning education, the evidence from Germany, France, the Netherlands, the UK and Ireland suggests that ethnic and cultural minorities are overrepresented in the lower levels of the education system, for example in schools for those with learning disabilities as well as in the group of early school leavers and dropouts. Migrant young people who finish lower secondary education are more likely to have 'low prestige certificates' and to opt for vocational training or apprenticeships. However, as in Germany, for example, their chances of obtaining an apprenticeship after lower secondary education is comparatively lower, which the high proportion of migrant young people participating in pre-vocational education and compensating measures confirms. Moreover, in upper secondary and in higher education the proportion of migrants is far below the average. Their underachievement is most often ascribed to individual language deficits that schools apparently fail to compensate for (see Bendit et al, 2000; Plug et al, 2002).

For the travellers and gypsies, their nomadic lifestyle, coupled with school admission policies and practices, have a direct incidence on the possibility for traveller children to participate in mainstream educational institutions. Consequently, their literacy rate is low and the rate of dropping out high. Many contributory factors are identified in the literature, including a perception of futility regarding academic education as well as racism and discrimination by schools, teachers and other pupils reproducing marginalisation (Plug et al, 2002).

Also, the occupational situation of ethnic and cultural minorities is more precarious than that of the indigenous population. Their employment is concentrated in manual work in construction, industry and those categories of the service and trade sector requiring low levels of qualification. In most countries, a so-called 'ethnic rotation' has taken place in the lower segments of the labour market, contributing to the discriminatory perception of foreigners as 'under-educated' and 'unskilled' (Bendit et al, 2000; Plug et al, 2002). Another peculiarity of the work condition of ethnic and cultural minorities is their proximity to the secondary and illegal labour market. In this area, they are more vulnerable to job insecurity, because of low wages and lack of contracts, and the fear of being reported to the police (as is the case of those staying illegally in the country). In the case of travellers, their economy has become obsolete as a result of socioeconomic changes, so that many have to rely on welfare in order to survive (Kiely, 1999).

Among the factors mentioned in the research literature as related to the disadvantaged position of the ethnic and cultural minorities are information, social and cultural capital:

- *Information capital* is related to the often limited knowledge of society by migrants, so that they cannot support their children sufficiently when it comes to choosing a certain job or apprenticeship (Braun et al, 1999; Hövels, 1999).
- *Social capital* refers to the capacity to access social networks that can determine the position on labour market. Often the effect of these networks is a segmentation of the labour market by ethnicity.
- Finally, *cultural capital* makes reference to the different value systems of migrants inasmuch as parents' expectations and desires can interfere with the future professional plans of their children (which is often the case with female migrants) (Bendit et al, 2000).

Women and (single) mothers

In general, women achieve better qualifications in school than their male counterparts, but they are less represented in vocational training. When they do enter vocational training, it is probable that they enter gender-related professional training and work in sectors such as care, health and social services, which leads to fewer employment positions with lower wages and fewer opportunities for mobility and further training. Such decisions are often influenced by vocational guidance contributing to the maintenance of disadvantage related to gender (EGRIS, 2002).

In Catholic countries in Southern Europe (and also Ireland), the expectancy that women are supposed to stay at home to take care of their children determined a low employment rate for women until recent years (Kiely, 1999; Plug et al, 2002). In Ireland, this has finally been overturned during the so-called Celtic Tiger economic boom of the past ten years or so. Even so, women are likely to earn less than their male counterparts. In the Netherlands as in Germany, and especially in the UK and Scandinavia, rates of women in the labour market are higher, but many of the jobs taken are part-time, which are usually more precarious than their full-time equivalents (EGRIS, 2002).

The main factor affecting young women's participation in the labour market is motherhood. The principal cause for this is the limited access to, or lack of, childcare facilities and the tendency of women to assume a greater share of responsibilities towards childcare in the home according to gender stereotypes and expectancies. This means that giving birth to a child increases the probability of leaving the labour market should other social support networks, for example the family of origin, be missing. The situation of young mothers is further jeopardised if they are single. In this circumstance, parental support or childcare facilities are essential. If they are missing, the risk of unemployment and poverty augments. Moreover, many measures that are intended to deal with unemployment do not include crèche facilities, so that young single mothers often cannot participate in appropriate programmes although they are very interested in being independent (Plug et al, 2002).

Regional disadvantage

Regional differences regarding training and work opportunities can be identified in most EU member states. On the one hand, this is the difference between rural and urban areas. Young people living in rural areas need to be very flexible and mobile in order to find apprenticeship or employment. Moreover, local conceptions of normality regarding work and gender stereotypes tend to be more traditional, which has the effect of stigmatising more easily those youngsters who do not fulfil normal expectancies. In countries such as Portugal, child labour tends to be a more serious problem in rural areas, where families need the support of their children in order to sustain family economy mostly based on agriculture (Pais and Santos, 1999). On the other hand, regional differences can occur on a larger scale, for example, between East and West Germany. Due to economic and labour market restructuring in the East, the supply of training and jobs is reduced, while the rates of young people dropping out of vocational training and the official unemployment figures, including those for long-term unemployment, are higher. This problem is aggravated by the disappearance of support settings in the East.

Disadvantaged by personal or biographical handicaps

Besides the groups mentioned earlier in this chapter, where structural aspects appear to play the central role in the generation of disadvantaged living conditions, there are other groups of young people for whom disadvantage seems to be more linked to personal (physical or psychological) and biographical factors. They include:

- pupils and school leavers with learning disabilities;
- physically and mentally handicapped young people;
- school leavers who can not be reached ('elusive','disengaged') due to negative experiences with formal education;
- young people in critical life situations needing partial or temporary support or care.

Also, in situations where there is a sufficient supply of training and/or jobs, these young people are considered to encounter problems in entering and maintaining sustainable careers without specific support.

The 'most disadvantaged' and their needs

In the context of the theoretical framework developed earlier, we can characterise the 'most disadvantaged' as those young persons who belong to vulnerable groups in society and are marked out by their susceptibility to be hurt, damaged or negatively affected in different ways. This category also refers to the structural and personal biographical factors influencing young people's possibilities of integration into society. In this sense, more or less vulnerable people can be distinguished depending on the psychological, physical and social resources that are available in the face of difficulty. From this perspective, vulnerability is a consequence of structural and personal disadvantage and should be applied to all situations in which a strong *accumulation of disadvantages* can be observed. This accumulated disadvantage may partially block educational, social, cultural, professional or political integration. It may generate a situation of social exclusion if the persons do not find the means and/or are psychologically unable to counteract the causes and effects of their accumulated disadvantages. This seems to be exactly the situation of those groups and persons defined institutionally as the most disadvantaged groups. In accordance with this, the official definition of the German Ministry of Education and Research includes all:

> who are not able to start and pursue their educational or professional career without specific aid .... On the one hand, they suffer from different weaknesses and deficiencies with regard to intellectual development and social behaviour, on the other hand (they) obtain many assets which normally are not sufficiently recognised and acknowledged. The disadvantaged mostly do not fit in the rigid patterns and models. (Quoted in Schulte, 2002)

Existing evaluations of programmes and measures for the disadvantaged strongly suggest that the 'most disadvantaged' are not being reached by 'normal' measures and policies designed for them. This is not an indictment of these programmes in themselves. As designed, they might well provide adequate support and indeed in many instances do. However, they are prone to colonisation by young people who have higher probabilities of success (the 'creaming off' effect). This phenomenon is observed but not tackled by administrative authorities or by pedagogical and social work teams. Therefore, experts increasingly call for special measures for the most disadvantaged; that is, for the most vulnerable, even though such special measures may be in contradiction with the principles of 'flexibility' and 'normalisation' and indeed may increase stigmatisation of the most vulnerable young people, as we have seen earlier in the chapter. Through such measures, they may be easily identified as 'losers', a status that would undermine even more their already low motivation and self-esteem. Therefore, a 'mainstreaming approach' by implementing social and pedagogical actions against disadvantage, vulnerability and social exclusion in all education and training programmes seems to be a more innovative and effective strategy, for example, where measures for the most disadvantaged are embedded into plans of local development.

Summarising the argument so far: it is possible to identify a wide range of situations in which accumulated disadvantages can be responsible for the partial exclusion of certain individuals or social groups from some aspects and spheres of social life, while at the same time being integrated in others. Policies and programmes for the most disadvantaged should consider this situation, focusing on those needs and skills that could contribute to empowering young people in extremely vulnerable situations, inhibiting their coming into a situation of social exclusion.

Framing Integrated Transition Policies to meet the needs of the 'most disadvantaged'

When we turn to the young people themselves, there is broad agreement in both research literature and practitioner experience about their fears and low expectations for themselves. Their ambitions are usually short-term, expressed in terms of immediate and tangible goals. It is as though they cannot really envisage a future, only an extension of the present (EC, 2000).

A number of general framework issues must be discussed in order to define policies and programmes for the most disadvantaged. First, a spectrum of disadvantages and problems is identifiable along which the position of the most disadvantaged can be defined as such. A second general issue refers to the questions of how their needs are to be identified and how these needs are to be addressed. It is imperative that researchers, policy makers and service providers generate processes of active and equal consultation, involving users in the definition of their own needs and the evaluation of measures intended for their benefit. A further imperative is the generation of an open dialogue between policy makers and representatives of youth organisations, youth associations, youth councils and non-organised young people to define more precisely the 'needs' of young people and innovative forms of intervention.

It is true that much good practice already exists in the fields of education, training, guidance and employment services, especially regarding standards, consistency, training and supervision and professionalism. To address the needs of the most disadvantaged, research experience suggests that these mainstream professionals must develop an outward-looking and dynamic approach, a set of networks and a physical presence in learning, family, community and employment settings. This will involve a change from a service *to which individuals come* to *one that goes to them*, and one that regards them as fellow actors, rather than clients. In effect, it involves the formal system incorporating models and methods from the informal system (see Chapter Ten of this volume). Within this general framework, a number of recommendations can be made:

- At the level of systems, *prevention and early intervention* are key priorities. This should be part of a *broad, active and continuing spectrum of support*. Such actions are likely to include social welfare and psychological services. Particular mention is made of the beneficial effects of mentoring and advocacy in helping individuals compensate for lack of knowledge, motivation and family and neighbourhood support networks as described above (see Chapter Three of this volume).

- *Intra-service and inter-service clarity and consensus regarding aims and objectives.* Helping the individual achieve social and economic independence and employability (that is, sustainability in the labour market and a viable personal and vocational identity) is a key objective of transition policy. Experience of successful transition measures indicates the *necessity* of an inter-agency approach and the *desirability* of inter-service consensus. Indeed, catering for the needs of the most disadvantaged demands the creation of a continuum of services and clarity regarding inter-service referrals, roles and responsibilities – in effect, a team approach at local level (Stokes, 2000).

- *Integration of services, systems and approaches* – it must also be acknowledged that implementing up-to-date, inter-agency collaboration has challenged the dominant service paradigms in education, training and employment services. A more active and assertive paradigm is necessary, one that emphasises integration on the basis of the needs of clients, not those of service providers. At the level of services, it requires effective multi-actor networks and mechanisms for cooperation between service providers, driven by a fundamental question: *do the services make sense to the users?* At the level of systems, the needs of the most disadvantaged demand links between formal and informal learning ecosystems, and between the worlds of school, training and work. This approach may be developed through joint projects and multi-agency training on common themes to build mutual understanding, terminology and operational gateways.

- *Linking the formal and informal* as the wider community of actors indicated earlier extends beyond the formal education, training, employment and social services. Organisations in direct contact with young people have evolved appropriate methodologies to work with them. So, it is important to promote the participation of these organisations as equal partners in all aspects of the planning and delivery of services. In the informal system, key players include family members, peer groups, youth workers and leaders in voluntary or non-governmental services. Other players in the formal system include local authorities, employers, social workers and police (see Chapters Eight, Nine and Twelve of this volume).

- It makes little sense to expect the most disadvantaged young people; that is, those who are hardest to reach, to present themselves to services. Rather, we may envisage a more *diverse set of delivery contexts*, including the home, the workplace, the sports ground, the street corner and the local shop or fast-food outlet – in other words, wherever the young person can most effectively be reached. These are best understood as starting points. While the location of the activity may subsequently change, the fundamental objective remains the same – to support the young person in making the transition to independent adult life.

- *Appropriate research and evaluation mechanisms* – a high proportion of the European experience in dealing with disrupted transitions and multiple disadvantages derives from action research processes. However, overall policy and research have been poorly integrated in the European discourse on changing patterns of transitions. The major frameworks for action have been political in origin, and have been set in relatively immediate time frames that have not allowed for substantial, objective research before, during and after the action. The importance of independent evaluation is also stressed, including the establishment of appropriate success and evaluation criteria. There is also a need to measure social effects/costs and to identify so-called 'sleeper effects' in persons and institutions by follow-up studies (of at least six months).

- *Appropriate resources for service providers* – successful approaches to working with the most disadvantaged are more intensive and longitudinal. They are often more expensive, therefore, than conventional approaches. However, such additional expenditure is rational in the context of the other forces in the lives of many users. Conventional services have not worked for them. Their situation demands greater targeted investment. This may be offset against income support that will not be required if such policies are successful.

- The need of *policy makers to take a long-term view* must be emphasised for two key reasons. The first of these is the degree to which the use of short-term interventions, based on projects, has infiltrated policy towards the disadvantaged (for example, due to funding criteria of the European Social Fund). The net effect, however, is to deliver services through projects delivered by mainstream systems. This creates a project infrastructure, as opposed to a service infrastructure. It ensures that services to the most disadvantaged are themselves marginalised and expendable. The second reason why a long-term view must be taken refers to previously cited 'sleeper effects' from active interventions that may not manifest themselves for a considerable period of time. At the systematic level changes do not take hold immediately. More of what has failed is not the answer for young people and others experiencing problems in the labour market. Many of their difficulties are structural issues and not short-term problems. Addressing their needs therefore requires a long-term view.

If we take the general line of argument presented above, what are the defining *characteristics of successful approaches* to working with the most disadvantaged? They are:

- individual, local, integrate;
- flexible, action-driven and solution-oriented;
- continuous, starting in compulsory schools and, if necessary, lasting until the first months of employment;
- holistic, combining different kinds of activities (vertical and horizontal) with permanent guidance at their centre.

They:

- incorporate formal and informal contexts and approaches;
- start 'where the young person is at', placing her/himself at the centre of action and treating him/her with respect and listening, involving, feeding back and giving time.

In multicultural Europe, cultural compatibility is appropriate.

These assets require large-scale cooperation and synergies between all relevant actors, primarily at local level and an integration of social work with educational and vocational training policies: Integrated Transition Policies (ITPs) (Stokes, 1999, 2000; EC, 2000; Schulte, 2002; see also Chapter Two of this volume).

A number of key issues arise regarding the employment of *professional staff* to work with the most disadvantaged. The first concerns new roles and jobs. In addition to teachers, trainers, social workers and guidance counsellors, a range of new roles and titles has emerged to describe the work conducted with disadvantaged individuals and communities. In the area of guidance, at least five approaches can be identified, such as personal care and encouragement, community-based guidance, peer guidance among young people, front-line guidance and pastoral care, and mentoring and advocacy by instructors, company supervisors, trade union personnel, or sports leaders for and with the young person in a range of contexts. There is also a pressing need for outreach actions. While these are not all the same, functional overlaps can be identified. In all cases, however, there are substantial issues regarding young people's status vis-à-vis their counterparts in the formal system as regards pay and conditions of employment (for example, job tenure, since many are hired on short-term project contracts). Support and professional supervision for those doing the most difficult work are important issues as well.

Conclusions

Transferring research findings into policy programmes and measures is a demanding and important task that must be improved. The central aim of this task with reference of this target group is not only to offer knowledge on specific issues characterising the most disadvantaged but to increase political awareness on the side of policy makers and authorities of the educational system about the specific needs, problems and the specific social significance of these disadvantaged young people.

Another aspect of this relationship refers to the policy makers' expectations towards research. They are time-driven and very short-term in orientation. In the frame of a more intensive cooperation between policy makers, administrators and researchers, this might be changed towards a more strategic perspective. Research, especially evaluative research, should mirror reality as much as possible in an unbiased way and also draw a more general picture of it so that specific developments can be better interpreted in this larger context. Research should also be accessible, practical and political, that is oriented towards real world problems. It is acknowledged that the relationship between research and policy will be always difficult. Nevertheless, regarding the problems of the most disadvantaged, there should be more research and it should be more central to policy formation. In a sentence, research should not only map the landscape, it should also help to plot the journey.

However, interpreted in terms of ITPs, such a journey cannot just be plotted by researchers for policy makers, it needs to be open for encounters with the addressees, the young men and women concerned. From a biographical perspective, disadvantage needs to be assessed in a dialogic way between authorities, individuals and research, starting from the assumption that destandardised transitions are vulnerable per se, uncertain and open to risks of exclusion. In this respect, disadvantage has to be regarded as the resources, opportunities and competencies – the support – needed to bridge the gap between subjective needs and aspirations on the one side and demands connected to the respective occupational and social positions on the other. Access to these, in the sense of sufficient time and place really to understand and actively cope with this gap in a meaningful way, must be viewed as a citizenship right that pertains to the participation of all young people in late modern societies that claim to reconcile capitalism and democracy.

References

Banks, M., Bates, I., Breakwell, G., Bynner, J., Emler, N., Jamieson, L. and Roberts, K. (1992) *Careers and identities*, Buckingham: Open University Press.

Bates, I. and Riseborough G. (eds) (1993) *Youth and inequality*, Buckingham: Open University Press.

Bendit, R., Keimeleder, L. and Werner, K. (2000) *Bildungs, Ausbildungs und Erwerbsverläufe junger migrantinnen im Kontext von Integrationspolitik*, Forschungsschwerpunkt "Übergänge in die Arbeit", Working paper 4/2000, München: Deutsches Jugendinstitut (www.iris-egris.de/egris/tser).

Bhalla, A.S. and Lapeyre, F. (1994) *A note on exclusion*, Working Paper, Geneva: IILS.

Braun, F., Lex, T. and Rademacher, H. (1999) *Probleme und Wege der beruflichen Integration von benachteiligten Jugendlichen und jungen Erwachsenen*, Expertise, DJI-Forschungsschwerpunkt "Übergänge in Arbeit", Working Paper 1/1999, München: Deutsches Jugendinstitut.

Doran, P. and Quilty, A. (1998) *Early school leavers*, Report by County Dublin VEC to Department of Education and Science, Dublin: County Dublin VEC.

Dubet, F. and Lapeyronie, D. (1992) *Les quartiers d'exil*, Paris: Editions du Seuil.

EC (European Commission) (1983) *Towards a Europe of solidarity: Intensifying the fight against social exclusion, fostering integration*, Luxembourg: Office for Official Publications of the European Communities.

EC (1996) *YOUTHSTART – A new commitment*, Luxembourg: Office for Official Publications of the European Communities.

EC (2000) *It's magic – A broader approach to guidance with the active involvement of young people*, Luxembourg: Office for Official Publications of the European Communities.

EGRIS (European Group for Integrated Social Research) (2002) 'Leading or misleading trajectories? Concepts and perspectives', in A. Walther, B. Stauber, A. Biggart, M. du Bois-Reymond, A. Furlong, A. López Blasco, S. Mørch and J.M. Pais (eds) *Misleading trajectories: Integration policies for young adults in Europe?*, Opladen: Leske+Budrich, pp 117-53.

Erikson, R. and Jonsson, J.O. (1996) *Can education be equalised? The Swedish case in comparative perspective*, Boulder, CO: Westview Press.

Fleming, T. and Kenny, D. (1998) *Early school leaving in mid-Kildare – A research report and review of Newbridge CTW*, Maynooth: Centre for Adult and Community Education.

Geurts, J. (1989) *Van niemandsland naar beroepenstructuur. Een studie over de aansluiting tussen onderwijs en arbeid op het niveau van aankomend vakmanschap*, Nijmegen.

Hannan, D.F. (1998) 'Early school leaving – its nature, consequences and policy identification', in *Prevention of early school leaving: The YOUTHSTART experience*, Conference proceedings, Dublin: YOUTHSTART National Support Structure.

Hannan, D.F. and O'Riain, S. (1993) 'Pathways to adulthood in Ireland', *General Research Series Paper*, Vol 161, Dublin: Economic and Social Research Institute.

Hövels, B. (1999) 'School leaving: the perspectives of qualification and labour market', in B. Hövels, H. Rademacker and G. Westhoff (eds) *Early school leaving, qualification and youth unemployment: Research and practice in Germany and the Netherlands*, Delft: Vidgeverit-EBURON, pp 12-52.

Jordan, B. (1996) *A theory of poverty and social exclusion*, Cambridge: Polity Press.

Kiely, E. (1999) *Irish National Report on misleading trajectories*, University College Cork (www.iris-egris.de/egris/tser).

McCoy, S., Doyle. A. and Williams J. (1999) *1998 Annual school-leavers' survey of 1996/7 leavers*, Dublin: Department of Education and Science, Department of Enterprise, Trade and Employment, ESRI.

O'Brien, M. and Penna, S. (1998) *Theorising welfare*, London: Sage Publications.

O'Sullivan, E. (1999) *YOUTHREACH social inclusion report – Early school leaving in Dublin City*, Dublin: County of Dublin VEC.

Pais, J.M and Santos, M.M. (1999) *Misleading trajectories: Portuguese Report*, Lisbon: ICS, Working Paper (www.iris-egris.de/egris/tser).

Plug, W., Kiely, E., Hein, K., Ferreira, V.S., Bendit, R., du Bois-Reymond, M. and Pais, J.M. (2002) 'Modernised transitions and disadvantage policies: Netherlands, Portugal, Ireland and migrant youth in Germany', in A. Walther, B. Stauber, A. Biggart, M. du Bois-Reymond, A. Furlong, A. López Blasco, S. Mørch and J.M. Pais (eds) *Misleading trajectories: Integration policies for young adults in Europe?*, Opladen: Leske+Budrich, pp 94-117.

Schnapper, D. (1996) 'Integration et exclusion dans les societés modernes', in *L'exclusion. L'etat des savoirs*, Paris: Edition La Recouverte.

Schulte, E. (2002) 'Comments on "Integration through training?"', Discussion paper to the European conference 'Young People and Transition Policies', 6-8 June, Madrid.

Stauber, B. and Walther, A. (in collaboration with E. Bolay) (1999) *Misleading trajectories in Germany: Traps of social exclusion in the system of school to work transition*, Tübingen, Working Paper (www.iris-egris.de/egris/tser).

Stokes, D. (1999) 'Guidance in the 21st century: a message from the margins', *Institute of Guidance Counsellors: Journal*, Dublin: IGC, pp 55-65.

Stokes, D. (2000) 'Youth unemployment: the experience of EU member states: Ireland', Paper delivered at the conference 'Youth unemployment in Southeast Europe: Access to education and training', Velingrad, Bulgaria.

Willis, P. (1977). *Learning to labour*, Hampshire: Gower.

Index

Page references for figures and notes are in *italics*; those for notes are followed by n

Also available from The Policy Press

Youth unemployment and social exclusion in Europe

A comparative study

Edited by Torild Hammer

Throughout the European Union, rates of unemployment among young people tend to be higher than among the general population and there is a serious risk of marginalisation and exclusion. This important new book presents the findings of the first comparative study of unemployed youth in Europe using a large and original data set.

Paperback £35.00 (US$59.50) ISBN 1 86134 368 X
Hardback £65.00 (US$99.00) ISBN 1 86134 369 8
234 x 156mm 240 pages July 2003

The right to learn

Educational strategies for socially excluded youth in Europe

Edited by Ides Nicaise

This book reports on a wide-ranging research study into education and social exclusion in Europe. It explores differing strategies to improve educational success among disadvantaged children. The countries studied, UK, Ireland, Belgium, the Netherlands, Portugal and Spain, reflect the diversity in systems and policies that currently exist. The book assesses their relative success, and makes suggestions for good practice.

Paperback £19.99 (US$34.50) ISBN 1 86134 288 8
234 x 156mm 432 pages November 2000

Losing out?

Socioeconomic disadvantage and experience in further and higher education

Alasdair Forsyth and Andy Furlong

Despite the recent expansion of higher education, representation, level of participation and likelihood of academic success remain highest among young people from affluent areas and lowest among those from deprived neighbourhoods. This report identifies the factors which impact upon the experiences of the minority of disadvantaged young people who enter higher education.

Paperback £14.95 (US$25.50) ISBN 1 86134 508 9
297 x 210mm 76 pages May 2003
Published in association with the Joseph Rowntree Foundation

Socioeconomic disadvantage and access to higher education

Alasdair Forsyth and Andy Furlong

The gap in representation in higher education between affluent and disadvantaged young people continues. Through a survey of school leavers, carried out both before and after leaving school, this detailed report explores the wide range of factors that affect young people's progress in this area. It concludes with policy recommendations for increasing disadvantaged young people's participation in higher education, making it vital reading for everyone interested in education and youth transitions.

Paperback £13.95 (US$23.50) ISBN 1 86134 296 9
297 x 210mm 64 pages November 2000
Published in association with the Joseph Rowntree Foundation

To order further copies of this publication or any other Policy Press titles please contact:

In the UK and Europe
Marston Book Services, PO Box 269, Abingdon, Oxon, OX14 4YN, UK
Tel: +44 (0)1235 465500, Fax: +44 (0)1235 465556,
Email: direct.orders@marston.co.uk

In the USA and Canada
ISBS, 920 NE 58th Street, Suite 300, Portland, OR 97213-3786, USA
Tel: +1 800 944 6190 (toll free), Fax: +1 503 280 8832,
Email: info@isbs.com

In Australia and New Zealand
DA Information Services, 648 Whitehorse Road, Mitcham, Victoria 3132, Australia
Tel: +61 (3) 9210 7777, Fax: +61 (3) 9210 7788,
E-mail: service@dadirect.com.au

Further information about all of our titles can be also be found on our website:

www.policypress.org.uk